Introducing African American Religion

This book offers a creative and unique approach to the history of African American religion. Tracing what it has meant to be African American and religious within the context of the United States, it provides a vital snapshot of some of the traditions that have shaped the religious imagination of the country. Major themes and problems encountered by African Americans involved in a variety of traditions are depicted in a clear and engaging fashion.

The chapters move from the period of slavery and the early arrangement of religious thought and practice within communities of enslaved Africans to the more recent growth in the number of African American "Nones". Drawing on cultural developments such as hip hop, Anthony Pinn links the language and activities of African American religious experience to the cultural worlds in which African Americans live.

Introducing African American Religion includes illustrations, summaries, discussion questions and suggestions for further reading as well as a glossary and chronology, helping students to become familiar with the main terms of the traditions discussed and to place their development in historical context.

For additional resources visit the companion website at www.routledge.com/cw/pinn

Anthony B. Pinn is Agnes Cullen Arnold Professor of Humanities and Professor of Religious Studies at Rice University, USA. His books include *Terror and Triumph: The Nature of Black Religion* (2003) and *Varieties of African American Religious Experience* (1999).

World Religions series

Edited by Damien Keown and Charles S. Prebish

This exciting series introduces students to the major world religious traditions. Each religion is explored in a lively and clear fashion by experienced teachers and leading scholars in the field of world religions. Up-to-date scholarship is presented in a student-friendly fashion, covering history, core beliefs, sacred texts, key figures, religious practice and culture, and key contemporary issues. To aid learning and revision, each text includes illustrations, summaries, explanations of key terms, and further reading.

Introducing Tibetan Buddhism
Geoffrey Samuel

Introducing Buddhism, second edition
Damien Keown and Charles S. Prebish

Introducing American Religion
Charles Lippy

Introducing Chinese Religions
Mario Poceski

Introducing Islam
William Shepard

Introducing Daoism
Livia Kohn

Introducing Judaism
Eliezer Segal

Introducing Christianity
James R. Adair

Introducing Japanese Religions
Robert Ellwood

Introducing Hinduism
Hillary Rodrigues

Introducing African American Religion

Anthony B. Pinn

Routledge
Taylor & Francis Group

LONDON AND NEW YORK

First published 2013
by Routledge
2 Park Square, Milton Park, Abingdon, Oxon OX14 4RN

Simultaneously published in the USA and Canada
by Routledge
711 Third Avenue, New York, NY 10017

Routledge is an imprint of the Taylor & Francis Group, an informa business

British Library Cataloguing in Publication Data
A catalogue record for this book is available from the British Library

Library of Congress Cataloging in Publication Data
A catalog record for this book has been requested

ISBN: 978-0-415-69400-1 (hbk)
ISBN: 978-0-415-69401-8 (pbk)

Typeset in Jenson and Tahoma
by HWA Text and Data Management, London

Printed and bound in Great Britain by
TJ International Ltd, Padstow, Cornwall

Contents

PART III
Issues and concerns in contemporary African American religion   **203**

Figures

Preface

For a good number of years I taught a course on the "Varieties of African American Religion" in which students were introduced to a good number of religious traditions embraced by African Americans. Students were often confused by the diversity of opinions and beliefs, and were a bit thrown by the tensions between these various traditions – particularly when they tried to view all the course materials through their own convictions. Class discussions revolved around at least one question: "How can all this be African American religion?"

A similar question has served as motivation for much of what I have taught and researched over the past two decades. I have been concerned with mapping out the nature and meaning of African American religion in part by exposing the complex religious landscape in African American communities. My effort has been to do so through attention to the history of various traditions, the theologies held by these traditions, the practices embraced by them, and the aesthetics or general style of expression and exchange marking them. I began with African American Christian churches, the major religious tradition within African American communities, but it did not take long to notice that these churches exist within the context of other traditions – responding to them, arguing against them, learning from them. In fact, for example, many Christians also give attention to root work, conjure and hoodoo. And African American Christians are aware of Voodoo (called Vodou in Haiti), Santeria ("Regla de Ocha"), and Islam among other traditions.

Furthermore, these various traditions have claimed the imagination and allegiance of African Americans. Granted, the number of adherents within these other traditions does not match the number of African Americans who claim some version of the Christian Church; but, they are important nonetheless and I wanted to learn something about them. And I wanted my students to learn something about them. I wanted my students to appreciate the importance of Christianity, but to place Christian churches within the context of other religious traditions present within African American communities.

In mapping out these traditions, Christianity and the others, I also needed to be sensitive to both their claims/beliefs and their practices – both the points of promise and their flaws. For example, I needed to give attention to their engagement with the larger world – the ways in which they mirrored the sexism and homophobia of society for instance, but also their efforts to combat racism and seek out economic injustice. It was important to give attention to how believers interact physically within the context of formal gatherings but also how they made use of technology to advance their faith claims.

Several things became clear to me through my work. For example, "movement" was clearly important for these various traditions. This included the Middle Passage, the Great Migration, and the reshaping of urban environments that informed and affected the teachings and practices of so many religious traditions. The human body – the bio-chemical reality that is born, grows, ages, and dies – has been a resource for these traditions, but it also has promoted tension and concern for some of these traditions, particularly churches. That is to say, for Christian churches, the body has been understood as the source of sin, the very thing that prevents closeness to God. Yet, it also serves as the place from which the religious worship and act out their faith in connection to others. Furthermore, spaces used for worship or practice shift and change; they are marked by particular symbols and images that represent key themes and points faith communities seek to communicate. And, these symbols and images are not disconnected from socio-political concerns within the larger society. For example, the civil rights struggles and black power philosophy generated new theologies but also encouraged a re-thinking of Jesus Christ (and God) as looking like African Americans. The Nation of Islam's understanding of God also privileges blackness in part as a corrective to the negative depictions of African Americans marking public and private conversations, policies, and social relations in the United States. The list goes on, but what has been clear through all of this exploring is the manner in which even these very different traditions have some basic concerns and goals that are shared. They differ in terms of discrete doctrine, creeds, and practices. That is to say, the ways in which they express their beliefs differ just as these beliefs differ. Yet, there is at least one commonality that cuts through these various traditions, that suggest a common human objective: African American religion – despite differences in expressions – is concerned with questions of life meaning, and works to forge greater life meaning.

Mindful of this, the following chapters do not provide an institutional history of particular traditions. There are plenty of books available to students that provide attention to the development of religious traditions in African American communities through an outlining of the creation of institutions, as well as the careful outlining of theologies, doctrines and creeds. Students have access to those books, but I wanted to do something different with this book. And this involves attention to a different theory of African American religion as well as an approach to this book involving the use of multiple methods of study, including theology, history, and cultural studies. This allows readers the ability to look at African American religion from a variety of angles, and using source materials that others might not consider important enough to consider. When pulled together, the goal of this book is not to provide outlines of the traditions that dominate African American communities – nor a mere rehearsal of the creeds and rituals that mark them. These things are mentioned at points throughout the various chapters, but I am much more concerned with providing a story of African American religion that seeks to show how the fostering of life meaning gets played out in relationship to slavery, continued discrimination, socio-political struggle and in connection to key issues such as sex, gender, sexuality, politics, key cultural developments, and so on. Much of this is filtered through a central question: what is it about the thinking and practices of these various traditions that tie them to the quest for greater life meaning? Answering this question does not always provide a positive story of growth and progress. There are just as many times when African American religion does damage to particular groups not part of the "in crowd." But neatness is not my concern; the nature of human need for life meaning and the messy effort to address this need is the point here. Humans who are capable of great good and great harm populate these traditions. The story of African American religion, as is the case for religion in other communities as well, must point out both.

Regardless of the particular perspective, religion matters; and it changes and shifts to address (not always well) human needs and wants. Belief and disbelief both fit into this framework.

This exploration of African American religion will not answer all questions. What study could? Instead, it is my hope this introduction to African American religion will point out the primary goal of competing faith claims and also, and this is important, demonstrate how religiosity – for good or ill – infiltrates and impacts all areas of human life.

Acknowledgments

Many individuals played a role in helping me complete this project, and I would like to take this opportunity to offer my gratitude. My family and friends remain a source of support and encouragement – thank you. I have enjoyed working with Lesley Riddle and Katherine Ong, and I am grateful for their patience and good humor during the process of bringing this book to its intended audience. My student, Christopher Driscoll, gave time and energy to reviewing the manuscript for typos and other difficulties – thank you. Finally, I would like to thank those who participated in the review process for this book. Their questions and comments made the project more precise and much better than it would have been otherwise.

Part I

The nature, origins, and historical overview of African American religion

1 *What is African American religion?*

In this chapter

This chapter presents the religious landscape of African American communities through a brief discussion of some of the competing faith claims of which it is composed. It provides a way of noting, exploring and addressing what this complex arrangement of practices means for a general definition of African American religion.

Main topics covered

- The traditional definitions of African American religion as centered on Christianity
- Challenges to Christianity-based definitions of African American religion
- An alternative understanding of African American religion sensitive to the diversity of experiences

Definitions

"That thing … ah, you know …that thing. What's it called?" How many times have you been in a conversation or you've looked for something and you've asked for help, but you can't think of what it is called. The thing you want or are looking for you can't name or define? In that situation the importance of definitions, of being able to describe or name something is clear.

Definitions are important in that they give us a way of thinking about the meaning of something, and in this way we are able to best describe and understand it. This is generally the case, and it is no less true for the study of African American religion. In a word, how does one study African American religion before we define what it is?

The history of major religious traditions in African American communities will be discussed in other chapters. However, that discussion can only begin after we have settled on a definition of African American religion: What do we mean when we say

African American religion? Everything else in this book rests upon our answer to this important and central question.

Religious diversity in early African American communities

The African American presence in North America is centuries old, and during these many years African Americans have practiced a range of religious traditions. Some of these traditions are unique to the "New World," and others like Christianity are older than the age of exploration that initiated the presence of Africans in large numbers in the American hemisphere. While African American religious traditions have been around for a long period of time, more recent is an effort to define what we actually mean when we say African American religion. If one thinks about it, one quickly realizes that it is not until the twentieth century that African American religion receives this type of academic attention. People from all walks of life have acknowledged the importance of religion for enslaved Africans and their free descendants in the United States, but most simply assumed there is a common understanding of the nature and meaning of African American religion. Scholars during the early twentieth century merely re-enforced this assumption when they began to define African American religion strictly in terms of Christianity. Casual observers and academics alike assumed that the most visible, most numerically significant, more dominant, and best organized form of religious experience – African American Christianity – could easily be used to name and categorize African American religion in general: to be African American and religious, they reasoned, was to be Christian. And while Christianity is a vital dimension of African American religiosity, its importance should be placed within a context of other traditions – albeit with smaller populations – that have importance for their followers.

The assumption noted above was based on the long history of African Americans involved in Christianity that easily extended back prior to the Middle Passage. For instance, the Portuguese worked to spread Christianity in Africa before the end of the fifteenth century. Hence, it is possible that some Africans taken to North America and other areas of the Americas might have been somewhat familiar with the Christian faith even if they didn't practice it. Even if this isn't taken into consideration, from the 1600s to the present, the history of Christianity in the United States has included African Americans. And for better than 200 years, African Americans have held and maintained their own Christian denominations. However, it is also important to note the longstanding presence of Africans within the Roman Catholic Church in North America. Catholics worked in North America, places like Maryland and Florida, to establish a presence. And, some of those brought into the faith were Africans. In fact, records indicate that an enslaved African named Esteban was converted in 1536, and lived in an area now represented by Florida, Texas, and Arkansas. Conversion to the Roman Catholic Church may have begun with Esteban but the numbers would expand in significant ways, with Catholics of African descent gaining positions of leadership in the church in the nineteenth century.

Many of the well-known leaders within African American communities during the period of slavery to the present have been members of Christian churches. Furthermore, the struggle for an end to racial discrimination in the United States has relied on Christian language of charity, equality, and concern for others. Think about figures like the Rev. Dr. Martin Luther King, Jr., (1929–1968) who as a Christian minister played a major role in changing the nature of justice in the United States. According to many, African American churches are the first and oldest organizations developed for and by African Americans, and the oldest organizations completely committed to the needs and wants of African Americans. Even earlier than King, legendary figures such as Sojourner Truth (1797–1883) fought for equal rights for African Americans and women across race, drawing principles and ethical commitments from their understanding of the Christian faith. Churches owned and managed by African Americans served as spaces for education, social equality, political organizing, and spiritual advancement. And the financial independence from white Americans made these churches prime locations for activism in that African Americans maintained them economically. Whether they were Methodist, Baptist, Pentecostal, or independent these churches understood themselves to serve the needs of the communities in which they existed. Even a quick glance at the history of African American churches as basic expressions of Christianity makes it clear these churches have played a major role in the struggles and advances of African Americans in the realm of religion, politics, and economics. However, does this alone mean one can (or even should) define African American religion strictly in terms of African American Christianity and the churches representing this religious tradition?

The careful student of African American history easily uncovers the presence of other religious orientations that makes very difficult the defining of African American religion in terms of the practices and beliefs of just one tradition. The evidence of these other traditions is found in the folk stories, folk wisdom, and narratives left to us by enslaved Africans as well as other colonists during the early years of the United States' development. For example, both white colonists and Africans mentioned the presence of some brought over as slaves who prayed numerous times each day in an odd posture, who gave their children foreign names, refused to eat certain foods, and did not practice the Christian faith. Over the course of time, scholars came to recognize these observations as references to the early presence of Islamic practices in North America amongst enslaved Africans. In fact, it is estimated that anywhere between 5 and 15 percent of the enslaved Africans brought to the Americas were Muslims. And while not all of these African

Muslims would have come to North America, we do know that some did. We have some biographical information on a few of these Muslims. One of these Africans was Bilali, who resided in Georgia and served as a religious leader on the plantation where he was held. In addition, documents left to us by overseers and other planters speak to black "Mohammedians" – an inaccurate naming of Muslims – being disciplined and unlike other slaves in certain ways based, for instance, on the scheduling of time entailed by their tradition of praying at various points during the day, etc. Not every aspect of Islam was present within these early Muslim communities of enslaved Africans; yet, there was enough about their practices separating them from Christians to make their stories important as well as making their tradition a reason to avoid defining African American religion strictly in terms of Christianity. Simply put, if the history of African Americans points out the existence of at least one tradition beyond Christianity, it becomes impossible to define the general category of African American religion in relationship strictly to Christianity. At this point we can say whatever the proper definition of African American religion, it must involve more than attention to the beliefs and practices of Christianity. The definition must take into consideration the existence of Islam – its beliefs and practices – held important by enslaved Africans and their descendants.

One might be tempted to think of a definition of African American religion based on overlap between Christianity and Islam, and say that African American religion can be defined by the common denominators between these traditions – things like belief in God, demand for moral and ethical living, devotion to scripture given by God, and so on. Even this, however, is too narrow a definition of African American religion in that the historical record points out the existence of religious practices not associated with either Christianity or Islam. The religious landscape of African American communities is more complex than just these two traditions, and our definition of African American religion must also be more complex than just these two traditions.

Some enslaved Africans arrived in the North American colonies committed to Christianity, others to Islam, and still others to African-based traditions that we have come to name using labels such as voodoo. (I use this term rather than Vodou to indicate a North Americanizing of the tradition over against what is practiced in Haiti or Africa.) Such labels are imperfect, but they do point out the existence of other religious practices that are not the same as Christianity and Islam, and in fact run contrary to some of the claims of those two traditions. For example, Christians believe that Christ is the savior of humanity – but practitioners of African-based traditions such as voodoo do not always believe that humans are guilty of an "original sin" committed by the first humans that requires salvation by Jesus Christ. Instead they argue that humans do things that require the restoration of balance through some type of action or sacrifice to one of the deities. And, unlike Islam, adherents of voodoo recognize the existence of more than one deity requiring devotion.

We typically associated traditions like voodoo with the Caribbean and with the descendants of enslaved Africans on islands such as Haiti, or with "Regla de Ocha" (or what many call Santeria) on the island of Cuba. However, while these traditions thrive in such locations from the period of slavery to the present, they are also present in the North American colonies and continue to have a home in African American communities in the United States. Archeologists, for example, have found household items that contain symbols associated with these traditions, and designs within quilts used during the period of slavery have symbols and colors that are associated with particular African deities. In addition to these bits and pieces of evidence, in locations such as New Orleans there are long-standing stories and reports of voodoo kings and queens like Marie Laveau, whose practice of voodoo took place openly, within the French Quarter of New Orleans as well as in more secluded swamp areas outside the city. Animal sacrifices to African gods, possession of devotees by these gods as well as ancestors, and practices used to communicate with these invisible forces are found throughout the literature of African American life in the colonies and early United States. These religious leaders like Marie Laveau have left us with strong evidence of a rich variety of African American religious practices associated with the continent of Africa and altered somewhat to fit the context of North America.

In addition to formal traditions such as voodoo, in North America there also emerged less formal sets of practices without clear ritual practices and doctrines and much more magic driven. We have come to reference them as hoodoo, conjure, and root work. That is to say, early folktales and stories speak to the presence of Africans in North America with a special relationship to the earth, the ability to use plants for example to secure particular wishes and wants. In addition, they could use hair or other personal items to do things such as secure the affections of a person, or gain control over them. In short, practitioners of hoodoo, conjure, or root work could use such items as a source of power by means of which to control people. For example, some accounts of these practices point to the use of root workers or conjurers to help young men secure the love interests of young women by collecting pieces of their hair prepared by the conjurer. The young men would be instructed on how to carry and store the women's hair in order to secure the love interests of these young women. Hair and other intimate items such as finger nail clippings associated with a person were believed to have special power that could be used to control that person, when that power is harnessed and turned against the person. That is to say, by controlling those items, a conjurer could control the person from whom the hair, etc., was taken. In other accounts people sought money or power through attention to invisible forces. What is clear, regardless of their reasons for seeking the aid of the conjurer, their requests point out the importance of a tradition beyond the Christianity and Islam that most typically captures our attention.

Religious diversity

- For centuries, North America has been marked by the presence of many religious traditions that combine African, European and North America elements.
- Enslaved Africans and their descendants practiced a variety of religious traditions during the period of slavery and beyond. No single tradition can serve as the general definition for African American religion.

Thus far the traditions used to develop a sense of what is African American religion have at least one common factor – a belief in invisible forces typically referred to as spirits or gods. However, the period of slavery also points out the presence of African Americans who are not interested in gods or god, and for whom theism in any form was inadequate. Within the blues and folktales, for example, African Americans have told the story of those whose movement through life is not premised on Christianity, Islam, African-based traditions, or any other theistic set of practices. And rather than developing ethics and morality (i.e., proper action and a set of values) in light of what sacred books outline, they depend on human ingenuity, creativity, and accomplishments. They are what we have more recently come to call African American humanists – those who replace allegiance to god or gods with allegiance to humanity as the "measure of all things." Recent studies have outlined the ways in which this humanism functions for African American humanists in ways similar to how Christianity, Islam or voodoo functions for their adherents. If this is indeed accurate, we must ask a question: Can one define African American religion in terms of worship of God or gods?

Growing complexity

The complexity discussed above only increases as African American history pushes beyond the nineteenth century into the twentieth century. With the end of slavery, African Americans began to move into cities (Northern and Southern) in search of greater social and economic opportunities. We call this movement beginning after the Civil War through the late twentieth century the "Great Migration." And as African Americans moved, they took with them their religious beliefs and transplanted them in new urban locations. Included in this cultural movement was the development of Gospel music – a blending of the theological content of Christianity and early Christianity-influenced songs called spirituals with the musical stylings of early secular tunes called the blues – in places such as Chicago. Key figures in this musical tradition born during this migration include Thomas Dorsey (1899–1993), often called the "Father" of Gospel Music, and one of its most widely recognized singers during its golden age – Mahalia Jackson (1911–1972).

Figure 1.1 Photograph of African American men, women, and children who participated in the Great Migration to the North, with suitcases and luggage placed in front (Chicago, 1918). Courtesy of Chicago History Museum/Getty Images.

As the music of Christianity shifted and changed, African American Christian churches grew thanks to these migrants. Further variations on traditional African American Christian churches developed. Spiritual churches combined elements of Christianity and African-based traditions, whereby prominent figures in Christianity such as Jesus Christ were combined with new invisible forces and spirits in an effort to make meaning.

They were called spiritual churches not because of a connection to the musical form – spirituals – but because of a deep concern with the well-being of the soul. Furthermore, Islam shifted and changed in a variety of ways – giving rise to the Moorish Science Temple and the Nation of Islam, as well as significant growth in the number of African Americans who have embraced Sunni Islam.

African American traditions on the move

- The Great Migration meant the transporting of African Americans and their religious practices to new regions of the country.

Figure 1.2   Portrait of Mahalia Jackson. Courtesy of the Library of Congress, Prints and Photographs Division, Carl Van Vechten Collection [LC-USZ62-102162].

In addition, conjure, hoodoo, and other African-based religious systems also took root in big cities where African Americans tried to make sense of a changing country, and tried to create new opportunities for their involvement in this new society. The urban geography supported an increasingly diverse religious world for African Americans. And within these new areas of the country – cities like Chicago, Detroit and New York – African Americans reshaped their religious practices and beliefs to fit their new environments and the challenges as well as opportunities provided by life in these cities.

New religious leaders developed who addressed continuing discrimination against African Americans as well as the changing political and economic realities facing African Americans by offering different ways of interrupting life as part of new religious communities. For example, the Reverend Major Jealous Divine or Father Divine (1876–1965) developed a peace community called the International Peace Mission Movement that included both African Americans and white

Americans. They lived communally with the understanding that Father Divine was God in human flesh. Despite continuing financial hardships for African Americans, he taught his followers how to manage their resources as part of their spiritual development. Around the same time Father Divine gained public notice, Bishop Charles Sweet Daddy Grace (1884–1960) developed the United House of Prayer for All People. Through this church he promoted the improvement of life for African Americans by means of a range of creative doctrines and religious practices. More will be said about these religious traditions in different chapters in the book, but for now it is enough to remember that all this attention to the practices of African Americans suggests the continually evolving nature of African American religious practices. And this recognition in turn points to a diversity of opinions as well as further bringing into question any effort to define African American religion in terms of any one tradition.

In response to these changes and new developments in what and how African Americans practiced religion, scholars adjusted what they said about the nature of African American religious practices. Many – but not all – moved away from thinking about African American religion in ways that privileged Christianity; and they began to describe African American religion in terms of its function – what it did for African Americans. In their writings and lectures they began to highlight the diversity of African American religious traditions and began to give increased attention to what African Americans said about the importance of their particular practices and beliefs. Yet, a solid definition of African American religion as a general category had not developed. And efforts to highlight diversity were challenged to some degree by the visibility of African American churches in the mid-twentieth-century political struggles for equality that we call the Civil Rights Movement. The presence of African American Christian ministers on the news, quoted in newspapers, and shown on television gave Americans the impression that African American religion was African American Christian churches. The importance of churches and Christian belief in America is certain; however, this is not enough to make African American Christianity the definition of African American religion. What about all those who do not practice Christianity? Are their beliefs unimportant? The fact that African American church membership began to decline in the 1970s and 1980s after civil rights activities ebbed speaks to a need to place both those churches and their former members into a larger context of African American religious practices.

A definition of African American religion

Every time scholars have assumed a particular tradition is *the way* to define African American religion, something has occurred or been discovered to call this into question. In response, some scholars began to talk about African American religion as the primary way in which African Americans orient themselves in life in relation to however they understand god or the divine. It is the way in which they struggle with the challenges of life. While this approach it useful, it still assumes the centrality of God or gods. But what about African Americans who consider themselves religious but don't believe in God or gods? Because it is important to think of a definition for African American religion that takes into consideration as many practices and beliefs as possible without privileging any one set of beliefs or practices, this book is based on a definition of African American religion that draws from the thinking given at the start of this paragraph, but it changes it in some ways.

Here is the definition guiding this book: African American religion can be defined as the quest to make meaning out of life. In this way, African American religion serves as a primary way by which African Americans wrestle with the huge questions of life – the "who," "what," "when," "where," and "why" questions. This involves a range of ethical practices, doctrines, rituals, customs, costumes, etc. It provides beliefs and practices that help African Americans understand who they are as human beings; understand what life means within the context of our world; come to grips with where humans fits into the larger scale of the existence of life in our world; and provide answers to the questions regarding why we exist. All groups have these questions and attempt to work out solutions that invest life with meaning. The uniqueness of African American religion as this quest for life meaning is the context for the quest and the range of historical encounters and developments associated with this community. In other words, African American religion as a quest for life meaning is unique to the extent it revolves around the uniqueness of the African American experience. To be sure, there are differences in how this takes place, but African American religion involves a process by which African Americans seek to make life meaningful, how African Americans make sense of life. And it does all this while being sensitive to the history of the African presence in North America – the legacy of slavery and continued discrimination, as well as the moments of successful transformation of socio-political and economic opportunities for African Americans.

This basic effort to make life meaningful takes many forms within African American communities, and all of them have importance and impact for segments of the African American population. And they do so in light of particular social, cultural, economic, political, and psychological needs of particular groupings of African Americans. In the same way not all African Americans are alike, the ways in which they act out this desire for meaningful life will have differences. Hence, African American religion will take a variety of shapes. Diversity is a key and central element of the religious landscape of African American communities. All the various traditions mentioned in this chapter and discussed more fully in other chapters have always been important and they remain so.

African American religion

- African American religion can be defined as the effort to make life meaningful, and to do so in response to the questions we ask about our existence and the world in which we live.

Based on this general definition, some African American traditions respond to these questions by connecting human life to the will of God or gods, who creates humans and the world and to whom humans owe worship and devotion. And these gods or this God requires believers to do certain things and believe certain things – including prayer, community worship, offerings, sacrifices, and reading of sacred scriptures. Others present humans as part of a larger matrix of life in the world, and they provide practices and beliefs that are meant to create harmony between humans and the rest of nature.

For those who make life meaningful in this way, particular practices and beliefs might center on fostering better connection to the natural environment as a way to better understand what human life is all about. This might include respectful use of the natural environment through ecological work, programs, and meditation. Still others answer these basic questions of life meaning by dismissing any talk of God or gods and simply relying on science to explain human existence, what the nature of our world is, and how we should behave in the world. While these approaches are different and at times are in conflict, they all share a basic concern – making life meaningful for individuals and individuals in community. It is this common concern – not any particular doctrine or practice, not any particular tradition – that defines the basic nature of African American religion.

Using this understanding of African American religion, we are able to appreciate the similarities and differences between religious traditions in African American communities. We are able to understand the importance of traditions that more narrow definitions would cause us to omit or downplay. In this way, we are able to better appreciate the rich and complex nature of what it has meant over the years to be African American and religious.

Every tradition mentioned or discussed in this book is seeking to accomplish this one fundamental thing: answer the questions about life that cut to our very humanity and in this way give life its elemental meaning. The remaining chapters discuss the development of particular traditions and major religious issues not highlighting their doctrines and practices, but rather suggesting how these developments involve an effort to render life meaningful.

Key points you need to know

- African American religion over the years has been defined typically in terms of the beliefs and practices of a particular and dominant tradition, usually Christianity.
- Defining religion in terms of one dominant tradition leaves out recognition of the diversity and complexity of what it means to be African American and religious.
- African American religion is best understood as the process for making life meaningful.
- This process for making life meaningful is expressed in many different ways based on the differences between African Americans and their particular needs.

Discussion questions

1. What is the most common way to define African American religion?
2. What type of features are highlighted typically through this common definition of African American religion, and what features are typically ignored?
3. What difficulty is created through the common way of defining African American religion?
4. What is a more useful way of defining African American religion?

Further reading

Lincoln, C. Eric and Lawrence Mamiya. *The Black Church in the African American Experience*. Durham, NC: Duke University Press, 1990.

Mays, Benjamin E. *The Negro's God: As Reflected in His Literature*. Eugene, OR: Wipf & Stock Publishers, 2010.

Paris, Peter. *The Spirituality of African Peoples*. Minneapolis, MN: Fortress Press, 1994.

Pinn, Anthony B. *Terror and Triumph: The Nature of Black Religion*. Minneapolis, MN: Fortress Press, 2003.

Raboteau, Albert. *Slave Religion: The "Invisible Institution" in the Antebellum South*. New York: Oxford University Press, 2004.

Savage, Barbara D. *Your Spirits Walk Beside Us: The Politics of Black Religion*. Cambridge, MA: Harvard University Press, 2008.

Sernett, Milton C. *African American Religious History: A Documentary Witness*. Durham, NC: Duke University Press, 1999.

Wilmore, Gayraud S. *Black Religion and Black Radicalism: An Interpretation of the Religious History of African Americans*. Maryknoll, NY: Orbis Books, 1998.

2 Africans in the Americas

In this chapter

With a definition of African American religion in place, this chapter discusses the slave trade and the establishment of the African presence in North America. It does so through a general presentation of what is commonly called the "Middle Passage," or the mass transportation by force of enslaved Africans into the Americas. It also presents information concerning the early formation of African American communities in the North American colonies and in the subsequent United States. Attention is given, as well, to the religious sensibilities brought by enslaved Africans to the Americas as a consequence of this forced movement. The chapter also addresses the ways these sensibilities were brought into contact with practices already present in North America.

Main topics covered

- The context and reasons for the African slave trade
- The way the slave trade was conducted and the locations for it in the Americas
- The religious practices and beliefs Africans brought with them to the Americas

Why and how the African slave trade began

There is some debate over when Africans made contact with the "New World" of the Americas – by "Americas" we mean North America, Central America, South America, and the Caribbean. Some scholars argue that long before Columbus (1492) and the development of the slave trade during the sixteenth century (and lasting for roughly 350 years), Africans had already made themselves known in the Americas – with evidence for this coming from artifacts like sculptures available in locations such as Mexico. While findings to support this claim are noteworthy, most agree that the largest movement of Africans into the Americas is the result of the slave trade that forced upward of 10 million Africans into locations such as North America, Brazil and the Caribbean to serve as labor for Europeans seeking wealth through agriculture and natural resources. Although there are written records that note the presence of "black" slaves in Europe, as early as the 1300s, it is in 1444 that we find Africans transported by a Portuguese sea captain for the purpose of servitude to Portugal. Spain allowed the transporting of small numbers of enslaved Africans to colonies in the 1500s. Initially the movement of enslaved Africans during this early modern period was small. This would change as European countries recognized the great wealth that could be secured in the "New World." One thing was clear: they needed laborers to work the land and aid in the production of items such as cotton, sugar and the mining of gold in the Americas. Some attention was given to the use of Native Americans as slaves and indentured European workers who labored for a set number of years in exchange for land. Early in the development of the colonies, it was actually less expensive to use indentured servants than to purchase slaves. However, neither of these two sources of labor – Native Americans and Europeans – proved sufficient. For instance, Native Americans knew the land well and controlling them and keeping them on plantations was difficult. Furthermore, periodic wars between colonists and Native Americans only added to the difficulties. There was also a growing interest in religious work amongst them and those interested in saving their souls questioned use of them as slaves. (Africans in North America would come to have a complex relationship with Native Americans in that they at times provided aid, but it was not uncommon for Native Americans to also own slaves.) Indentured Europeans servants couldn't be physically distinguished from landowners, and this could make maintaining them as servants difficult. In addition, and more importantly, European servants did not come to the colonies in sufficient numbers to meet the labor need, and they only worked for a fixed (and often legally arranged) period of time. However, as the number of Africans brought to the Americas increased, the cost of securing them became more easily absorbed. Africans seemed a plentiful source of laborers – ones who had agricultural skills and could easily adapt to the environmental conditions found in South America, North America and the Caribbean. Nonetheless, it is important to note that not all of the first small groupings of Africans brought to North America were slaves for life. This arrangement changed as the need for and benefits associated with their labor became increasingly apparent. They were made slaves for life.

Religion provided an important rationale for this development. Readers should keep in mind that many Europeans who came to the colonies left their homes in search of religious freedom, believing that God has something special for them in the "New World." In this way, religious language and commitment provided a rationale for leaving their homeland, and for assuming the geography of the Americas was theirs to do with as they pleased. Religion, however, performed another task in that it also provided a rationale for their treatment of Native Americans and Africans. Europeans made selective use of the Bible and theological ideas about the nature of humanity to provide religious grounding for the socio-political and economic need for free labor. That is to say, religious ideas about original sin, the curse of Ham's son, and so on, provided talking points for justifying the enslavement of Africans.

The largest numbers of enslaved Africans were brought to places like Brazil and the Caribbean, but North America also received many shipments from West Africa. According to many historians, the first Africans brought to North America arrived in Virginia in roughly 1619. And although most of the enslaved Africans brought to North America worked on plantations in the Southern colonies, growing rice and tobacco, the Northern colonies in New England also received so many slaves that, by 1775, they accounted for something like 10 percent of the total population in the region. However, on most plantations the number of Africans remained relatively small, but the total number of enslaved Africans brought to North America would with time reach roughly 500,000. Those who did not secure enslaved Africans directly from slave traders tried to increase their labor force through the birth of babies by slaves.

Enslaved Africans

- Enslaved Africans from West Africa were brought to the Americas as early as the 1500s.
- The first Africans brought to the North America colonies arrived around 1619.
- The total number of enslaved Africans brought to North America during the period of slavery was roughly 500,000.
- The slave trade lasted in the Americas for roughly 350 years.

There was a great deal of money to be made in the capture and transportation of enslaved Africans to labor markets in the Americas. It was a dangerous journey, but the financial rewards for those willing to undertake this travel were substantial. The trip involved equipped ships leaving Europe. Those Africans brought to the Americas were at times sold to slave traders as prisoners of tribal wars but traders, who moved into West Africa, stole the vast majority of Africans forced into the slave trade. These traders worked their way inland as far as they could and used their firepower to subdue and control Africans who were then made to travel by foot from where they were to the coast of countries like the Gold Coast. Those that did not die along the way were placed in dungeons in coastal fortresses until they could be loaded onto ships. There could be a substantial amount of time before a ship arrived, and so due to poor conditions, some Africans who survived the walk to the dungeons would die while awaiting transport. The men, women, and children who survived this ordeal were loaded onto ships and taken away. They resisted as best they could, and some jumped out of the smaller boats that took them to the ships.

When our slaves were come to the seaside, our canoes were ready to carry them off to the longboat ... if the sea permitted, and she convey'd them aboard ship, where the men were all put in irons, two and two shackled together, to prevent their mutiny or swimming ashore. The negroes are so willful and loth to leave their own country, that they have often leap'd out of canoes, boat and ship, into the sea, and kept underwater till they were drowned, to avoid being taken up ...

(Captain Thomas Phillips as quoted in Hugh Thomas,
The Slave Trade: The History of the Atlantic Slave Trade, 1440–1870.
New York: Simon & Schuster, 1997, 404)

Still others struggled in different ways once loaded on the ships and once the ships were away from land, but subduing their captors was difficult at best.

Abroad these vessels one typically found a captain in charge of the journey; a doctor to care for the crew and the enslaved Africans; a small group of people responsible for the business records; a crew to work the ship as well as weapons to protect the boat from attack. Ship crews experienced harsh conditions and physical challenges, but this is nothing in comparison to what Africans on the ships encountered. While we do not have direct records from enslaved Africans concerning the journey, we do have historical documents from Europeans that give us some sense of what was involved. The boats were neither designed nor arranged for the comfort of enslaved Africans in that the captain's financial profit was based on the number of slaves transported. The more loaded on each ship, the greater the chance for a big payday. Male slaves were loaded below deck and typically secured to prevent them from harming the crew, or destroying the ship in order to secure their freedom. Males were positioned head to foot in order to get as many on board as possible. Women and children posed less of a threat and so they had a greater range of motion. It was assumed women and children could be overpowered should they attempt anything, and they could be controlled using whips and other tools of punishment.

The air below deck quickly became hot and the floors became littered as Africans experienced seasickness, and developed other illnesses. Their clothes would be taken away to help lessen sickness and to make cleaning them easier. Periodically, men were brought above deck for exercise in order to make certain the captain could make good money through the arrival of somewhat healthy slaves. Those who did not voluntarily dance and move around when above deck would be beaten to get them "dancing," as the crew labeled it. And those who refused to eat were forced to eat in order to maintain their strength, size, and financial potential. This forced feeding was not without damage in that the devices used to hold open their mouths could easily break teeth and cause other problems. The crew kept a careful eye on

THE AFRICANS OF THE SLAVE BARK "WILDFIRE."—[FROM OUR OWN CORRESPONDENT.]

THE SLAVE DECK OF THE BARK "WILDFIRE," BROUGHT INTO KEY WEST ON APRIL 30, 1860.—[FROM A DAGUERREOTYPE.]

Figure 2.1   Africans on the deck of the slave bark Wildfire, brought into Key West on April 30, 1860. Courtesy of the Library of Congress, Prints and Photographs Division [LC-USZ62-41678].

the slaves to make certain healthy slaves did not jump overboard or throw their small children overboard in order to end their pain and free them from the pain and terror of the "Middle Passage." Those who became ill without perceived possibility of improvement or those who died on the ship would be thrown off the ship.

The journey could take a good deal of time. But, the enslaved Africans who survived the voyage were oiled down, dressed and prepared for the slave market where they would be sold to the highest bidder and transported to plantations to begin their slave labor. On plantations and other locations of slave labor, treatment varied. However, what remained consistent was the fact that enslaved Africans were not free like European colonists. The labor they provided was too important to have slaves questioning the justification of their enslavement, and planters certainly couldn't afford to have slaves seeking freedom. One way to avoid this was to deny them the Christian faith that might spark disruptions to the colonists' way of life.

Selling slaves

The slaves are put in stalls like the pens used for cattle – a man and his wife with a child on each arm. And there's curtain, sometimes just a sheet over the front of the stall, so the bidders can't see the "stock" too soon ... Then, they pulls up the curtain, and the bidders is crowdin' around. Them in back can't see, so the overseer drives the slaves out to the platform ...

(Quoted in James Mellon, ed. *Bullwhip Days: The Slaves Remember*, New York: Weifenfeld & Nicholson, 1988, 291)

During these early years, the vast majority of colonists had limited access to religious communities; however, this was extended to enslaved Africans in that supporters of slavery assumed they did not have the intellectual ability – and perhaps not a soul – necessary to appreciate and accept the gospel message. It was recognized that part of what God wanted accomplished in the "New World" was the conversion of sinners to the Christian faith, but they weren't convinced this included their African slaves. Embedded in this thinking was a fear that efforts to convert Africans once they were in North America might also cause slaves to question their status and seek freedom.

Figure 2.2   Slave sale in Charleston, South Carolina. From a sketch by Eyre Crowe c.1856. Courtesy of the Library of Congress, Prints and Photographs Division [LC-USZ62-49867].

Attention to the souls of Africans

While some Africans in North America were free because they had either escaped slavery, purchased their freedom, or had been granted their freedom, the vast majority of Africans in North America were enslaved. Regarding those enslaved, there is a tension in the argument concerning religion: if enslaved Africans were actually meant for slavery based on the scriptures, how could efforts to address their spiritual needs alter this status? Other colonists believed that Africans might be inferior, but this did not rule out their ability to understand and embrace the Christian faith. In fact, they reasoned, colonists had an obligation to bring enslaved Africans into the Christian community. This work, however, had to take place based on an agreement that spiritual salvation did not alter the physical condition of enslaved Africans. They were to remain slaves. It was even hoped embrace of the Christian faith would make enslaved Africans better slaves because they would understand their servitude as part of God's will for their lives and the lives of their descendants.

Christians concerned with the spiritual health of enslaved Africans were not simply Protestants, but Roman Catholics as well. In fact, Roman Catholicism had a presence in the Americas as early as the 1500s, and this included Southern portions of North America where Catholic missionaries worked. More to the point, the first reported African Catholic in North America was Esteban in 1536.

> Catholic masters of course are taught that it is their duty to furnish their slaves with opportunities for being well instructed, and for practicing their religion.
>
> (Quoting William Henry Elder in Cyprian Davis, *The History of Black Catholics in the United States*, New York: Crossroads, 1991, 44)

The willingness of slaveholding Catholics to baptize slaves made their involvement in the Catholic Church more feasible, and this was particularly true in Florida. Even though this did not affect their legal status in most cases and did not involve complete involvement in the church, there is evidence of an African presence in Roman Catholicism. For example, before 1800 there was a reported 100 African Catholics in Pensacola, Florida, alone. The Catholic Church was also present in the middle colonies, in locations such as Maryland. However, travel was difficult and a limited number of priests to conduct missionary work made mass conversion of whites and Africans unthinkable. This, one might imagine, was not a situation only affecting the Catholic Church.

Although ministers were in short supply, some Protestant Christian churches put resources into the development of organizations with the purpose of taking the gospel to slaves – while mindful of the restrictions imposed by slave owners. Beginning with limited conversions in the 1660s, some effort was made to take Christianity to slaves throughout the colonies with enslaved Africans being told that a redeemed soul was worth the price of perpetual servitude. There, however, were limitations to the success of early efforts. For example, in the Northern colonies the emphasis on the Bible and reading the Bible made attention to slaves difficult in that slaves, by law, couldn't be taught to read or write. But Protestantism in those colonies assumed access to the written word. Generally speaking, the results of missionary efforts were only minimally successful because the need to safeguard slavery hampered the work of ministers.

Questions arose: how do preachers avoid harming the slave-based economy and still bring the gospel of salvation to slaves? Did the first concern contradict the second concern? In the South, efforts were also made on a limited scale to convert enslaved Africans, but these activities took place under the watchful eye of plantation owners and their staff who made certain the preachers and missionaries didn't say anything that might result in rebellion on the part of slaves. The intimate relationship between Christian churches and the system of slavery was often portrayed in graphic ways through the presence of Christian ministers who were also slaveholders. Some slave owners were willing to open their plantations to missionaries as long as their activities did not challenge their authority and the religious instruction did not involve teaching slaves to read or write. And all efforts to Christianize the slaves had to take place on the only day they weren't in the fields – Sunday. However, the fact that Sunday was their only day to take care of their own needs often made religious services that simply celebrated their enslavement less than appealing to the enslaved.

Efforts to convert slaves simply limped along without much success until there was a general change in the attitude of colonists toward their own spiritual needs. This came in the 1730s when services highlighted fiery preaching and energetically expressed concern for the saving of souls. This period, called the Great Awakening, brought people back to a strong sense of the need for personal salvation. Through the preaching of ministers such as George Whitefield (1714–1770) there was expressed an equal excitement for converting whites and Africans, and the churches felt that God could make use of anyone in this ministry who was willing to serve God. As a consequence, Baptist and Methodist churches allowed enslaved Africans (and free Africans) to preach, and on some occasions they preached to mixed audiences of whites and Africans. Sermons were passionate and straightforward in their message as black and white preachers told audiences that salvation was answer to all human problems. Whitefield and those like him captured the imagination of huge crowds – preaching the importance of salvation and the joy it provided. This was matched by warnings to those rejecting the Christian faith that they would experience the pain of hell. The passion and energy of these preachers, typically called evangelists because of their effort to convert people to Christ through energetic preaching about personal salvation, was matched by an emotional response from their listeners. The numbers of Africans in Christian churches was once small, but it exploded during the Great Awakening, with tens of thousands joining Methodist and Baptist churches. While slavery continued, within these churches there was shared worship.

The success of the Great Awakening sparked a second Great Awakening in the early 1800s, in the middle of the country, marked by large revival services. These services, led by preachers such as Charles G. Finney (1792–1875), took place over the course of days and drew those seeking salvation. The second awakening had the same energy, the same demand for surrender to God, and access to pulpits for enslaved Africans who felt called to preach. This only served to further increase the number of enslaved and free Africans involved in Christian ministry as well as the number who made their home the churches offering these services. The Great Awakenings brought enslaved Africans and free Africans (those who were not slaves) into churches but conversion did not mean social or political equality. Africans remained subject to abuse and discrimination in that they remained a necessary source of free labor.

Converting enslaved Africans

- The First Great Awakening, beginning in the 1730s, brought large numbers of enslaved Africans into the Methodist and Baptist churches.
- The Second Great Awakening was also composed of revivals and energetic camp meetings that brought colonists and Africans to the Christian faith, but this one in the 1800s took place further south.

These two Great Awakenings worked so well because the camp meetings and revivals allowed missionaries and evangelists to travel with fewer restrictions than pastors would have. It is also believed by many scholars that Methodist and Baptist practices appealed to enslaved Africans because they served as a reminder of practices going back to Africa. For example, many African religious practices involved the importance of water and water spirits. And baptism within Baptist and Methodist churches placed a similar importance on water and spiritual change resulting from being in the water. In addition, being filled with the Holy Spirit within these churches may have reminded some Africans of spirit possession they had encountered in Africa. These are just two of the reasons for the appeal of Baptist and Methodist forms of Christianity in particular. However, this argument also points to the presence of other religious traditions within the newly forming African communities in the North American colonies and later within the growing United States. It is reasonable to believe some Africans, rather than embrace practices and a religious faith offered by colonists, simply continued to practice their original religious traditions as best they could under the conditions of life in North America. Put another way, to the extent Christianity helped Africans in North America make sense of their new world, and develop meaningful life that provided answers to the major questions of life, they embraced the tradition. But this was not the case for all, and those Africans for whom Christianity did not address their concerns embraced other practices and beliefs.

What Africans brought with them

By the time Africans embraced Christianity in significant numbers during the first Great Awakening, they had been in North America for almost 100 years. We should not believe that Africans were simply waiting around for their captors to provide them with religious rituals and beliefs. These were people who had come from areas with rich and longstanding religious systems and practices, and they did not forget all they knew of these systems just because they were no longer in Africa. Memory and even limited opportunities to practice based on these memories kept traditions beyond Christianity alive.

The Middle Passage was harsh, and no real attention was given to making certain that Africans from particular cultural groups were kept together, and the ability to maintain their religious practices developed in Africa was hard. However, there is no reason to believe that the trauma of being transported to a new land, where the language is unknown and the social arrangements are foreign, was enough to wipe out *all* practices and beliefs associated with their homes in Africa. Certain things were maintained – words from their languages, artistic practices, social norms, and some elements of their religious traditions. Some religious practices and beliefs were maintained during the period of slavery because they continued to be useful and the elements necessary to keep them in place were available around plantations. For instance, in the French Quarter of New Orleans in what was known as Congo Square, Africans both free and enslaved were allowed to gather, dance, and sing. During these gatherings it was not uncommon for voodoo practices to take place as the centerpiece of the community activities, with whites present. Drumming and songs spoke to the presence of African gods. In the bayous and swamps even more of these activities took place, organized rituals conducted by voodoo priestess and priests. A creative blending of their African religious heritage and the Catholicism encountered in the colonies allowed for the growth of a rich and complex religious landscape composed of a growing African Christian presence as well as the continuation of African traditional practices from West Africa. In addition to ceremonies, small bags of dirt from the cemetery called gris-gris were believed to have particular powers for protection and good luck, and would be carried by Africans for such purposes. These bags and other charms are signs of the existence in North America of West African religious practices. Furthermore, the practice of voodoo in the United States – as attested to by these bags and ceremonies – only intensified when the revolution in Haiti freeing the island from French rule brought slaveholders and their slaves to

By means of song, news of the meeting of a voodoo society would be carried from one end of the city [New Orleans] to another and upon the appointed night Negro men and women would slip from their beds before midnight and would assemble for their ceremonies.

(Quoted in Robert Tallant. *Voodoo In New Orleans*, New York: Collier Books, 1946; Macmillan, 1971, 35)

the United States. Of course, they brought with them their religious practices and blended with those already in place.

Even efforts to end the practice of voodoo served only to force Africans to hide their practices, but attention to voodoo gods and spirits continued. In addition, with time, some of the particular elements of voodoo were lost, but specialists with recognized abilities would still be sought out by Africans in North America to provide rituals or powerful items that could be used to change their circumstances or secure something they really wanted – such as avoidance of harm by slave holders or the overseers who controlled the plantations on a day-to-day basis.

Outside Louisiana in other Southern locations such as North and South Carolina and Georgia, Africans maintained traditional practices in a somewhat looser manner through systems of magic and conjure that we often call hoodoo, root work, or simply conjure. The signs of these practices could be detected in conversation, and were also represented in items found in the possession of Africans. At times, however, practices could be maintained without a great deal of interference. In particular, the islands off the coast of the Carolinas were the home to slaves but there was a limited white presence that made them ideal locations for the preservation of African practices. Africans were able to conduct themselves in accordance with the beliefs and rituals that had marked life in Africa and they could do this without interference from whites that might find these African retentions a threat to the slave system and the dominance of white slave owners.

Signs of more than just Christianity

- Similar rituals involving water and possession by God were similar to activities in Africa and this made Methodist and Baptist churches somewhat appealing, but this also pointed to the continued presence of African religious practices despite efforts to destroy them.
- Practices similar to Vodou in West Africa are present in North America in the form of voodoo, hoodoo, conjure and root work
- Roman Catholicism's attention to saints provided a way for Africans to maintain traditions brought from Africa without slaveholders being fully aware of what they were doing.

Figure 2.3   Umar Ibn Said (ambrotype). Courtesy of Documenting the American South, the University of North Carolina at Chapel Hill Libraries.

The African gods survived the Middle Passage and found new homes in the Americas, including North America, where Africans continued their devotion, rituals, and requests to the cosmic forces they knew in Africa. But in addition to this, some enslaved and free Africans maintained another tradition brought with them from Africa. Islam had been an important religious tradition on the continent of Africa, moving from East Africa to West Africa long before the slave trade began. By the time ships loaded Africans to take them to the Americas, Islam was firmly established and it was the tradition of many on those ships. While not all of these African Muslims would have landed in North America, there is evidence that some of them did and they maintained as best they could the elements of their faith. The evidence of their presence isn't as readily available as it is for Christianity within African communities in North America, but there are signs nonetheless. For example, there were advertisements for the capture of runaway slaves that described them using Islamic names. Muslims we do know about, such as Umar Ibn Said (1770–1864) from North Carolina provided a sense of the religious practices maintained in North America.

> When I came to the Christian country, my religion was the religion of Mohammed, the Apostle of God – may God have mercy upon him and give him peace.
>
> Quoted from Umar Ibn Said's autobiography

There are five fundamental elements of Islam, referred to as the five pillars of Islam – (1) affirmation that there is only one God, Allah; (2) prayer five times each day; (3) giving of alms; (4) fasting during Ramadan; (5) pilgrimage to Mecca. Clearly, some of these could not be done because of the restrictions of slavery, but others including prayer, feast days associated with the religion, and dietary restrictions were observed.

Other Africans found all forms of theism – Christianity, Islam and African traditions – problematic. For them only attention to their own humanity without reliance on God or gods would work. Evidence for this type of thinking is found in the cultural production of the early period of slavery in things such as work songs, folktales, and the blues that critique reliance on the supernatural and instead celebrate human creativity and ingenuity. This approach to life represents the early signs of what we have come to call African American humanism.

> I prayed for twenty years but received no answer until I prayed with my legs.
>
> Frederick Douglass, abolitionist, political leader, and writer

The religious landscape

Prior to the nineteenth century, Africans both free and enslaved developed a rich and complex religious life. It was composed of humanism, Christianity, Islam, and a host of African-based traditions all meant to provide life meaning within a troubled and troubling world. Africans brought many of these traditions with them to North America and they were exposed to others once enslaved. In both cases, they made these traditions work for them; they made these practices their own and blended them in ways meant to meet their particular needs and address their concerns. It was easier for African-born slaves, who did not know English but communicated in indigenous African languages, to maintain African practices and pass elements of these traditions to their children. However, North American-born slaves, who spoke English and were familiar with the North American context, were further removed from African practices. When they maintained them, they did so in ways that reflected their new location. In all cases, however, they thought about religion in light of their needs and tried to shape practices and beliefs so as to fit their circumstances. Some of this involved holding onto what they could remember and maintain of their African home, but it also involved a creative manipulation of what they discovered in their new land. We see some of this developing during the 1600s and 1700s, but it is within the 1800s – the nineteenth century – that the practice of these traditions really grows amongst Africans and takes on unique and creative aspects and dimensions. Efforts to control how, where, and when Africans practiced their various faiths failed. And they failed in large part as Africans shaped their own versions of religion and used it as an increasingly visible tool for struggle against oppression. In the next chapter, we explore some of the major episodes in this on-going development of what it means to be African American and religious in North America, and we do so through attention to the more secret activities of Africans within the context of what we call hush arbor meetings and the Invisible Institution.

Key points you need to know

- Both Catholics and Protestants participated in efforts to Christianize enslaved Africans.
- Successful Christianizing of Africans takes place in large part because of two religious Great Awakenings.
- African gods were brought to the Americas, and there are reports concerning voodoo in North America that date back to the 1700s.
- Africans brought Islam to North America, and there are clear indicators of its presence.
- Religious conversion did not affect the status of Africans because they remained slaves.
- Some Africans rejected theism altogether and instead relied on an approach to life centered on human creativity and ingenuity.
- Diversity defines the religious landscape of African life prior to the nineteenth century.

Discussion questions

1. Why did some slaveholders oppose efforts to convert Africans to Christianity?
2. What were the reasons provided by those who were interested in missionary work amongst enslaved Africans?
3. Why did Methodist and Baptist churches appeal to Africans?
4. What are some of the signs of Islam's presence in North America?
5. What were some of the early practices in North America related to African gods?

Further reading

Allen, Norm Jr. *African American Humanism: An Anthology*. Buffalo, NY: Prometheus Books, 1991.

Austin, Allan D. *African Muslims in Antebellum America: Transatlantic Stories and Spiritual Struggles*. New York: Routledge, 1997.

Balmer, Randall and Lauren Winner. *Protestantism in America*. New York: Columbia University Press, 2002.

Davis, Cyprian. *The History of Black Catholics in the United States*. New York: Crossroads, 1991.

Holloway, Joseph E., ed. *Africanisms in American Culture*. Bloomington, IN: Indiana University Press, 1990.

Pitts, Walter F. *Old Ship of Zion: The Afro-Baptist Ritual in the African Diaspora*. New York: Oxford University Press, 1993.

Tallant, Robert. *Voodoo in New Orleans*. New York: Collier Books, 1946; Macmillan, 1971.

Turner, Richard. *Islam in the African-American Experience*. Bloomington, IN: Indiana University Press, 1997.

3 Beginnings of African American religion

In this chapter

This chapter explores ways in which enslaved Africans combined various activities and sensibilities in open practices as well as in secret gatherings referred to as "hush arbor" meetings. Because Chapter 4 addresses the nineteenth century, this chapter is more concerned with developments during the seventeenth and eighteenth centuries. The goal of this chapter is to present the early formation of the unique African American religious landscape, and to do so by giving attention to the process by which enslaved and free Africans reshaped religious traditions to meet their particular needs.

Main topics covered

- What scholars assume took place within secret meetings
- The impact of secret meetings on the diversity of the religious practices of Africans
- The efforts of slaveholders to expose and destroy these secret meetings
- The importance of these secret meetings for later religious developments

Africans under surveillance

In previous chapters, we discussed religion as a quest for life meaning, an effort to give life meaning. And, we discussed the roots of the diversity of African American religious traditions in North America. In exploring that diversity most of our attention was turned to what Africans brought with them and what they received within their new context, and new arrangements of communal life. This chapter begins our consideration of what Africans did with all this religious material, and it centers on how they shaped it into something uniquely their own prior to the nineteenth century. We will call this the beginning of African American religion. This is not to say Africans had no religious practices prior to this point. They certainly did – as was shown in the first two chapters. Instead, calling this the beginning of African American religion is meant to mark out and highlight the time during which and the locations where Africans began to shape in significant ways these borrowed and owned religious practices in ways that spoke to their new situation. And we discuss this beginning of African American religion through attention to what they accomplished when whites weren't supervising them. But to understand the importance of the secrecy surrounding those activities, it is important to first give attention to the many efforts to monitor the thinking and activities of enslaved Africans.

The system of slavery – the "peculiar institution" as it was called – required continual observation of Africans to make certain their behavior did not threaten the system of free labor upon which so much of the North American economy was based. And the need to observe and control only increased as the size of the slave population grew and as opposition to slavery in some quarters became more vocal. To accomplish this, there were nightly patrols composed of whites that volunteered for the duty. These patrols searched the woods and road to make certain slaves were not wandering around.

> Owners dictated where and how the slaves lived, how they worked and played, and with whom they associated. Slaves learned this fact early in their lives, and their owners never allowed them to forget it.
>
> (Quoted in Ira Berlin et al. *Remembering Slavery*, New York: The New Press, 1998, 3)

Every movement during daylight hours (and after dark) required slaves to carry passes from the owner of the plantation indicating that he or she was authorized to be off the plantation for a period of time. Punishment for being off the plantation without permission could be severe, including the lashing of a slave's back, the loss of a limb, or being sold away from friends and all that was familiar.

> If we went off without a pass we allus went two at a time. We slipped off when we got a chance to see young folks on some other place. The patterrollers cotched me one night and, Lawd have mercy me, they stretches me over a log and hits thirty-nine licks with a rawhide loaded with rock, and every time they hit me the blood and hide done fly. The drove me home to massa and told him ...
>
> (Quoting a former slave, in Ira Berlin et al. *Remembering Slavery*, New York: The New Press, 1998, 173)

Figure 3.1   'The Lash' – card showing bound African American slave being whipped. By H. L. Stephens c. 1863. Courtesy of the Library of Congress, Prints and Photographs Division [LC-USZ62-41839].

Drastic punishment was meant to deter slaves from trying to escape. In addition, overseers on plantations would monitor the activities of slaves to make certain they were in line with the wants of the slave owner. Those found guilty of poor behavior, including inadequate work performance, were punished.

There were also laws in place that limited the ability of slaves to meet in a group, and this was meant to prevent them from having opportunities to plot revolts and rebellions. Overseers would also make use of willing slaves called "drivers" who – in exchange for privileges or items like additional food or treats – made sure work was completed and who also at times served as spies in the slave quarters, reporting back on the conversations and actions of their fellow slaves. Planters at times would undertake surveillance on their own by sneaking around the slave quarters, paying attention to what was being done and said inside the thin-walled slave cabins. It was also common for slaveholders and their agents to ask young slaves about the happenings in the cabins, but all slave children were trained early to give little direct information to whites about the activities of adult slaves. Hence, not even children could be easily tricked into providing information that would cause adult slaves physical harm. Without doubt, the serious nature of secrecy and the importance of these private meetings were impressed upon slaves of all ages. But even without a consistent ability to gather information, slaveholders knew that slaves weren't happy, and they took every precaution to prevent them from acting out of this discontent in ways that would damage the slave system. There was reason to fear, however, that enslaved Africans acted out against the system of slavery in all the ways available to them – slowing down work, destroying tools, running away, and harming whites through poisoning them for instance. Related to this, planters and their families feared voodoo, conjure, and hoodoo because these religious practices might be used to cause harm to whites, and they tried to prevent this by attempting to stop the practice of these religious activities to the extent possible. Despite such efforts, on many occasions Africans sought the assistance of root workers and conjurers to gain assistance in securing freedom, or in punishing whites for actions they'd taken against that slave.

Slaveholders did not want Africans on their plantations gaining any type of power – real or imagined – that might allow them to gain the upper hand and damage the control whites had over them. And while some hoped Christianity would make slaves more content with their plight, others realized spiritual health might foster a desire for physical freedom. It made sense to them to bring slaves into the Christian faith, but their practice of that faith had to conform to acceptable standards. With respect to Catholicism, there was a general concern that Catholics gave greater allegiance to the Pope than to the political leaders of the colonies and the United States. Whites believed this was the case amongst them and that African Catholics might pose an even greater problem. Furthermore, Islam was foreign to whites and as a result it met with suspicion whenever it surfaced – despite claims that African Muslims made for good and disciplined workers. Things unfamiliar remained a source of fear and prompted a desire to monitor and control them. After all, rebellions and revolts had been reported amongst slaves long before the nineteenth century that re-enforced for white slaveholders the need to maintain a vigilant watch. But slaves and free Africans made use of the inconsistencies and shortcomings in the slave system and its protective devices, and worked these defects to their advantage.

Techniques for surveillance

- Written passes were required for Africans when moving between plantations.
- Overseers used Africans as spies to report on what took place in slave quarters on the plantations.
- Africans were not allowed to have meetings of more than a couple of people without whites present.
- Certain religious practices were prohibited.
- Severe punishment and whippings were used to enforce the system of slavery.

The religious landscape was diverse, but the most significant tradition numerically within African life in North America was probably Protestant Christianity. Its growth was based on an agreement between preachers, missionaries and the slave system: nothing would be said or done with slaves that would call into question the correctness of their servitude. This meant only select scriptures from the Bible could be a part of Christian education for Africans – only those passages that supported slavery such as the famous "slaves, obey your earthly masters with fear, trembling, and sincerity, as when you obey the Messiah," drawn from Ephesians 6:5 in the New Testament. Preachers gave sermons based on these sorts of principles. In other cases, slaves would be invited to Bible studies, etc., led by slaveholders to make certain the proper message was provided.

> They always tell the slaves dat if he be good, an' worked hard fo' his master, dat he would go to heaven, an' dere he gonna live a life of ease. They ain' never tell him he gonna be free in Heaven. You see, they didn't want slaves to start thinkin' 'bout freedom, even in Heaven.
>
> (Quote from a former slave in Ira Berlin et al. *Remembering Slavery*, New York: The New Press, 1998, 192)

On top of this, enslaved Africans, as was mentioned earlier, were not allowed to read and write and this was to keep them from reading the Bible for themselves and coming away with different – slavery questioning – interpretations. Outside religion, this restriction also prevented enslaved and free Africans from writing passes and other documents that would allow them to escape. In addition to controlling the content of the Protestant faith presented, the slave system also put in place opportunities for surveillance. For instance, slaves were not to have religious services without whites present in the room. The slave owner might pay someone to attend and monitor the content of such services. The cost was worth it to slave owners because this observation was to prevent anyone from preaching a version of Christianity that increased the slaves' sense of themselves as equal to their masters and consequently as having this increased sense of self-importance encourage plotting against their masters. This surveillance also prevented these church gatherings from serving as a smokescreen for meetings that really involved schemes to do harm to whites through escape or destruction of plantations. It goes without saying that slaveholders also favored preachers they believed were clearly on their side and encouraged ministers who would preach the type of gospel message that made plantations safe and productive for whites. Corresponding to this preaching, slaveholders who believed themselves to be Christians did not oppose preaching that required them to treat slaves with some compassion in light of the demands of the gospel of Christ, but this shouldn't be taken so far as to suggest any type of equality.

There was a delicate balance between the spiritual health of enslaved Africans and the preservation of their status as slaves. Slave owners understood this balance could only be preserved through careful observation and unsparingly and rigorously enforced rules, combined of course with a slavery-friendly type of religion.

Religion when whites aren't looking

Christianity

It is important to remember that both Africans and Europeans in North America brought cultures (including religious sensibilities) with them, and over the course of time they exchanged elements of these cultures. So there were Europeans from various locations – even those in the British colonies of North America came from different areas of Great Britain – and Africans from a variety of regions of West Africa and representing a variety of cultural worldviews. In addition to this, both Africans and Europeans encountered cultural worlds endemic to the Americas. All this is to say North America was not a blank cultural slate, but rather there were people populating this portion of the globe with their preferred ways of making life meaning. In important ways, how Africans worked through these cultural materials, including religious options, took place in the public life of plantations and in urban areas as well. However, some of this work, and a great deal of the religious work, also took place in more secluded and private spaces of life.

Although an effort was made to control the activities of enslaved Africans, this could not be accomplished fully. For example, while laws prohibited teaching slaves to read or write, a small percentage of them did gain some abilities in these two areas either from sympathetic whites who worked against the formal rules, or by tricking whites into teaching them bits and pieces of their spelling books. Those who could read and/or write even in a limited way would share these abilities with others. On plantations approximate to wooded areas, slaves would sneak away late evenings and they would hold informal schools where basic lessons were taught. It remained key, however, that slaves who could read and write or were learning to do so in these informal schools did not let slaveholders know about their skills. Doing so put them at risk of severe punishment or death. The same level of secrecy was used with respect to slaves practicing creative versions of Christianity.

Slaves attended public and monitored services both with whites and in services organized exclusively for slaves. Yet, late evenings and during time away from work on Sundays, holidays, and sometimes on Saturdays when they weren't forced to work the full day, the enslaved would get to themselves and develop religious practices and beliefs more in keeping with their perspective on slavery as unjustified and in light of their deep desire to preserve their personhood despite the violence of the slave system. For example, slaves would hold Christian worship services in their quarters

Figure 3.2   African American prayer meeting in a log cabin – 1800s (woodcut, nineteenth century). © North Wind Picture Archives / Alamy.

and would protect themselves from observation through the use of buckets of water into which worshippers would speak to capture sounds and keep loud noises from getting away from them.

When not in their quarters, slaves often went deep into the woods to what were referenced as "hush arbors" to conduct religious services free from the restrictions in place when whites were present. (For slaves living in cities, secret meetings could take place in root cellars, for example, as opposed to the woods.) Coded announcements of these secrets meetings could be spread to enslaved Africans and free Africans through song. For example, "Go Down Moses" could be sung as code for the announcement of a meeting to take place in the slave quarters, or in the woods.

Out in the woods and the swamps they would gather after alerting each other in covert ways of the meeting, and after indicating the location for the secret service by leaving subtle signs only the most observant would notice. However, they also made an effort to move far enough into the swamps and woods to avoid slave patrol parties that were reluctant to go in that deep because of the animals and other dangers they might encounter. Yet, just in case, enslaved Africans might also hang wet blankets from the trees to absorb the sounds of their meetings, and keep it from attracting the attention of whites. The dangers in the swamps, snakes and other creatures, paled in comparison to what they gained from the time together away from whites. These hush arbor religious meetings would allow them some opportunity to speak their mind without punishment. In these secret services, slaves would preach a different version of the gospel, one that highlighted God's desire that they be freed. These sermons were also laced with calls for justice and righteousness, and with a critique of slaveholders who claimed to be Christians but yet treated other humans – Africans – as less than human. How was this consistent with the gospel's call for love? It was also within these secret meetings that Christian slaves developed the spirituals – a unique form of American music developed by slaves that told biblical stories and spoke of their desire for salvation and physical freedom. The spirituals are still with us, and they have influenced more recent musical developments such as gospel music. These meetings, of course, would not have been approved had they been known by slaveholders and their overseers because of the potential for revolt at worst, or the mere fact that keeping late hours would hamper their work performance at the other end of the spectrum of concern. If discovered by slave patrols, those gathered – particularly the preacher – would receive a beating or worse depending on what the patrol heard or saw taking place. The simple way to put it is this: the more threatening the activity, the more severe the punishment.

This is an opportunity to emphasize the preacher within the Christian communities forming within these secret meetings. Slave preachers had an important status, and whether they could read or not (and not is most likely the case) they were relied on to interpret the scriptures in a way that rang true to those listening. In addition, they led prayers, baptized new believers, and led others to Christian fellowship as well as oversaw rituals meant to mark all the major happenings in the lives of slaves. In short, they served as a primary means by which slaves processed the Christian faith. But how were they selected, and upon what was their authority based? It was commonly the case that slave preachers became religious leaders because they expressed a call to preach, but to be successful they also had to have demonstrated ability as a preacher as well as a general talent for leadership. That is to say, their preaching had to inspire reaction; it had to ring true, and it had to offer hope. When preaching a sermon, it was common for those listening to speak their agreement through shouts of "amen," "preach," or other words of encouragement. This practice continues beyond the period of slavery and we refer to it as the "call and response" tradition. Preachers, through their demonstrated talents, had to gain the confidence of fellow slaves but also be wise enough to avoid the suspicion of slaveholders and their agents. In these meetings, slaves could listen to their own preachers, people they recognized as being called by God to preach, and what they heard was meant for their advancement as opposed to encouraging contentment with servitude. And it is within the context of these meetings, within these early Christian communities, that the role of the preacher is refined prior to the more public presence of black preachers in the nineteenth century.

Some of the activities taking place in these secret gatherings were also done in modified form in open services. One example is the "ring shout," which is rhythmic movement in a circle, taking place during a service. While outsiders might mistake it for dancing, the ring shout didn't qualify as such for participants because the slaves did not cross their feet. (To dance, from the perspective of many Christians, would have involved sin.) Those involved in the "ring shout" would gather, and some would sing a spiritual or some type of song considered appropriate for the occasion, and they would keep time with the music by patting their hands. The others would remove any obstacles and form a circle. They would begin moving in that circle consistent with the music, and they would continue to speed up the movement of the circle of people until Christians in the circle began to feel the spirit of God. They would keep singing, clapping, and moving until eventually everyone in the circle would "catch the spirit."

> Us ... used to have a prayin' ground down in the hollow and sometime we come out of the field, between 11 and 12 at night, scorchin' and burnin' up with nothin' to eat, and we wants to ask the good Lawd to have mercy. He puts grease in a snuff pan or bottle and make a lamp. We takes a pine torch, too, and goes down in the hollow to pray. Some gits so joyous they starts to holler loud and we has to stop up they mouth.
>
> (Quote from a former slave in Ira Berlin et al. *Remembering Slavery*, New York: The New Press, 1998, 197–198)

Those who participated believed it was only through the ring shout that people could fully praise God, and it was only through the energy of the ring shout that sinners could be called to salvation. People would move in and out of the circle, shuffling until the spirit of God made them shout, and this process could go on for the better part of the night and early morning. However, it had to end before their absence would be detected and they were late for the morning call to the fields. Nonetheless, times of worship during those secret meetings gave enslaved and free Africans opportunity to connect their religious practices to a desire for physical freedom.

There was some carry over between hush arbor meetings and public services. Outside these secret meetings, slaveholders might observe energetic movement in services held for slaves, but they thought little of it. If anything it appeared an odd but relatively harmless activity that did nothing to question the system of slavery and the dominance of whites over life in their communities. They might not like the ring shout but this was because of the emotion involved, not because it gave some indication of any involvement in a real plot against them. But even the spirituals, for those who listened closely, called into question the injustice experienced by enslaved Africans.

Constituting an early unique mode of North American music, the spirituals drew on the musical practices of the Methodists and Baptists who made some inroads with respect to the conversion of slaves, and blended this with African sensibilities and stylistic elements such as beats and rhythms. In this music, through the lyrics and the movement of their bodies, slaves wrestled with the Bible – read themselves into the stories of the Children of Israel and understood themselves, like the Jews, to be the chosen of God who would one day experience freedom. For white slave owners, the songs were haunting, and they might even request certain songs be sung, not knowing that the songs they requested raised questions concerning the system of slavery. It was not until the nineteenth century that slave holders became somewhat aware of the ability of slaves to use music to communicate subversive messages, but prior to that the larger concern for the slaveholder tended to be overseers avoiding any work slowdowns due to singing that was too energetic or continued for too long. Only through the secrecy of private gatherings did the full impact of the ring shout and the spiritual songs as a source of personhood and contact with God come out.

Ain't gonna let nobody turn me "roun"

I promised the lord that I would hold out
Hold out
I promised the Lord that I would hold out
Wait until my change comes.

(Lyrics from a spiritual song)

The ability for one set of words – the lyrics of the spirituals for example – to have more than one meaning involves a process we have come to call "double-talk" or "signifying" by which slaves could say something that contained a critique of slaveholders and the slave system, but those listening thought they heard something much less harmful in the meaning. These songs could be used to tell a different version of the Christian faith, one in which the slaves are made free. In other cases, the songs could be used to simply warn other slaves that an overseer or owner of the plantation was nearby. In either case, whites might hear the song but not fully grasp the way it was functioning in that context. This "double-talk" had other implications. For example, slaves often believed that it was not always sinful to steal things. For example, it was not sinful to furtively take food from slave owners, but it was sinful to take things from other enslaved or free Africans. They reasoned that slaveholders were sinning by making African slaves, and therefore anything slaves did to make their lives tolerable had to be justified. Furthermore, "double-talk" also involved re-envisioning shared concepts. For example, slaves weren't the only Christians who expressed a desire for heaven, or for changed life circumstances; they weren't the only ones who claimed to represent the new people of God. In fact, the establishment of the initial North American colonies was based on the assumption that the colonists are the people of God who, like the Jews, had been given a new land. However, when slaves sang of heaven, they meant not only spiritual closeness to God. They were also expressing a desire for physical freedom as being tied to spiritual freedom. Finally, the "double-talk" extended to include the very reasons enslaved Africans embraced the Christian faith in significant numbers during the eighteenth century. For some, it was a matter of genuine conversion and a belief that the Christian faith was best for them. Others embraced it because doing so might lessen the demands of labor by providing time away for religious services and revivals. Along these lines, it also provided a pragmatic way to gain some control over their circumstances: if whites had power and were Christians, perhaps, some enslaved Africans reasoned, becoming a Christian would expose slaves to this same power.

Before moving on, it is important to provide a bit more information concerning our understanding how religion functioned with respect to double-talk and in relationship to surveillance. While many of the songs and religious practices of slaves were about physical freedom couched in the language of spiritual health, this wasn't the case in all circumstances. It would be a mistake to assume all materials should be read this way. For some slaves, spiritual salvation was enough, and their circumstances on earth were considered temporary and not deserving of much attention. Heaven would be their reward regardless of their lot on earth. Scholars typically consider the first perspective – physical freedom and spiritual health – as a "this-worldly orientation" and the latter – spiritual salvation is enough – is referenced as an "other-worldly orientation." Both have had adherents, and both would find expression as the slaves gave more visible expression to their covert religious activities and beliefs. There were a few who made public their disregard for the system of slavery and the incompatibility of slavery and the Christian gospel. They met with resistance. In addition, they gained the ire of slavery sympathizers by framing religion as being against slavery. This had limited consequence apart from some minor revolts, some attempted escapes, and a call for greater surveillance by slave owners. However, taking such a public stance could be bad for one's health – resulting in severe punishment if not death. Mindful of this, it was more likely that slaves and free Africans would be more careful and less public, in most cases, in their challenges to slavery and their use of Christianity to critique and hopefully compromise the "peculiar institution."

These secret Christianity-based meetings taking place prior to the nineteenth century gave shape to what scholars call the "Invisible Institution" – the early form of African American churches. Within these meetings, slaves began to perfect elements that have come to define institutionalized African American Christianity: the sermonic style of the African American preacher; the musical tradition of the spirituals that eventually gave raise to various gospel genres; styles of worship including possession by the Holy Spirit promoting unique bodily movement, and interaction between worship leaders and the audience known as "call and response"; the African American prayer tradition; and, a particular understanding of the Bible that places slaves in the position of God's chosen people to whom freedom (at times understood spiritually and at other times understood physically) will come. And while we must wait until the nineteenth century for significant representations of independent churches for free and enslaved Africans in North America, as early as the eighteenth century there are examples of the "Invisible Institution" becoming visible. In the North, in Philadelphia, Pennsylvania, a group of free Africans formed a religious meeting. These particular African Methodists had up until 1787 participated in services at St. George's Methodist Church. However, racism at the church became unbearable and they left to form their own worship opportunities. Within a short period of time, they established a religious organization called Mother Bethel African Methodist Episcopal Church. This denomination took shape in 1816, and according to many scholars it was formed roughly three years after the Union Church of Africans (African Union Church) denomination, in 1813. The "African" in the name African Methodist Episcopal Church was meant to speak loudly about the links of its members to their African heritage. This was a statement of pride and history in a context where all things of African descent were considered inferior. "Methodism" connected the denomination to the larger Methodist Church coming out of England and associated with John and Charles Wesley. And, "Episcopal" meant the church had a hierarchy run by bishops. Further south, black Baptist churches would begin to emerge in the mid-eighteenth century with Silver Bluff Church (1775) in South Carolina typically considered the first of these Baptist churches, although there were others formed in places like Kentucky and Virginia. These churches, however, weren't entirely free during the eighteenth century in that whites in their supervisory roles typically arranged management and appointment of ministers for those congregations. And in some areas of the country, laws were put in place that prohibited the ability of Africans to construct places of worship for fear they would be used to organize violent revolt. Despite this, in other locations these churches emerged in the form of prayer houses authorized by slaveholders. Nonetheless, these early independent churches put in place the building blocks for what would become the most significant Christian denominations within African American communities. And by the turn of the century, the impact of organized religion on African communities in North America was certain. Some scholars argue that churches with mixed congregations of whites and Africans had a degree of equality not found outside the context of church community. For example, enslaved and free Africans within these churches could hold whites accountable for their spiritual shortcomings and could exercise some leadership within these churches based on a sense of spiritual equality. However, this does not necessarily mean that this sense of equality extended beyond the doors of the church, nor did this situation replace a desire on the part of many slaves and free Africans to create spaces of worship that they controlled and that were geared exclusively to their particular needs. It became quite clear that independent African churches, combined with a growing number of other organizations such as mutual aid societies and Masonic lodges, provided infrastructure for communal life. However, the reach of religious concern and development during the eighteenth century extended beyond North America.

The disruption of the Revolutionary war and its aftermath resulted in some colonists loyal to Great Britain relocating to the Caribbean and establishing Christian ministries there. As early as the 1780s there was some movement of Africans to Canada to preach and establish churches in places like Nova Scotia. More pressing for some, though, was a concern for Africans on the continent of Africa. Shouldn't they receive the gospel of Christ? Wasn't that the responsibility of their kin who'd been taken away to North America? Many of these churches and organizations held an interest in the continent of Africa and some expressed this through a desire to send representatives to West Africa who would spread the Christian faith and other cultural and social mechanisms they'd come to know in North America. This concern for Africa would grow in the nineteenth century to constitute a widely recognized movement – worked on by whites and Africans – to return Africans to Africa. There were a variety of reasons for this, of course. Some whites wanted to simply remove Africans once their usefulness was questionable. Others saw it as part of a responsibility to spread Christianity and civil forms of government to the continent of Africa.

Humanism

Not all the songs sung by slaves were about their commitment to the Christian faith. There were also secular songs that championed human activity and found the meaning of life not in worship of God but in the fulfillment of human potential and the securing of human wants as individuals and within the context of communities. These songs became part of the language of slaves and their descendants who embraced humanism as their primary life orientation. Some of the more popular and long-lasting examples of this more humanistic genre of music during the period of slavery are work songs, the field holler and then the blues. Work songs developed as enslaved Africans expressed through music their plight and discussed the joys and sorrows of a life filled with labor for the benefit of others.

And, the blues, we tend to mistakenly think about in relationship to the twentieth century and the production of "race records" which were recordings of blues tunes by some of the more popular singers of the period. They were called race records because they were primarily for distribution to African Americans. Although important, these records do not constitute the beginning of a blues tradition. The documentation of the blues through sheet music and later records speaks to the evolution of the blues, but not the origins of the blues. As many scholars note, in the same way we cannot

Shuck that corn before you eat

Caller:	All dem purty gals will be dar
Chorus:	Shuck dat corn before you eat.
Caller:	They will fix it for us rare
Chorus:	Shuck dat corn before you eat.
Caller:	I know dat supper will be big
Chorus:	Shuck dat corn before you eat.
Caller:	I think I smell a fine roast pig,
Chorus:	Shuck dat corn before you eat.
Caller:	I hope dey'll have some whisky dar,
Chorus:	Shuck dat corn before you eat.
Caller:	I think I'll fill my pockets full
Chorus:	Shuck dat corn before you eat.

(Slave Work Song http://www.history.org/history/teaching/)

accurately date the emergence of the spirituals, we do not know the exact time when the work songs and blues are first created. And, as is the case with the spirituals, most of our examples were recorded post slavery, after the civil war. Both of these musical forms – one theistic and the other a critique of many theistic claims – emerged early and were intertwined as the blues drew some of their nature from the spirituals, but their content was more clearly related to the thematic structures of work songs and field hollers (used to establish the rhythm of fieldwork and performed as individuals whereas the work songs might be sung by groups of workers). One can go further and say that as the spirituals were developed and refined in the context of secret meetings, there were likely other meetings unknown to slave holders and overseers during which the work songs and blues were also developed and refined. Not every slave had the musical talent necessary to develop and perform the spirituals and the blues. Both involved a degree of creativity as the spirituals and blues rehearse episodes in the daily activities of slaves, and only those songs that spoke best to the wants, needs, and beliefs of the slaves survived. In both cases, the goal was to express musically the content of and challenges to a meaningful life. And, the blues and the spirituals are performed in ways that require the active use of the body; whether to keep time through clapping or other movements to accent the lyrics and music, or as the subject of the song – the enslaved African's body and its plight received attention in the music as it did in the slave preachers' secret sermons. In some cases, this attention tied Africans to a Christian god, and in other cases it tied Africans more closely to humanity without any real concern for anything more than that. The latter points in the direction of those we would come to call African American humanists and the African American humanism they practiced – an approach to life that centers *not* on trans-historical beings but on human reason and human activity.

African-based traditions in North America

There was movement between religious traditions in slave communities and there was a blending of traditions to the extent the basic concern was the fostering of a better sense of themselves and a greater life meaning over and against strict attention in most cases to orthodoxy. This willingness to draw from particular traditions was present in Africa and continued as one of the mindsets found within the descendants of the first generation of African slaves.

The written record concerning these traditions is small in comparison to what is available regarding Christianity, yet it is safe to say that Christianity was not the only tradition spreading roots, so to speak, in the years prior to the nineteenth century. And while Christianity did not necessarily promote closeness to the earth, other traditions practiced by Africans did. Weeds, berries, herbs and other items grown around the plantations and readily available in the woods were used to get rid of headaches, deal with animal bites, and ease other pains and aches. Use of these items for these medical purposes could be undertaken in full view of slave owners and overseers, and at times these whites would request use of the herbal knowledge of slaves to fix their problems. However, items found in nature were also used away from the gaze of whites for more subversive purposes. For example, it was also during these secret gatherings that slaves maintained practices such as conjure and hoodoo. For example, Roman Catholicism in places in the Americas allowed enslaved and free Africans to maintain their allegiance to certain African gods because they resembled Catholic saints. That is to say, some enslaved Africans would hide their interests in African gods through a turn to Catholic saints with similar abilities and outlook. Enslaved Africans could mask their African practices behind the saints and avoid detection of their true intent and purposes. For instance, Shango, a Nigerian god, is associated with lightning and the color red, and Saint Barbara for Catholics is also associated with lightning and fire, and images of her depict her wearing red. Her relationship to artillery also linked Saint Barbara for some Africans to Shango who is associated with battle. The difference in gender wasn't important because it was believed cosmic power isn't restricted to any particular gender. Although slave society – as controlled and promoted by slave holders – feared the practice of African traditions and worked to prevent it in many cases, enslaved and free Africans could maintain their allegiance to the belief in and rituals associated with gods like Shango by associating them with Catholic saints. In the woods, or other secluded areas, slaves could practice these traditions and use them to inflict harm on oppressive whites – to get even as best they could with those who abused them. A good number of enslaved Africans continued to practice versions of the religious traditions associated with their ancestors in Africa. Hush arbor meetings provided an opportunity to refine and spread these traditional practices and beliefs, and through these efforts African-based traditions move from the early years of slavery to the nineteenth century in discernable and definable ways.

Secret meetings

- Were used by slaves to teach each other to read and write.
- Slaves also used these meetings to plot against the system of slavery through the hatching of escape plans.
- Involved energetic worship in the form of the ring shout.
- Slave preachers gave sermons that critiqued slavery and promoted freedom as part of God's plan for slaves.
- A form of music called the spirituals was refined in these meetings and also served as a way to announce upcoming meetings, and also to warn slaves of approaching whites.
- African-based traditions such as voodoo were practiced with greater attention to protecting slaves from whites as well as helping them secure power needed to escape.

Although we typically think of New Orleans when considering these African-based practices, it is more accurate to say such traditions had adherents well beyond Louisiana, most notably in areas where there were more slaves than whites. This difference in population allowed for less observation from overseers and for more interaction between slaves. When most complex, there was more than magic involved in these traditions; there was recognition of a host of gods and spirits including ancestors who exercised some concern with and influence over human activities. And through the use of proper items and proper rituals, these spirits could be convinced to provide aid or to harm one's enemies. Both whites and Africans were aware of these practices, and spoke both privately and publicly about the ways in which this magic could help and harm, which made necessary the exercise of care and clear attention to the signs that hoodoo or conjure had been worked. Such practices reflected an African world view; but, as the fear of witches by Europeans in North America through these early centuries would suggest, there was also something about these hoodoo and conjure, or voodoo and root work practices that spoke to a system of magic also familiar to Europeans. While conjure or voodoo and witchcraft as understood by Europeans were not the same, they all pointed to a sense of power lodged in the natural environment that could be manipulated for good or harm. There are ways in which this attention to magic might have been further supported by similar beliefs held by Native Americas in the surrounding areas where "medicine" drawn from the natural environment was used to provide aid or harm. Secret organizations would form as a way to bring together adherents to these various practices, and to provide the rituals necessary to bring others into the traditions. If nothing else, these secret groups helped to preserve these traditions in a land where there was often hostility toward them. Such practices and structures begin to develop beforehand, but it is in the nineteenth century that they gain impressive structure.

Figure 3.3   Louisiana planter showing a voodoo charm to apprehensive plantation workers (engraving, 1886). © World History Archive / Alamy.

Conjurers and others working within the context of these African-based traditional practices gained stature (as either famous or infamous) with time, as both whites, free and enslaved Africans heard stories – and had personal encounters – with their knowledge and power. However, this is not to suggest that there was no conflict between Christians and practitioners of conjure, hoodoo, and voodoo. To the contrary, Christians were at least rhetorically opposed to these practices, labeling them backwards if not demonic in nature. If Christianity provided salvation, they reasoned, what good purpose was there behind the use of these non-Christian activities? If the Bible was a book full of information that brought about the welfare of believers to the extent its lessons were taken to heart, of what real benefit could one find in roots, herbs, and other mundane items? If the preacher was called by God and had answers to life's pressing questions and concerns, of what importance was the root worker or conjurer? These questions point to the type of pressure that made important covert practices of and conversation concerning these traditions. Such pressure wasn't consistent in that some of those Christians who publicly denounced conjure and hoodoo privately sought out the assistance of these root doctors and conjurers. To say the least, we must acknowledge that there was tension and paradox in the public conversation and private response to these practices.

Islam

In some areas, such as Florida and French Louisiana, the historical record indicates the presence of Islamic communities. As historian Michael Gomez notes, as of the eighteenth century, there is a substantial group of Muslims in St. Augustine, Florida. Whereas these locations – Florida and Louisiana – housed communities able to maintain certain connections to the practices and beliefs of Islam, other groups in Virginia for example, claimed a historical and ideological connection to an early Muslim presence in the colonies. Information concerning such communities is rather limited.

Ultimately, Christians and practitioners of these other theistic traditions all recognized that the world was a complex place, layered with various forces and powers that have bearing on human existence. Whether through prayer and commitment to the requirements of Christ, or through careful and knowledgeable engagement with forces through rituals reflecting their African past, enslaved and free Africans in North America attempted to produce meaningful lives that pushed against the boundaries and limitations of their social existence in a country that considered them inferior because of the color of their skin. Even early humanists for whom talk of supernatural forces made no sense shared nonetheless a commitment to the development of greater life meaning and a greater range of freedom for enslaved and free Africans.

Key points you need to know

- To protect the system of slavery, slaveholders developed strategies for monitoring the activities of slaves.
- Some allowed slaves to hold worship services or incorporated them into services for whites, but slaves also held covert religious gatherings.
- Covert gatherings in "hush arbors" gave slaves an opportunity to worship consistent with their personal style and also gave them opportunity to plot against the system of slavery.
- Visible African churches begin to develop around the same time as these secret meetings shaped and gave rise to various aspects of tradition such as spirituals.
- Missionary activities on the part of blacks begin to develop before the nineteenth century and include Canada and the Caribbean.
- Secret meetings also serve as locations for the continued growth of African-based traditions as well as early practices we now associate with humanism.

Discussion questions

1. Why did slaveholders fear secret gatherings of slaves, and what did they do to try to prevent them?
2. What are the "hush arbor" meetings, and what took place during them?
3. What are some of the elements of African American Christianity that develop prior to the nineteenth century?
4. What is "double-talk" and how did it function in slave communities?
5. What are the blues and how do they differ from the spirituals?
6. How would you describe some of the other traditions that gain some form in the years prior to the nineteenth century?

Further reading

Anderson, Jeffrey E. *Conjure in African American Society.* Baton Rouge, LA: Louisiana State University Press, 2005.

Berlin, Ira, Marc Favreau, and Steven F. Miller, editors. *Remembering Slavery: African Americans Talk about Their Personal Experience of Slavery and Emancipation.* New York: The New Press, 1998.

Chireau, Yvonne. *Black Magic: Religion and the African American Conjuring Tradition.* Berkeley, CA: University of California Press, 2006.

Epstein, Dena. *Sinful Tunes and Spirituals: Black Folk Music to the Civil War.* Urbana, IL: University of Illinois Press, 1977.

Levine, Lawrence. *Black Culture and Black Consciousness: Afro-American Folk Thought from Slavery to Freedom.* New York: Oxford University Press, 1977.

Lovel, John. *Black Song: The Forge and the Flame; the Story of How the Afro-American Spiritual Was Hammered Out.* New York: Macmillan, 1972.

Mitchell, Henry H. *Black Church Beginnings: The Long-Hidden Realities of the First Years.* Grand Rapids, MI: Wm. B. Eerdmans Publishing Company, 2004.

Newman, Richard. *Freedom's Prophet: Bishop Richard Allen, the AME Church, and the Black Founding Fathers.* New York: New York University Press, 2009.

Pinn, Anthony B. *By These Hands: A Documentary History of African American Humanism.* New York: New York University Press, 2001.

4 African American religion in the nineteenth century

In this chapter

Whereas the last chapter was concerned with select seventeenth- and eighteenth-century developments, this chapter outlines the significant increase in the formal and institutional presence of African American religion during the nineteenth century. It describes the organizations that develop and explains some of their major beliefs and practices. Special attention is given to the rise of independent black church denominations, the changing shape of African-based traditions, and the persistence of Islam. It also places these activities in the context of the Civil War, Reconstruction, and the Great Migration. There is an important shift that takes place during this period. Prior to the freeing of slaves connected to the Civil War, I have referred to enslaved Africans and free Africans because there was little about the United States that suggested deep inclusion of this population. However, with the end of the system of slavery and the legal inclusion of the descendants of slaves into the workings of the nation, I begin to refer to that population as African Americans as recognition of their greater place in the life of the United States. Much of the discussion in this chapter and those after it is guided by a tension between spiritual and secular concerns. While some will disagree with this approach, I think it provides a good sense of the ways in which religious organizations approached the range of challenges confronting them.

Main topics covered

- The rise of independent African American churches and denominations
- Religion as source of visible protest, including bloody slave revolts and rebellions
- Development of voodoo and hoodoo community structures and leadership
- Increased presence of non-believers or humanists
- Persistence of Islam in areas such as Georgia
- Continued blending of religious traditions to foster new ones
- Impact of the Civil War, Reconstruction, and Great Migration on the look of African American religion

Establishing a visible presence

The nineteenth century marked a major change in the religious landscape of African American communities. The colonies transformed into a country during the eighteenth century, and the next century was marked by the turmoil and eventual collapse of the slave system. Whether one attributes the decline of slave labor to increased moral and ethical outrage over such dehumanizing practices, or to its declining economic significance as the means of production become more industrial, what remains important is the way by which debate over slavery and its aftermath shaped the nineteenth century. Advocates of slavery worked hard to secure it, and those opposed to it worked equally hard to usher in its demise. Social and political shifts and changes were initiated not only by debate over slavery but violent slave revolts and rebellions involving both whites, free Africans and enslaved Africans determined popular perceptions of the changing nature of life in the United States. David Walker's *Appeal* in 1829 which critiqued the system of slavery and called upon people of God's will to fight against it, combined with the revolts led by figures such as Denmark Vesey, Gabriel Prosser, Nat Turner, and John Brown pointed to the manner in which religion could serve to both pacify and prompt aggressive effort to end injustice.

African-based practices

Readers will recall that from the very beginning of the colonies through the end of the eighteenth century, the country was marked by religious diversity – a series of competing faith orientations and effort on the part of whites, enslaved Africans, and free Africans to manage these traditions. At times, this involved blending traditions, and at other points the approach involved either ignoring counter practices or seeking to destroy them. There was no clear winner in this struggle until the Great Awakenings and the massive movement of both whites and Africans into Christian churches. While this made Christianity numerically dominant and made it the centerpiece of histories regarding the religious life of North America, it did not mean the complete destruction of other traditions. They remained important, but just with fewer adherents and less public attention. In fact, with respect to traditions that challenged the status quo, African-based traditions were proven. People living in the United States were well aware of the impact voodoo had on the revolution in Haiti that freed it from French control and made it the first independent nation in the Caribbean. It was believed those who fought the French made use of the power of voodoo's more aggressive (petwo) spirits to secure their victory, and it was feared African-based traditions in the United States could have the same impact. If Christianity was used to religiously and theologically back rebellions, wouldn't African practices of which less was known – and secrecy generates suspicion –

be capable of the same? Variations such as hoodoo and conjure of African-based traditions provide alternate readings of life in the United States that centered on unseen forces, and also played an active role in efforts to overthrow the system of slavery. It wasn't simply a matter of conjure or voodoo, or hoodoo being used to secure relief for an individual by safeguarding an escape plan or gaining revenge on a cruel overseer. These traditions also had the potential to effect larger types of change. One need only keep in mind conjurers like "Gullah Jack," who was part of Denmark Vesey's (1796–1830) 1822 rebellion. In this way, these traditions had spiritual, social, and political impact on life in the nineteenth century. While many sought to wipe out these practices and in turn advance the Christian faith, the distinction between these various religious traditions wasn't always so clear and neat. The religious landscape was complex and the overlap between traditions points to it also having a plastic, or flexible, quality to it. The changing political, social, and economic climate of the United States during the nineteenth century due, for example, to the Civil War, the end of slavery, Reconstruction, and the Great Migration gave African Americans continued reason to seek assistance from whichever religious means seemed most useful and productive.

Figure 4.1   Reading the Emancipation Proclamation. H. W. Herrick, del., J. W. Watts, sc., *c.* 1864. Courtesy of the Library of Congress, Prints and Photographs Division [LC-USZ62-5334].

Efforts to destroy these practices were unsuccessful as these forces, for the knowledgeable, could be used to great effect. People held on to them as best they could, and in spite of the danger inherent in doing so. To help with preservation of these practices and beliefs, secret organizations existed in areas of the South where this knowledge was shared and used. During this century, the emergence of strong religious leadership within these traditions also had an impact on their practice and viability. For example, Marie Laveau (1782–1881) was recognized as a voodoo queen during that century and she had the attention of both blacks and whites in Louisiana.

She and others like her organized the religion of voodoo, with a clear hierarchy of deities and other forces as well as with systematized rituals and ceremonies. There was complexity to these practices in the nineteenth century. And figures outside Louisiana, throughout the South, provided – for a fee – services to those seeking assistance for various life problems and concerns.

Although there were mixed feelings concerning traditions such as voodoo and conjure, those with proven ability in these traditions – proven through the success of their potions, charms, etc. – tended to have significant influence in their communities and tended to avoid too much interference from whites. Being on the wrong side of a powerful conjurer could result in great harm, if not death. In short, their powers generated both great interest in their services and fear of what might happen if they were angered. Through newspapers, and by word of mouth, members of various communities heard about the abilities and exploits of these figures.

Whereas Christian preachers were the center of the African American churches, for voodoo and conjure, hoodoo and root work, the center was the voodoo queen or king, the conjurer and the root doctor. As the preacher was assumed to have spiritual power and authority, the same was the case for the ritual expert in these other traditions. However, stories of how power was secured by these various religious

African-based traditions

- Secret organizations preserved beliefs and practices associated with these traditions.
- During the nineteenth century there was a growth in the social importance of religious leaders associated with traditions such as voodoo, hoodoo, and conjure.
- Involvement as a leader in one of these traditions could result from being born with special gifts or acquiring spiritual power through a deal with spiritual forces.
- They played a role in slave rebellions.
- Some practiced elements of these traditions and held membership, for example, in a Christian church.

Figure 4.2   Hypnotic trance induced during voodoo dance rites – Louisiana (engraving, 1886).
© World History Archive / Alamy.

leaders differed. For example, it was assumed Christian ministers at best were called by God to preach, or at worse they appointed themselves. For conjurers and voodoo leadership, one might be called into the tradition through birth – perhaps being born with a caul, a membrane, over their eyes. It is not uncommon for this caul to be called a "veil." And, some believe this means the baby will grow into a person with the ability to see into the spirit world as one with a special relationship to the unseen forces. In addition, some stories tell of those who secure conjure power by selling their souls to the devil. In either case – called by God, born with the gift, or acquiring it through the selling of one's soul – what results from this is a similar structure of authority that provided different paths for spiritual fulfillment and social status. The flexibility of their beliefs allowed them to make use of the dominant Christian culture, but shape it to fit the basic structures of hoodoo, conjure and voodoo.

Islamic practices

It wasn't just these traditions that showed this type of flexibility. For example, there are some accounts suggesting that Islam was also brought into contact with Christianity in ways that entailed adherents blending some of the beliefs. In part, this is because although Islam had a presence in the United States, it was more difficult to maintain its ritual practices in a country more heavily marked by opportunities for Christianity or even African-based traditions. Nonetheless, within the nineteenth century there are clear examples of Islam's continued presence, including portions of an autobiography by a slave (Omar Said) who practiced Islam.

Figure 4.3   Believed to be the earliest known portrait of a practicing American Muslim. Yarrow
Mamout, 1819 (oil on canvas), Peale, Charles Willson (1741–1827) / Philadelphia
Museum of Art, Pennsylvania, PA, USA / The Bridgeman Art Library.

Additional accounts recorded after the end of slavery provide comments on Islamic
practices from the descendants of early slaves. They speak in clear terms about the
adherence to a schedule for prayer, the naming of children, and the celebration of feasts
associated not with Christianity but Islam. Memories of particular Islamic practices
within families persisted, and these memories yield the names – such as Omar ibn
Said, Belali Mahomet, Phoebe Mahomet – and the activities of these Muslims.

But more than a few elements of religious practice can be associated with Islam,
something more along the lines of an intact set of practices and stated beliefs, does
not emerge until the twentieth century. Prior to that, in a few select locations of
the South, in communities composed of free Africans, there were Muslims and
they maintained elements of the Islamic faith. However, it is also important to note
that the late nineteenth century also marks the rise of new Islam-based religious
communities in Northern cities, as well as the presence of Muslims from places
such as Turkey who introduced Islam to a US population that included African
Americans. In addition, there are records of Muslims fighting in the Civil War, and
immigration of Muslims from the Ottoman Empire is documented.

African American Islam

- During the nineteenth century individuals maintained the tradition of prayer, fasting, and observation of feasts.
- A few prominent African American Muslims authored texts discussing their personal stories of faith.
- Descendants of African Muslims in the United States provide much of what we know about the presence of Islam in the nineteenth century.
- Immigration of Muslims to the United States increased the practice of "orthodox" Islam in the nineteenth century.

Like African Americans moving into major cities in search of economic opportunities, Muslims arrived with the same hope and in the process they planted greater awareness of and attention to Islam as a religious option.

The spread of Christianity

While African-based traditions continued to develop organizational structure and patterns of leadership, and as Islam maintained at least a shadow presence on the African American religious landscape, African American Christians increased in visibility and complexity. Related to this growth, the nineteenth century bridges two conditions – i.e., the slave system and the freedom of African Americans – and two perspectives. One perspective supported the system of slavery and the other was an abolitionist perspective that sought to end slavery. Religious developments reflected this tension: missions amongst slaves continued, as white denominations worked to better arrange and conduct their efforts to convert slaves consistent with the demands of the slave system as others sought to convert slaves and end the system of slavery. This was a difficult balancing act – support of the slave system and claims to the moral and ethical demands of the Gospel of Christ. However, that century also marked increased presence of churches developed by African Americans. While, as noted in the previous chapter, independent churches began to develop during the eighteenth century, it was during the nineteenth century that these independent churches radically increased their membership and began to develop regional and national organizations. At times, these independent congregations and denominations developed with some cooperation from whites, but it was just as likely that they developed in spite of white resistance. These religious organizations built on the effort of societies and associations developed by free Africans to aid their advancement through financial assistance, social coordination, and religious instruction. For example, the early African Methodist congregations developing in the Northeast under the leadership of figures such as Richard Allen – a former

Figure 4.4   Portraits of Richard Allen and other African Methodist Episcopal (A.M.E.) bishops, surrounded by scenes including Wilberforce University, Payne Institute, missionaries in Haiti, and the A.M.E. church book depository in Philadelphia. Courtesy of the Library of Congress, Prints and Photographs Division [LC-USZ62-15059].

slave and minister – organized themselves into a denomination in 1816 through legal action granting them independence, with Allen (1760–1831) serving as its first bishop.

They maintained for some time a connection with the white Methodists in various ways including relying on Bishop Francis Asbury to ordain their ministers and also seeking recognition of their churches from the Methodists. In large part this was because those involved in the formation of the African Methodist Episcopal Church continued to understand themselves as Methodists, maintaining the Methodist Episcopal Church's book of rules and regulations called *The Book of Discipline*. Yet, they were Methodists who saw a need to develop congregations in which African Americans could worship in the Methodist way with a major change – freedom from the racial discrimination they encountered in predominantly white congregations. They believed it important to demonstrate not only their religious commitment through this new denomination but also through their appearance and conduct to demonstrate to the larger society that they were capable of full citizenship with all its rights and responsibilities. Not long after 1816, other African American Methodists in the New York area developed another denomination – calling it the

African Methodist Episcopal Church Zion. The last word in the title was meant to distinguish them from their Philadelphia neighbors. However, they shared an understanding of themselves as people of African descent (African), Methodist in their structure (Methodist), and run by bishops (Episcopal). Both denominations developed as a result of racism faced in the Methodist Episcopal Church and a deep desire to worship and live as Christians without experiencing discrimination within the context of their religious commitments. These two denominations were interested in expanding, but they worked best on a soft agreement not to intentionally do harm to each other. Although useful in theory, they did not always abide by this agreement. Both denominations believed in membership to anyone willing to abide by its regulations; however, one such regulation prevented supporters of the system of slavery from membership in the congregations. (This including both black and white slaveholders. It is important to remember that some free Africans had the financial resources necessary to purchase slaves.) By the end of the nineteenth century, these African American Methodist denominations claimed large memberships.

These developments must be put in the context of emerging and growing Baptist churches and conventions, such as Silver Bluff Church (Silver Bluff, South Carolina), founded between 1773–1775 (although the cornerstone reads 1750); the numerous Baptist churches founded in the 1800s in locations such as Massachusetts, Pennsylvania, and New Jersey. As Methodism was growing in African American communities, Baptist churches were also multiplying in the North and South. In fact, African American Baptists outnumbered their Methodist counterparts. Some of these Baptist churches belonged to regional, white associations. Yet, it was difficult to work within these arrangements in that the issues of racial discrimination and slavery were always present, and always played a role in shaping levels of participation available to African American Baptist churches. Participation could easily mean oversight by white congregations and ministers, and this worked against the basic premise of the independent African American congregation and their desire to forge greater life options for their members. The size of the African American congregation did not safeguard it from this type of interference. Nonetheless, the number of African American Baptist churches continued to grow over an expansive section of the country. Unlike Methodists who operated based on a centralized structure of authority, the authority of the local congregation was the basic arrangement of power and governance. While fear of rebellion prior to the end of slavery made impossible the development of independent Baptist conventions within African American communities, the situation in the North was a bit different which allowed for the unifying of Baptist churches into association by the mid-nineteenth century. With time, efforts to participate in associations formed by white Americans would be replaced by African American Baptist regional and eventually national associations that strengthened their ability to conduct missions and maximized the use of their limited resources. Yes, they began forming associations that connected local congregations across regions, but these were voluntary associations that did not trump the independence and authority of local churches to hire and fire ministers, and arrange local church organization as they saw fit. Recognizing the need for partnerships alone was insufficient to maintain those connections. The independence of local congregations often made it extremely difficult to maintain regional associations prior to the late nineteenth century when the National Baptist Convention, USA, Inc., was formed (1895). This convention was the result of a merger between three conventions and it took place for the purpose of unified action on issue of racial oppression and missionary efficiency. Through its missionary organizations and its publishing board, this convention was in a position to impact both the spread of the gospel and the spread of information on pressing issues. Nonetheless, before the nineteenth century was over, there would be a split in this convention over issues including whether or not to form partnerships and collaborative work with white Baptists.

The issue of race served as a common concern for African American churches regardless of doctrinal differences. In most cases, in forming new churches, denominations and conventions, African Americans were not separating themselves from the religious creeds and doctrines of whites but rather they were making a clear statement concerning the need for consistency between racial policy and Christian faith practice. Yet, the vast majority of African Americans during this period who were Christians affiliated with independent African American Methodists and Baptists, where they were free from white influence. This is because African American churches in predominantly white denominations were financially and doctrinally dependent on white Americans. Although the vast majority of African American Christians were to be found in Baptist and Methodist churches in the nineteenth century, it is also important to note that during that century there is also the emergence of the Holiness Movement.

The Holiness Movement involved Christians, typically Methodists, concerned with salvation and proper moral behavior in terms of what they referenced as "sanctification." By that they meant living a holy life after one experiences salvation. The idea was to avoid all forms of evil and to live a life completely consistent with the will of God. There was a tension between secular concerns and spiritual concerns. While Pentecostals were involved in issues such as temperance and women's rights, there was a greater emphasis placed on "holiness" as a spiritual quest than one typically found in African American Baptist and Methodist circles. This is because salvation and spiritual warfare against spiritual enemies were of such great importance. Methodists who held this view pushed a sense of Christian life beyond what was typically required within their denominations and conventions. And using revival services and camp meetings, those involved in the Holiness Movement spread their religious viewpoint in both the North and the South, and in opposition to more traditional Methodist thinking.

Figure 4.5   African American outdoor prayer meeting in the South – 1870s (woodcut, nineteenth century). © North Wind Picture Archives / Alamy.

By the late nineteenth century, the Holiness Movement generated African American congregations such as the Church of the Living God founded in Arkansas in 1889. Churches such as this one developed because some within the Holiness Movement believed that holiness could not be fully achieved in churches that weren't completely committed to that perspective on Christian faith. This push to leave Methodist churches if they couldn't be transformed was fought through denominational regulations that granted Methodist ministers permission to restrict who could speak from the pulpit and what activities could take place in the church. Nonetheless, Holiness churches and denominations would grow through incorporation of Methodists and Baptists who wanted a more spiritual intensive and more restrictive social existence than the traditional denominations could offer. In addition, before the end of the nineteenth century, some within the Holiness Movement would push even further and argue that sanctification was not enough in itself because a proper relationship with God and with humans required new tools and talents. Scripture, they argued, spoke of the indwelling of the Holy Spirit as a third development: salvation, sanctification, being filled with the Holy Spirit. Debate and further transformations in the religious life of the United States would result from Holiness and a new development called Pentecostalism.

Some African Americans remained in predominately white churches, often forming predominately African American congregations within denominations such as the Episcopal Church, the Presbyterian Church and so on. Furthermore, the role of African Americans in the Roman Catholic Church also increased, with African American males gaining recognition as priests and African American women as nuns. The number of people of African descent in the Roman Catholic Church in the United States was relatively small in comparison to the numbers claimed by Protestant churches. Yet, in 1854, James Augustine Healy (1830–1900) was ordained a priest. Patrick Francis Healy (1830–1910), who was ordained in 1864, eventually became the head of Georgetown College (in 1874), now known as Georgetown University. In 1886 Augustus Tolton (1854–1897) was the first priest publicly recognized as black. Several African American priests would advance in the hierarchy of the church and gain status as bishops and leaders of institutions. An increase in the number of African American men ordained priests was matched by growth in the number of African American parishes. Furthermore, by the mid-nineteenth century, groups of African American nuns were operating – e.g., Oblate Sisters of Providence, Sisters of Holy Family, and Third Order of St. Francis. Formed around 1828, the Oblate Sisters, the first group of nuns, was recognized by the international leadership of the Church for its educational work with young women. Like African Americans in Protestant denominations, African American Catholics experienced their share of discrimination. But a commitment to the value of Catholicism served as inspiration for some Catholics to push for large-scale conversion concerning the status and meaning of an African American presence in the Roman Catholic Church, and this concern was expressed before the end of the nineteenth century.

Whether talking in terms of Catholics or Protestants, significant growth of Christianity within African American communities marked the nineteenth century. However, the most significant expansion took place near the end of the century as a result of the Civil War. Although the Methodist denominations had begun their work in the South before the Civil War, independent churches were hard pressed to secure access to plantations for fear they would promote rebellion. This fear was well founded in that both Baptist and Methodist ministers – such as the Baptist preacher Nat Turner (1800–1831) and the Methodist minister Morris Brown – had been implicated in plots against the slave system. Turner was executed for his efforts, and Morris Brown had to leave South Carolina to avoid a similar lot. It was also dangerous for free African Americans to journey south in that their freedom could be ignored easily and they could be sold into slavery. However, with the Civil War and the ending of the slave system, the way was opened for African American Methodists and Baptists to conduct missionary activities amongst the formerly enslaved. The message of their ministers and missionaries was clear: you are now physically free, shouldn't you affiliate with a church that is also African American and free from white control? Why connect yourselves to the churches of your former slave owners? Southern white Methodists tried to counter this (while maintaining their preference for a segregated structure) by financially supporting the development of an affiliated African Methodist denomination that was philosophically distinct from the two Northern African American Methodist denominations that had moved South and were disrupting the social and religious landscape. This third African American Methodist denomination was named the Colored Methodist Episcopal Church. It had African American bishops supported by the larger, white Methodist denomination. The Methodists from the North critiqued this third denomination and sought to limit its growth by arguing it was the handiwork of racist whites, and it wasn't a truly independent African American denomination. Whether accurate or not, in key ways this argument worked in that of the three it experienced the least amount of growth, and it remains the smallest of the three.

Physical freedom should be matched by religious affiliation marked by autonomy. This strategy worked and, when combined with the tensions amongst white Methodists over the race question that had resulted in a split between Southern and Northern Methodists, it only strengthened the reason to join with other African Americans. Tens of thousands of former slaves in the South joined these independent African American churches and denominations, swelling their numbers and testing their resource base. As their numbers grew, their organizational structures became larger and more complex. For the Methodists, this meant the appointment of new bishops, and new conferences composed of churches in a given region meeting annually to discuss finances, growth and address pressing issues. For Baptists, this meant new regional associations and national conventions to unite African American Baptists in their common causes. Both Baptists and Methodists expanded their church structures to accommodate their domestic missionary work, and they attempted to match this concern with a similar commitment to foreign missions in the Caribbean and Africa. This work was done through missionary organizations formed by these independent organizations, and financed by local churches within the larger organizational frameworks. These denominations, associations, and conventions understood it as their Christian duty to bring the gospel of Christ to people of African descent in the Caribbean and to Africans on the continent. The rationale for doing this was found in Psalms 63 – "And Ethiopia shall soon stretch forth her hand unto God." But this was not the only piece of scripture significant to African American Christians. The Exodus story in the Hebrew Bible (or what is known as the "Old Testament") was understood as being played out in the modern world through the movement of African Americans metaphorically into proper relationship with God and physically through a movement from slavery to new cities and towns, and new international destinations such as Canada and Africa. For them, both Psalm 68:31 and the Exodus account (in the Book of Exodus) were a matter of prophecy, a stating of the redemption of Africans. And they saw themselves as being the best means by which to share this Gospel with Africans and African Americans in need. Some took this argument further and saw scripture as the basis for new types of nationalism – e.g., a new nationalistic philosophy based on equal participation; or the rise of a new, black nation as God's favored people. Regarding the first – a new model for national involvement – some African Americans argued the United States faced destruction as a consequence of its treatment of African Americans, and that the country would only prevent this fate and survive by treating African Americans properly and granting them full citizenship with all accompanying rights and responsibilities. In line with this argument African Americans – particularly ministers – sought to play a role, during the period of Reconstruction following the Civil War, by running for elected office. Several won elections on both the local and regional levels. Such markers of Reconstruction were made possible by changes to laws and amendments to the Constitution that sought to recognize African Americans as full citizens. However, these changes to formal laws and regulations did not necessarily modify informal customs. So, regarding the second formulation of nationalism, African Americans saw little hope that the United States – despite the Civil War and Reconstruction – would ever treat African Americans properly, and instead of fighting for rights here they determined that God wanted them to relocate to Africa. We typically call this philosophy and its resulting actions the "Back-to-Africa" movement, supported by both African Americans and white Americans – but typically for different reasons. The former wanted to fulfill their potential and expand the greatness of people of African descent, and many in the latter group simply wanting to remove from the United States what they considered a problematic population. Amongst African American nationalists wanting to expand the greatness of African peoples are notable figures such as Alexander Crummell (1819–1898), an Episcopal minister, who worked in Africa until his health required a return to the United States. Martin Delaney, a doctor and author (1812–1885), touted the importance of African American churches but more importantly served as an early advocate of African American nationalism. For example, his novel *Blake* (1862) used religion and culture in general as a way to celebrate the significance of people of African descent and to explore the possibilities of a black nation.

His was not simply nationalism on paper, Delaney also traveled to Africa in hopes of finding a place where African Americans might return to start a new nation. Instead, however, he returned to the United States and continued his efforts on behalf of oppressed African Americans. In addition, Paul Cuffee (1759–1817), a businessman and preacher, blended religious commitment and politics to forge a sense of purpose for African Americans that involved the reconstitution of a great, black nation. He did this by establishing a shipping business connecting North America and Africa, as well as establishing a religious society in Sierra Leone. Despite his efforts, a mass movement of African Americans to Sierra Leone never occurred.

African Americans interested in emigration were often aligned with the American Colonization Society, founded by white Americans to aid the movement of African Americans back to Africa. This organization played a major role in the founding of Liberia (1822) as a colony for African Americans in Africa. With time, some African Americans who initially supported the American Colonization Society criticized it for pushing emigration based not on the welfare of African Americans, nor Africa, but rather based on racist positions that rejected African American contributions to the United States. In short, they wanted to push African Americans out based on a desire to claim the United States for white Americans. In opposition to this racism, African American advocates of emigration believed it was part of the destiny of African Americans to return to Africa, where they would spread the Christian faith and democratic governmental system. They believed it was for this eventual return with new information and skills that God had allowed the enslavement of their ancestors in the first place. What they lamented, however, was the presence of white colonial structures in Africa. From their perspective the presence of whites pushed against God's will for Africa worked out through its children in North America moving back home. Whites on the continent could only perpetuate the harming of Africans and a denial of the destiny of African Americans. This sense of nationalism also played out in the United States with the formation of black towns by African Americans moving west to advance themselves economically and socially in accordance with a philosophy of self-determination.

Whether migration across the country, or emigration to Africa proved practical or not, and regardless of continued discrimination encountered by African Americans, African American church members believed themselves to be in line for a special blessing from God. And they held to this perspective despite the backlash against them coming after Reconstruction efforts to produce new socio-political opportunities failed. If nothing else, churches provided communities for the likeminded who appreciated the importance and human value of African Americans. Even titles used within the context of churches – "brother," "sister," "saint," "pastor," and so on – ran contrary to the derogatory ways in which they might be addressed in the larger society. In the context of the churches they ran, churches with a primary concern for their members, African Americans had respect, appreciation, and a degree of protection. This generated a sense of self-importance and worth much needed as African Americans made their way through a changing world. Manifest Destiny, an idea lodged in the very founding of the colonies, was taken by enslaved Africans to do a different type of work. Rather than supporting slavery, the idea was used to promote a link between enslaved Africans and God. This was done through the idea that God has a special plan and purpose for African Americans, and this plan will eventually include their freedom. They believed God was going to usher in new opportunities for them, if they remained faithful and persistent in their work. How could the Civil War, their freedom, public policies associated with Reconstruction, and the Great Migration point in the direction of anything less than this?

Movement serves as a good way to describe what was taking place both religiously and physically for African Americans following the Civil War and continuing through the mid-twentieth century. As ministers and missionaries were moving into the South and into foreign countries, large numbers of African Americans were packing up and moving into Northern (and some Southern) cities in search of greater life options and better employment. Opportunities in Southern agriculture were slim and often resulted in African Americans being sharecroppers whose annual income didn't typically cover their expenses; so, from year to year they remained in debt to white landowners. This, combined with the ever-present threat of racial violence such as lynching in the New South (and Northern locations as well, although we typically associated this form of violence with the South), made leaving Southern locations promising. This movement was further encouraged through recruiters from the North who moved South promising African Americans greater freedoms and financial opportunities in the industrial North.

African American Churches in the nineteenth century

- Major growth as result of mission work in the South following on the heels of the Civil War and Reconstruction.
- New denominations form to meet the needs and styles of various African American needs and desires.
- The Holiness Movement adds attention to sanctification as the requirement of Christian life beyond initial salvation.
- Ministers get involved in politics, holding political offices at least for short periods of time in certain locations.
- Great Migration carries certain styles of worship and practice to Northern and Southern cities.
- Churches undertake international missions in addition to domestic mission efforts.
- Churches debate their proper orientation: this-worldly or other-worldly, or salvation and socio-political/economic programs vs. salvation as sole responsibility.
- Schools, newspapers and journals develop and serve as resources for discussing important issues and incorporating African Americans into the workings of the United States.
- The Book of Exodus and Psalm 68:31 were understood as speaking to the redemption of people of African descent.

The movement of African Americans as a result of these factors, called the Great Migration, involved a significant population shift, although the majority of African Americans remained in the South (with more in Southern cities than had been the case before the Civil War and Reconstruction). African Americans took more than their personal property and high hopes; they also took with them their religious commitments and desire for religious community. Records and narratives indicate that Southern churches felt the financial and membership pain – as many of their members relocated. In some instances, ministers sent word requesting their ongoing financial support; in other cases, ministers decided to move with their members and re-establish themselves in Northern cities.

The promise of a new life in the North held unanticipated challenges, including tension with Northern religious organizations and institutions, as well as new types of social issues and new forms of racial discrimination. Once in the cities, African Americans typically found fewer economic opportunities than had been promised. Often confined to inner city areas with limited outlets for recreation and poor housing, African Americans involved in the Great Migration often relied on their religious commitments as a source of assistance and peace of mind. Some were able to integrate into the established African American churches in Northern cities. However, many found themselves the victims of social isolation and misunderstandings as Northerners rejected the cultural ways of Southerners moving north. Northerners in African American churches often considered themselves more refined and more sophisticated than African Americans migrating north from the South. On one hand, existing members of the congregations did not want to be associated with what they considered the "country behaviors and attitudes" of the migrants. It was believed by many such an association would only hamper the progress Northerners had already made. On the other hand, there were some differences in religious outlook and styles of worship that ran contrary to what Southerners often brought with them. The ring shout, for example, was an unwelcomed addition to Northern churches seeking to gain the appreciation and acceptance of whites as a way of gaining greater social and political status. And some Northern churches rejected the spirituals in favor of more refined hymns also as a way of pushing beyond the legacy of slavery and thereby gaining greater status. That is to say, there were social and cultural differences that made integration into Northern African American society difficult at times. So, those who were unable to find homes in Northern churches – which would include the ability to gain leadership positions in these churches – developed their own.

During this period there was also a more pronounced conversation concerning the role of churches in the socio-political struggles of African Americans. While this debate had been in place for some time, it was only in light of the Civil War, Reconstruction, and the Great Migration that it took on a highly public and charged tone. In the scholarship related to African American religion we have come to refer to the ensuing debate as entailing the tension between a "this-worldly" orientation and an "other-worldly" orientation. Regarding the former, churches understood themselves as having an obligation to meet the spiritual and physical needs of African Americans. This might entail the creation of educational opportunities, political involvement to fight discrimination, job training, and missions. In terms of the latter, other churches perceived themselves as having the sole purpose of saving souls. This position at times stemmed from recognition that the limited resources of individual churches, conventions or denominations could not meet the deep needs of the migrants and the existing membership in a way that was sufficient. So, it was better to restrict attention to what they could do without limitation – preach the gospel to save souls. Ministers and congregants debated the merits of these perspectives, and often did so in the church-based journals and papers that developed during the nineteenth century. These media outlets became a major means by which to exchange opinions and concerns not simply related to the structure and beliefs of a particular denomination or to report on services and projects of local congregations. They also served as a way to address issues involving national politics and economics, as well as affording commentary on social trends in the United States beyond church communities. In addition, schools for African Americans – including Wilberforce University founded by the African Methodist Episcopal Church in 1856 and Livingstone College founded in 1880 by the African Methodist Episcopal Church Zion – and secular journals and papers also developed during this period. The latter pushed political issues and the former were meant to provide intellectual growth and skills by means of which African Americans would advance their position in the United States.

It is safe to say that the nineteenth century was a time during which African Americans further developed their communication infrastructure, political platform and participation, as well as promoted social organizations and further enhanced religious institutions. All this was meant to address the overall desire for full inclusion in the life of the country. African Americans were legally free – although discriminated against – and every social organization, including churches, was involved in discussions and activities concerning what this freedom meant and how it might be enhanced and safeguarded.

African American humanism

African-based traditions, Islam, and Christianity grew during the nineteenth century, but this does not mean these were the orientations of choice for all African Americans. Rather than embracing one of these God-based traditions, some African Americans maintained an allegiance to human capacity and responsibility. They rejected the idea of supernatural assistance and placed little importance on the sacred books of these traditions. Instead, they celebrated life – the small and large moments of triumph – and recognized without great frustration the shortcomings of human life. The folktales, music and folk wisdom of African Americans continued to tell this alternative story of non-theistic African Americans. In fact, even those involved in theism – such as Christians – recognized the existence of those who didn't believe in God and who gave the churches no great importance in their lives. For instance, Daniel Alexander Payne (1811–1893), one of the great leaders of the African Methodist Episcopal Church, comments on this very thing. In the nineteenth century, before leaving the Lutheran church he lamented the impact of the evil of slavery on African Americans. He said that he encountered a slave, during his missionary travels in the South, who claimed there were those like himself who did not go to Church and wouldn't be Christians because of the relationship between slavery and Christianity.

> They hear their masters professing Christianity; they see their masters preaching the gospel; they hear these masters praying in their families, and they know that oppression and slavery are inconsistent with the Christian religion; therefore they scoff at religion itself – mock their masters, and distrust both the goodness and justice of God. Yes, I have known them even to question his existence. I speak not of what others have told me, but of what I have both seen and heard from the slaves themselves.
>
> (Daniel Alexander Payne, 1839)

Furthermore, Payne notes that those like this gentleman even mock or deny God. Payne wrote about this episode in 1839 as a warning and as a call to end the system of slavery. There were no formal organizations associated with this perspective. That type of infrastructure for African American humanism would not emerge until the twentieth century. However, there is a body of materials, a type of canon of literature that speaks to the existence of this religious position. (The blues and folktales are probably the best examples of this.) This position was frowned upon by most within African American communities because of its denial of the supernatural and its tendency to mock the religious beliefs of Christians. At times those who held to beliefs that play into the development of twentieth- century humanism would make use of voodoo and conjure, or at least sing in the blues about their prowess regarding these things. Yet, this was not a deep embrace of the supernatural leanings of these traditions. Rather, it was much more pragmatic – a tendency to demonstrate the power of humans to manipulate earth and other humans. It did not entail a fear of cosmic powers, but rather it involved a deep concern with human creativity and ingenuity. They discussed cosmic forces as a way to tame them by including them in human history as ideas worked by humans. That is to say, even when talking about these things, they maintained the dominance of humans. These African Americans appealed to other humans, and limited themselves to what could be understood and explored within the context of physical, human life.

Key points you need to know

- African-based traditions developed societies and other organizational features that gave these traditions more structure and reach.
- Islam continued through the presence of small communities in some Southern states and through the writings and activities of a few prominent figures.
- The first African American Methodist denominations and Baptist conventions developed through the collaboration of independent African American churches.
- Churches undertook foreign missionary work in addition to domestic missions in the south
- Reconstruction results in ministers moving into political positions for the short term.
- The Holiness Movement resulted in the development of churches that extended their doctrine and practices beyond salvation to a call for sanctification or holiness.
- Humanism continued to grow in African American communities and was visible in the blues and in folktales, as well as in the testimony of missionaries working in the south.

Discussion questions

1. How did the Civil War affect the development of independent African American churches?
2. What is meant by a "this-worldly" orientation? What is meant by an "other-worldly" orientation?
3. What is the Great Migration and how did it affect the development of African American religious traditions?
4. What role did religion play in African American slave rebellions?
5. What is meant by Manifest Destiny, and what did African American churches make of this idea?
6. What is the relationship between black nationalism and African American religion?

Further reading

Boles, John. *Masters and Slaves in the House of the Lord: Race and Religion in the American South, 1740–1870.* Lexington, KY: University of Kentucky Press, 1988.

Diouf, Sylvaiane. *Servants of Allah: African Muslims Enslaved in the Americas.* New York: New York University Press, 1998.

Fandrich, Ina J. *The Mysterious Voodoo Queen, Marie Laveaux: A Study of Powerful Female Leadership in Nineteenth Century New Orleans*. New York: Routledge, 2005.

Foner, Eric. *A Short History of Reconstruction*. New York: Harper Perennial, 1990.

Giggle, John M. *After Redemption: Jim Crow and the Transformation of African American Religion in the Delta, 1875–1915*. New York: Oxford University Press, 2007.

Gomez, Michael A. *Exchanging Our Country Marks: The Transformation of African Identities in the Colonial and Antebellum South*. Chapel Hill, NC: The University of North Carolina, 1998.

Greenberg, Kenneth S. *Nat Turner: A Slave Rebellion in History and Memory*. New York: Oxford University Press, 2004.

Harding, Vincent. *There Is a River: The Black Freedom Struggle in America*. New York: Vintage Books, 1983.

Jacobs, Sylvia. *Black Americans and the Missionary Movement in Africa*. Cleveland, OH: Greenwood Press, 1982.

Johnson, Sylvester. *The Myth of Ham in Nineteenth-Century American Christianity: Race, Heathens, and the People of God*. New York: Palgrave Macmillan, 2004.

Miller, Randall M., Harry S. Stout, and Charles Reagan Wilson, editors. *Religion and the American Civil War*. New York: Oxford University Press, 1998.

Martin, Sandy D. *Black Baptists and African Missions: The Origins of a Movement, 1880–1915*. Savannah, GA: Mercer University Press, 1998.

Montgomery, William E. *Under Their Own Vine and Fig Tree: The African American Church in the South, 1865–1900*. Baton Rouge, LA: Louisiana State University Press, 1993.

Sernett, Milton. *Bound for the Promised Land: African American Religion and the Great Migration*. Durham, NC: Duke University Press, 1997.

Smith, Edward D. *Climbing Jacob's Ladder: The Rise of Black Churches in Eastern Cities, 1740–1877*. Washington, DC: Smithsonian Institution, 1988.

Stowell, Daniel W. *Rebuilding Zion: The Religious Reconstruction of the South, 1863–1877*. New York: Oxford University Press, 2001.

Washington Creel, Margaret. *A Peculiar People: Slave Religion and Community-Culture Among the Gullahs*. New York: New York University Press, 1989.

5 *African American religion in the twentieth century*

In this chapter

This chapter follows the Great Migration of African Americans out of rural areas into cities and explores the ongoing development of religious traditions and religious activism from the start of the twentieth century through the end of that century. It argues that much religious innovation was made possible in part through the blending of traditions that occurred as result of the Great Migration, and also because of the Great Depression that wreaked havoc on the economy of the United States during the third decade of the century. The chapter also places these developments in the context of major socio-political struggles against injustice such as the Civil Rights Movement and the Black Power Movement. Some attention is also given to trends in the twentieth century that inform African American religion during the first decade of the twenty-first century.

Main topics covered

- Development of new Christian denominations such as Church of God in Christ
- Growth in the number of Sunni Muslims, and the formation of Islam-based traditions such as the Moorish Science Temple and the Nation of Islam
- Expansion of African-based religious traditions through contact with the Caribbean, Africa, and Brazil
- Involvement of religious organizations in social justice movements
- Critiques of African American religious organizations in the late twentieth century and the strengthening of non-theistic orientations
- Globalization of African American religion

Expansion of Islamic communities

Lingering interest in Islam and the creative manner by means of which some maintained pieces of this faith gave rise to new and highly syncretistic or blended

Figure 5.1   Attendees of the 1928 Moorish Science Temple Conclave in Chicago. Noble Drew Ali is in the front row center. Courtesy of http://www.themoorish sciencetempleofamerica.org/

practices and belief systems during the twentieth century. Most notable of these developments during the early twentieth century is perhaps the work of Noble Drew Ali (1886–1929), who argued African Americans were really Moors from Morocco (descendants of Muslims in that region) and that their true religion was Islam not Christianity. In fact, he argued that African Americans were really Moorish Americans, and that those who followed his teachings have a good understanding of their nationality, history, and cultural heritage. In 1913, he founded the Canaanite Temple, eventually renamed the Moorish Science Temple.

Members of his organization dressed to reflect their identity and to express the Temple's sense of life meaning. They wore distinctive clothing they believed to be associated with the Middle East (such as the Fez) so as to distinguish themselves from others in African American communities. In addition, they carried a card identifying themselves as Moors so as to not be confused with African Americans who did not have such clear connections to an identity beyond slavery and Christianity. These outward appearance distinctions spoke to an inner change, and to a different understanding of themselves and their place in the world. That is to say, the Temple taught that followers of Noble Drew Ali have proper knowledge, a firm sense of who they are, whereas African American Christians have embraced a religion that encourages their destruction. Beyond their appearance and their claims to citizenship outside the United States, many of their religious practices involved elements of Islam such as daily prayer. These practices also borrowed from nationalist philosophies, positive thinking traditions, and Freemasonry. But other elements seemed to be North American developments such as Noble Drew Ali's identity and role that are similar to that of the Prophet Muhammad in Islam. More to the point, according to some of his followers, Noble Drew Ali is understood as being the incarnation of the Prophet Muhammad (570–632). He died before all the work in establishing the Moorish Science Temple was complete; however, the organization has continued and remains important in locations such as Washington, DC, and Detroit, Michigan. The total membership of the organization has always been somewhat uncertain, and this was part of the mystery surrounding it and its teachings. With the death of Noble Drew Ali there was a struggle for power that compromised the strength of the organization, but it remains an important religious orientation for an unspecified number of people. This religious tradition and its blending of Islamic sensibilities and United States racial politics served as an early model for other Islam-based organizations such as the Nation of Islam. In fact, some argue that the Nation of Islam's teachings borrowed directly from Noble Drew Ali in that the early leadership of the Nation of Islam included followers of Noble Drew Ali. These claims, however, are still debated.

In 1930, in Detroit, a man made his way through the African American communities. He was selling various items, but more important than that he engaged people in conversation concerning their true home outside the United States, their greatness as a people, and the proper way to care for themselves – eat no pork, for example. Word spread about this man, Master Fard Muhammad (1893–1934), and larger groups of people expressed interest in hearing what he had to say than could be accommodated in homes. The Nation of Islam resulted from this interest in and devotion to his teachings. Master Fard Muhammad's lectures blended elements of Islam – such as references to Allah, dietary restrictions and mention of the Qur'an – with elements of Christian thought. The latter is included because Master Fard Muhammad understood it was the dominant tradition within African American communities, but it can even be used to demonstrate the truth of his claims. Those who come to Nation of Islam meetings are told that African Americans are members of the original people, and that Master Fard Muhammad had been sent to provide them with proper knowledge that would enable them to free themselves from the bondage of Christianity and white society. During a time of economic decline represented by the Great Depression and segregation, the teachings of the Nation of Islam had appeal. African Americans who embraced these teachings developed a sense of themselves as important, with a history that extends beyond slavery. One of those joining the Nation of Islam was Elijah Poole from Georgia.

The leader of the Nation of Islam recognized Elijah Poole (1897–1975), despite his limited education, as having something special to offer. As a result, he became a key minister in the Nation of Islam; his name was changed to Elijah Muhammad, and upon Master Fard Muhammad's disappearance in 1934 he became the leader of the organization. As one might expect there was a power struggle, and Elijah Muhammad was forced to leave Detroit. But during his absence he further developed the teachings of the Nation of Islam in line with what he'd been given by Master Fard Muhammad. To further clarify the Nation of Islam's structure, the Honorable Elijah Muhammad taught that Master Fard Muhammad was God incarnate: Allah always existed in physical form as opposed to Christian teachings that God is a spirit. Furthermore, he positioned himself as the final prophet sent to the African Americans in North America – the "lost, found nation" – to provide them with information necessary for their redemption and the restoration of their proper relationship with Allah. He imposed strict discipline including limiting members to one meal per day, business attire for men and clothing that fully covered women. Classes were developed to teach members their true history and importance as the creations of Allah, while re-enforcing the importance of self-sufficiency. Separation from whites was key for members of the Nation of Islam. Members were not to participate in politics because the United States was to be destroyed because of its sins and the original people – African Americans – who knew their true history and had knowledge of self would be restored to their greatness. Why participate, then, in a dying society? What really gained this religious tradition public exposure were the more charged elements of its theology. For example, the Honorable Elijah Muhammad taught that white Americans were "the devil." That is to say, they were made a long time ago through a grafting process involving the enhancement of recessive genes in the original people that lightened skin, while refining and strengthening aggressiveness and mischievousness. Allah allowed the making of whites in order to use them to punish the original people who'd strayed away from their original religion of Islam. As one might imagine, the idea that white Americans were demonic in nature caused quite a stir in a society marked by white supremacy.

The Nation of Islam grew during these years, but it was not until the 1950s, with Malcolm X (born Malcolm Little) joining the organization and becoming a major spokesperson, that the Nation of Islam gained national attention and expansion in Northern and Southern cities. Why X rather than another name for Malcolm X (1925–1965)? The "X" was given to new members of the Nation when their slave names (i.e., European names associated with slaveholders that were given to enslaved Africans in the colonies – "Smith," "Jefferson," and so on) were taken away. It demonstrated the unknown and served as a reminder that African Americans are not a part of this US culture.

Figure 5.2   Malcolm X. Courtesy of the Library of Congress, Prints and Photographs Division
[LC-DIG-ppmsc-01274].

In some cases, the X was replaced by a new last name that reflected the true self
and their membership in the Nation. The Honorable Elijah Muhammad provided
these new names. His not receiving a new name should not be read as a negative
statement concerning Malcolm X's importance to the Honorable Elijah Muhammad
and the Nation of Islam. To the contrary, Malcolm X's rhetorical gifts allowed him
to spread the teachings of the Honorable Elijah Muhammad more effectively than
any other minister, and consequently his rank within the Nation of Islam increased
to include the title of national spokesperson. He remained a faithful member of the
Nation of Islam until the last few years of his life. But new situations made staying in
the organization extremely difficult. For example, he became disillusioned with the
personal behavior of the Honorable Elijah Muhammad.

On top of his disappointment with the Nation's leader was the pain of his decreased
role in the Nation of Islam based in part on punishment for critiquing the United
States at the time of President John Kennedy's assassination. The situation was even
direr when one also takes into consideration growing jealousy over Malcolm X's role

in the Nation of Islam, combined with suspicion concerning whether he wanted to replace the Honorable Elijah Muhammad which resulted in threats on his life. He would eventually leave the Nation of Islam, converting to Sunni Islam in 1964. He traveled to Africa, went on pilgrimage to Mecca, and worked on the development of two organizations (the Muslim Mosque, Inc., and the non-religious Organization of Afro-American Unity). In large part, his goal was to provide new structures by means of which to address African American human rights in light of the United Nation's Universal Declaration of Human Rights (www.un.org/en/documents/udhr/). For Malcolm X – who changed his name to El-Hajj Malik El-Shabazz – his travels and pilgrimage demonstrated how far the Nation of Islam was from the world community of Islam's beliefs, and how wrong it was to assume whites were incapable of proper conduct and inclusion in the community of Muslims. He was assassinated in 1965. Questions remain concerning the circumstances surrounding his death.

The Nation of Islam continued under the leadership of the Honorable Elijah Muhammad until his death, in 1975. Minister Louis Farrakhan (1933–) assumed he would be appointed head of the organization at that point; however, prior to his death the Honorable Elijah Muhammad surprised many people by making his son, Wallace Deen Muhammad (Warith Deen Muhammad, 1933–2008), head of the Nation of Islam. Farrakhan attempted to work with the Honorable Elijah Muhammad's son, but changes to the Nation being made in an effort to bring it in line with other Islamic communities proved more than he could stand. Movement away from the Honorable Elijah Muhammad's teachings and policies, along with a demotion in his rank, resulted in Farrakhan leaving and reconstituting the Nation of Islam under the original teachings. Over time, Farrakhan modified the more charged elements of the Nation's doctrines as a way to downplay separatist elements and address charges of reverse discrimination and anti-Semitism. For example, the Nation of Islam no longer considered whites devils, but instead argued that white supremacy was demonic. Furthermore, instead of a demand for land that would allow African Americans to develop a "nation within a nation" – a separate nation within the territory of the United States – Farrakhan began encouraging members of the organization to involve themselves in the political life of the United States, and this included running for public office. Such alterations may have made the Nation of Islam more attractive to a US audience. However, the Nation of Islam's total membership has never been clear. And while it continues to exist in the United States and in other countries, there are questions concerning its ability to survive a transition from Minister Farrakhan to another leader.

While Farrakhan restored the original teachings, Warith Deen Muhammad moved those who remained with him into Sunni Islam by removing teachings inconsistent with Sunni Islam. Warith Deen Muhammad would rename his organization several times – the World Community of Al-Islam in the West (1976), American Muslim Mission (1981), and eventually the American Society of

Figure 5.3   Nation of Islam leader Louis Farrakhan, right, with Iman W. Deen Mohammed
prior to Farrakhan's speech at Saviours' Day 2000 in Chicago (February 27, 2000).
Courtesy of Tim Boyle/Getty Images.

Muslims. In a surprise to some, prior to his death, Warith Deen Muhammad began
to dismantle his organization, and he actively encouraged its members to become
involved in existing mosques. According to recent statistics, there are roughly 3
million African American Sunni Muslims in the United States. His importance
within Sunni Islam continued to increase as he gained, for example, the authority to
certify Americans for participation in pilgrimage – or Hajj – which is the journey to
Mecca required of all Muslims physically and economically capable of doing it.

It, however, would be a mistake to believe that Warith Deen Muhammad was
the only point of entry into Sunni Islam for African Americans. To the contrary,
as of the second decade of the twentieth century, Shaykh Dauod Ahmed Faisal's
Islamic Mission of America, Inc., was working to spread the teachings of Islam to a
North American audience, including African Americans, and to provide community
for immigrant Muslims. In locations such as New York, Imam Faisal provided
information concerning Islam as well as language training so that new Muslims in

the United States would have access to Arabic, the Qur'an, and the Sunna. African Americans Muslims associated with the mosques developed by Imam Faisal were trained in the basic practices and beliefs of Islam in counter distinction to what they considered the flaws in the practices of organizations such as the Nation of Islam. As might be expected, natural tensions and disagreements surfaced through the cultural differences between African Americans and immigrant Muslims, and Imam Faisal's mosque in New York – State Street Mosque – experienced a schism. African Americans and immigrant Muslims each had their own relationship with the United States that informed its understanding of Islam. Resulting from this friction in 1962 was the emergence of a new Muslim community led by Yahya Abdul Karim, called Darul Islam. According to some sources, Darul Islam grew to encompass some 30 mosques – a development stemming from belief that bringing people to Islam was a basic and necessary expression of one's faith. Members of these mosques were expected to separate themselves through their moral code, ethics, knowledge of Islam, and association primarily with other Muslims – but these mosques didn't embrace the political separatism advanced by organizations such as the Nation of Islam. In addition, the aesthetic of this community ran contrary to the European suits worn by male members of the Nation of Islam. Those in these mosques were expected to dress as best they could in a manner that represented traditional, Islamic sensibilities. By 1980, friction and schism would result in Yahya Abdul Karim announcing the end of Darul Islam. Yet, Sunni Islam would continue to grow in African American communities, and by the beginning of the twenty-first century, some would estimate the number of African American Sunni Muslims in the United States to be roughly 3 million.

Despite the media attention given the Nation of Islam, and the significant number of African American Sunni Muslims, one of the greatest impacts on popular culture in the United States has come through the Five Percent Nation (i.e., Nation of Gods and Earths). This organization was started in the 1960s by Clarence 13X, a former member of the Nation of Islam. According to some accounts, ethical and moral misconduct including gambling resulted in him being removed from the Nation of Islam by the Fruit of Islam, the division of the Nation responsible for discipline. Others argue that he recognized the shortcomings of the Nation's teachings, and left the organization in protest. In either case, Clarence 13X had a significant following amongst young men in Harlem, and they formed the core of his alternative movement.

In organizing the Five Percent Nation, or the Nation of Gods and Earths, he argued that the Nation of Islam failed to provide a complete understanding of the nature of African American men and women. The former are not simply created in the image of God; they are gods. In addition, women are earths to be respected for their ability to produce a nation. Clarence 13X – also called Father Allah by his followers – constructed divine mathematics as a way of interpreting and deciphering knowledge for the benefit of the members of the new organization. Through these teachings, members of the Five Percent Nation were able to unpack language in ways that revealed the true meaning of words. For instance, knowledge was said to involve *knowing* the *ledge*; or the library was said to be the place where lies are buried. Furthermore, disregard for the Nation of Islam is clear in the teachings: 85 percent of the African American population is ignorant and blind to the true facts of their purpose and status; 10 percent of the African American population has proper knowledge but fails to share it (i.e., the Nation of Islam); and, 5 percent of the population constitutes the poor righteous teachers, the members of the Nation of Gods and Earths who spread proper teachings. Appeal to young people and the organization's commitment to sharing information have been played out largely through the presence of Five Percent representatives in Hip Hop culture. In their lyrics and other aspects of the culture, artists provide the teachings first offered by Clarence 13X.

African American Islam

- The Moorish Science Temple is the earliest formal organization associated with Islamic belief and practice, and it was followed by the development of the Nation of Islam.
- Efforts were made to link African Americans historically and religiously to Africa and the Middle East.
- Attention was given to issues of health, appearance, and proper relationships as part of religious commitment.
- Both the Moorish Science Temple and the Nation of Islam changed names of followers to indicate a new identity and new sense of personal and community history.
- Doctrine provided a critique of white supremacy and replaced it with the superiority of African Americans.
- An effort was made to separate as much as possible African American Muslims from engagement in the social and political dimensions of life in the United States.
- Popular culture, particularly Hip Hop, has been used to spread Islamic teachings.

Caribbean and South American influence on African-based traditions

Islam is not the only religious orientation to gain greater visibility and organizational status during the twentieth century. Traditions such as voodoo also grew. During the early twentieth century, practitioners could easily gain information on voodoo experts through newspaper advertisements. Those with proven abilities also developed a strong clientele that purchased special items and paid for consultations. Even after the period dominant by Marie Laveau (and those claiming the name), voodoo's importance and power remained in place. However, with time, a distinction would be drawn between voodoo practices meant for tourists in locations such as New Orleans, and actual practices and beliefs available only to those willing to make a clear commitment. Those involved in more than superficial appeals to some of the more basic elements of voodoo were involved in a complex and rich system composed of a wide range of gods and other spirits, many of which were developed in direct response to the condition and needs of African Americans in North America. Rituals were in place that appealed to particular gods and spirits, and in exchange for proper attention to these invisible forces practitioners were able to have their wants and needs addressed. Conjure and hoodoo – which are understood as typically interchangeable terms for the same attention to spirits and the magical practices (differentiating them tends to be a matter of personal preference for one term over the other) – also continued their role as sources of magical aid to those wanting assistance. During the late twentieth century, these traditions received more media attention, some of it for instance in the form of films telling fantastic stories of zombies and spirit possession. Other films provided a more balanced presentation of these practices. In either case, African-based traditions during the twentieth century captured the imagination of Americans in a much more public way. In part increased attention dates back to the popular writings of anthropologist and folklorist Zora Neale Hurston. Based on her fieldwork, including personal experience with African-based traditions in Florida, Hurston wrote books and articles providing information on hoodoo and conjure beliefs and practices during the twentieth century. Recognition by the World Order of Congregational Churches in 1945 only served to further the tradition's public recognition. And while hoodoo and conjure continue to this day, there are also African Americans who have worked to maintain the full scope of voodoo belief. They include leaders such as Ava Kay Jones of New Orleans, who seeks to maintain a distinction between the authentic practice of voodoo and the superficial and sensationalized materials made available to tourists in that city. Jones attempts to accomplish this through public education on voodoo.

While the movement of practitioners of African-based traditions into North America goes back to the period of slavery and the arrival of Haitian slaves during the Haitian revolution, during the twentieth century the movement also goes in the opposite direction with African Americans going to the Caribbean, South America, and Africa for training. It is reasonable to believe African Americans were aware of traditions such as Santería – "the way of the saints" – because of the movement of Cubans and Puerto Ricans to the United States in significant numbers. For example, botánicas, or shops selling ritual items associated with this tradition, were present in major cities such as New York and Los Angeles by the mid-twentieth century. Some scholars argue that these shops were established to provide ritual supplies for

Figure 5.4   Voodoo priest with her snake – French Quarter, New Orleans. © LOOK Die
Bildagentur der Fotografen GmbH/Alamy.

practitioners whose presence dates back to the 1940s, perhaps with Francisco Mora
being the first to organize the tradition when he arrived in the United States in 1946.
Practices and communities revolved around the Spanish language, and this posed
a barrier for African Americans who might be interested in learning more about
the tradition. This, however, did not mean the full exclusion of African Americans,
but it did result in rather limited participation and minimal understanding of the
activities and supporting belief system. It was typically the case that these traditions
were safeguarded and assumed to be relevant only to those who knew the languages
of the traditions, and who had been introduced to the religious community by one
of its members. Based on this system of introduction, the Jazz played by figures
such as Tito Puente referenced the beliefs of "the way of the saints" and was a major
source of contact sparking the interest of African Americans. Some heard him play
and wondered about the figures named and celebrated in his music. Connecting to
this type of introduction was an interest on the part of some African Americans to
connect to their African heritage and to reject what they considered a religion of

enslavers – Christianity. These practices, influenced by Africa in a number of ways, provided a way of doing precisely that.

According to many, African Americans were initiated into "the way of the saints" within the first few years of the 1960s, and as of the 1970s African Americans were moving beyond participation in Spanish-speaking *iles* – or houses composed of practitioners – to form their own. In some cases this level of independence also played out in the way in which the tradition was described, with some African Americans referencing it as "Yoruba religion," or "Ifa" rather than calling it Santería. In addition to African Americans entering the tradition from the United States, others traveled. In fact, one of the most prominent examples involves African Americans going to Cuba to gain initiation. In 1959, Walter King (1929–2005) was initiated in Cuba. He brought back to the United States what he learned and used this information to establish a cultural society as well as other related organizations. His efforts to highlight the African nature of the tradition met with some resistance and critique from members of the larger Santería community. Unable to gain in the North the type of traction he needed in order for his work to thrive, King relocated and founded Oyotunji African Village in Sheldon, South Carolina. He served as the King of the Village with the title of Oba Efuntola Adefunmi I. This village is committed to the practice of Yoruba culture, including its religious dimensions, and Oba Efuntola Adefunmi I claims adherents across the country, many of whom spent time in the Village being initiated into the tradition.

The African nature of the tradition – in the context of the Village it was initially called "Orish-Vodou" – should be in the forefront, this includes the clothing worn, the work done, the rituals observed, the language used, great attention to the ancestors, and so on. The teachings within the Village remove the Catholic elements found in Santería, arguing that masking the African gods was necessary during the period of slavery to protect the traditions and their practitioners, but this is no longer the case. From the perspective of members of this community, the tradition is for people of African descent and must be safeguarded in line with this belief.

Other African Americans have made their way to Brazil to participate in traditions such as Candomblé, and they brought their practice back to the United States with them. In addition, others spend time in West Africa to secure initiation into African traditions. They make this journey reasoning that one can best understand African traditional practices by going to their place of birth and learning from those who have been able to maintain these traditions without the type of interference experienced by enslaved Africans in the Americas. Whether one thinks in terms of Spanish-speaking adherents or African Americans, practices developed in the United States or brought from elsewhere, it has often been the case that they have met with discrimination and suspicion based on animal sacrifices and other practices that trouble many Christians. However, the late twentieth century saw the arguing of court cases that safeguarded the religious freedom of those practicing African-based traditions. In this way, one sees some traditions gaining the freedoms and protections that had once been the almost exclusive holding of Christian churches. All this points to the globalization of African-based traditions and the blending of various elements from these traditions by African Americans and others who look to these traditions for aid with the deep questions of life.

African-based traditions

- Travel to the Caribbean, South America and Africa result in the expansion of these practices.
- New organizations and communities emerge with African American leadership.
- Effort was made in some cases to highlight the African nature of these traditions through removal of any signs of Christianity from associated beliefs and rituals.
- Legal cases guarantee free practice without interference.

Buddhism and African Americans

African Americans are not only looking to Africa for religious guidance. While the numbers are smaller in comparison to some other traditions, roughly 30,000 African Americans claim Buddhism as their religion of choice. With some limited attention to Buddhism stemming back to the 1800s, attention in the United States to Eastern tradition began in earnest during the mid-twentieth century as part of an effort to find comfort in a world marked by war (World War II) and destruction. While African Americans in general were suspicious of these developments, the support for civil rights that leaders from Buddhist communities demonstrated over the years made it particularly appealing. Concern for equality and a downplaying of race as significant gave African Americans a way to think about Buddhism as a resolution to the conflicts and problems facing them in a society so very concerned with race. Furthermore, it avoided the limitations of the Christian faith, but allowed African Americans to address both their individual development and the needs of the larger community. This was particularly true with respect to Soka Gakkai International-USA and its efforts toward tolerance. The "Four Noble Truths" – life is marked by suffering; suffering is caused by our desires for false happiness; suffering ends when desire ends; the eightfold path offered by Buddhism ends suffering – could be embraced along with one's sense of identity as an African American. For example, Buddhist teachings on the nature of suffering aided African Americans attempting to understand socio-political and economic developments and to put them in perspective. Meditation allowed African Americans an opportunity to center themselves and focus on the importance of inner life and balance. Buddhism's visibility within African American communities was enhanced when celebrities such as Tina Turner and Herbie Hancock embraced the tradition. The frustration with Buddhism, however, has often involved the inability of African Americans to gain positions of leadership within the organizational structure of the tradition in the United States.

Buddhism

- The vast majority of African American Buddhists are affiliated with Soka Gakkai-USA, an organization first present in the United States as of the 1960s.
- Support for the socio-political issues important to African Americans served as an entry point for Buddhism.
- Attention to peace and education gave the tradition added appeal.

Variations on Christian themes

The Civil War resulted in a variety of shifts and changes in the make-up and arrangement of religious organizations. However, the trauma of war also produced other practices. For example, death – over 600,000 killed during the Civil War – raised questions for remaining family members concerning what happened to their loved ones after their physical death. While traditional churches offered answers, they failed to provide opportunity to hear directly from the spirits of departed loved ones. What emerges in response to this perceived shortcoming is the tradition of Spiritualism, which involved a series of practices and rituals such as séances that allowed for communication with the dead. These activities eased the pain of loss by suggesting that there are links between physical life and spiritual life. Drawing on teachings coming from France and elsewhere, Spiritualism offered religious relief from the misery of life in a country at war. However, the importance of this tradition did not end with the Civil War, but rather remained viable into the twentieth century.

Some of the alterations involved African Americans taking elements from Spiritualism and combining them with elements of Christianity and voodoo. Black Spiritual churches emerged as a result of this blending of belief systems. Spreading from Northern cities such as Chicago and Detroit, to Southern cities such as New Orleans, Black Spiritual churches provided a structure that allowed for spiritual well-being and the tools necessary for material success. They were called "spiritual" over against "spiritualism" because the churches wanted to highlight their deep connection to the inner self; they were spiritual people. Initiated by the efforts of noteworthy figures such as Mother Leafy Anderson (1887–1927), King Louis H. Narcisse (1921–1989), and George Willie Hurley (1884–1943), Black Spiritual churches combined attention to a vast spirit world with a style of worship connected to Holiness and Pentecostalism. In addition to belief in God, these churches believe a series of spirits, including spirit guides such as the Native American Black Hawk, provide answers to questions and general assistance with life challenges. The basic framework of Black spiritual church beliefs and practices centers on an effort to harness the powers of the spirits to address pressing issues of life, and in this way contribute to the formation of rich life meaning. These churches had the look of traditional African American churches, with a few clear exceptions: status of saints and spirit guides, and tables with rituals items for key spirits. In addition, the attire of ministers in spiritual churches combine Protestant robes with Roman Catholic items associated with bishops and cardinals. Most of these churches have small memberships, but they can have supporters beyond members in that ministers in these churches who claim to have strong connections to the spirit world provide consultations with a range of people including members of the larger denominations.

Strong connections to the spirit world were of importance to more than just members of spiritual churches, and a blending of spiritual and material concerns marked a variety of traditions emerging during the twentieth century. In important ways, the socio-political and economic challenges of the twentieth century meant an audience for anyone who could demonstrate unique powers or insights that improved life conditions. One such figure was Reverend Major Jealous Divine (1876–1965), or more commonly referred to as Father Divine. Emerging on the scene in the 1920s when he was first affiliated with a Baptist Church, he then worked as the assistant to a minister named Samuel Morris who referenced himself as "Father Jehovah." By this time, Divine was well aware of a positive thinking philosophy known as the "New Thought Movement." His relationship with Morris would end, and he would combine his Christian sensibilities, positive thinking, and claims to divinity into a unique belief system and organization. He was God – a source of authority and divine knowledge not represented by others. Father Divine preached a strict lifestyle to his small group of fellows. And he was able to establish a multi-racial community in which all things were held in common.

People were particularly impressed by his ability to feed, clothe and house people during the Great Depression when so many Americans were suffering. His social ministry served to separate him from many of his contemporaries who were less "worldly" in their thinking and practices, and the claims made by his followers resulted in the spread of his movement across the country, from New York to Los Angeles. There was also knowledge of his movement in Europe. Some estimate that the membership of his organization rivaled that of some of the major African American denominations. The size of his movement and his economic resources made him popular with politicians and community leaders as well as the general population. Confrontation with other religious leaders over theological issues (e.g., some objected to the claim that Father Divine was God) resulted in the Peace Mission leaving New York and relocating to Philadelphia. After his death in 1965, his wife –

Figure 5.5   Father Divine's Peace Mission, New York City. Courtesy of the Library of Congress, Prints and Photographs Division [LC-USF34-012896-D].

Mrs. S. A. Divine – controlled the organization. And while it no longer maintains the numbers once associated with it, the Peace Mission continues to operate.

Father Divine was not alone in his interest in New Thought. Reverend Frederick J. Eikerenkoetter (1935–2009), simply known as Revered Ike, was a minister who preached a message framed by a commitment to proper thought generating material results. He started preaching early, serving as an assistant pastor of his father's church at 14, and he would go on to found churches in South Carolina and Massachusetts. Reverend Ike was best known for the church he developed in Harlem – the Christ United Church. Connected to this church are various educational programs offering degrees related to New Thought. Through his personal wealth, he sought to demonstrate the way in which thought and action connected, and on both television and radio he used testimonials as a way to verify his claims. Reverend Ike had a personal style that was flamboyant and distinctive, yet he wasn't the only minister during this period with a unique aesthetic.

As Father Divine's reach declined, that of Marcelino Manuel da Graça (1881–1960), better known as Sweet Daddy Grace, increased. After arriving in the United States from the Cape Verde Islands, he began a preaching career and built his first church before 1920. He traveled the United States preaching a message that hinged on the understanding that while he was not God, he was God's primary instrument. His teachings were also based on practices associated with the growing tradition of Pentecostalism. This basic principle is played out in the structure of the ministry, which is composed of a variety of positions, such as bishops, but with everyone answering to the ultimate authority of Sweet Daddy Grace.

Much of the church's doctrine involved forms of holiness that promoted strict and proper behavior. Through services marked by music, energetic worship, the United House of Prayer for All Peoples grew under his leadership, expanding both the number of physical locations and the reach of his teachings even beyond the physical churches he built. For example, its organizational structure included a variety of products such as those for personal hygiene and foodstuff all speaking to the importance and power of Sweet Daddy Grace. And while Sweet Daddy Grace was the ultimate authority in the church, there were leadership opportunities for talented members that encouraged the further development and expansion of his vision. Because of its structure, the organization survived the death of its founder. And while the actual number of members is uncertain, it has maintained its presence in major cities such as New York and Washington, DC.

The religious connection between church and political nationalism is perhaps most clearly presented in the emergence of the African Orthodox Church associated with Marcus Garvey's Universal Negro Improvement Association (UNIA), and organized in 1921 by George Alexander McGuire who served as the chaplain of the UNIA. Garvey's movement to restore the greatness of people of African descent through relocation to Africa was the largest mass movement to ever take place regarding the socio-political condition of African Americans. This strategy was linked to a theological assumption readers will remember from other contexts: African Americans are a chosen people by God, designed for greatness that can only be fulfilled outside the context of the Americas. And more to the point, he believed African Americans should envision a God who looked like them, just as white Americans spoke of a God who physically favored whites. But ultimately these theological changes would have little significance unless they motivated people of African descent to return to their African home. Many Methodist and Baptist ministers – including Malcolm X's father who had also been a minister – and laypersons embraced his teachings and rolled them into their thinking and activities within their churches and denominations. The impact of Garvey's movement was felt across the globe, from the United States, the Caribbean to places such as South Africa and Ghana.

Diversification of African American denominations

All of the traditions noted above pushed against traditional African American churches, providing critiques of what these churches offered theologically and practically. And in response to these perceived shortcomings, these new traditions

Figure 5.6   Marcus Garvey. Courtesy of the Library of Congress, Prints and Photographs
Division [LC-USZ61-1854].

offered themselves as alternatives. There is every reason to believe some African
Americans embraced these critiques and selected alternatives to the African American
Christian Tradition as a way to engage the large questions of life. Some African
Americans remained members of predominately white denominations, and in many
cases, they are part of substantially African American congregations within these
denominations. For example, African American Catholics, while a small component
of the worldwide church, still represent a noteworthy percentage of African American
Christians. However, the Methodist and Baptist denominations continued to grow in
size and popular importance during the first several decades of the twentieth century.
Before the end of the century, African American Methodism and Baptists would
be dominated by the African Methodist Episcopal Church, the African Methodist
Episcopal Church Zion, the Christian (formerly Colored) Methodist Episcopal
Church, the National Baptist Convention, USA, the National Baptist Convention of
America, and the Progressive National Baptist Convention. Participation within the

political struggles of African Americans differed in these various denominations, but the Progressive National Baptist Convention was unique in that it was organized due to the desire of some Baptists to participate more fully in the civil rights activism that was sanctioned by the National Baptist Convention, USA.

In their own ways, these various denominations developed domestic and international mission efforts resulting in new churches and new programs meant to meet the spiritual and material needs of African Americans. Added layers of administration and new techniques for responding to the changing socio-political and economic environments mark Baptist and Methodist denominations during this period. This starts from the very beginning of the twentieth century. For example, the Reverend Reverdy C. Ransom developed the Institutional Church and Social Settlement House in Chicago in 1900 as a way of providing spirituality, educational opportunities and social programs. He, like several others, attempted to blend their Christian beliefs and socialism so as to transform socio-political and economic relationships consistent with their perception of Jesus Christ's development of communal existence. In short, Ransom and a few like him embraced socialism (i.e., as a political and economic system). Within Baptist circles, schisms produced new strands of theological thinking due to disagreements over doctrine and resources. However, each of the conventions gained membership.

The formation of Pentecostal churches, particularly the Church of God in Christ, shifted the make-up of the most widely recognized churches. Within the Holiness Movement discussed earlier, some insisted on a step beyond sanctification. This involved speaking in tongues as evidence of believers receiving the Holy Spirit. For these Pentecostals, such a sign of sanctification was consistent with the story of Pentecost in the New Testament. While many African American Christians rejected both Holiness and Pentecostal teachings, other Methodists and Baptists embraced the demand for a more structured and disciplined religious life. For them it offered a way to make sense of the seeming socio-political, cultural and economic turmoil of the twentieth century.

Figures early in this movement included Charles Parham (1873–1929), a white person who taught Pentecostal doctrine in various locations, established a school in Topeka, Kansas, and who maintained Jim Crow regulations. His students claimed to have received baptism in the Holy Spirit during worship, and they spread word of this event to all who would listen. The school did not last long, but Parham would duplicate it in Houston, Texas. And while racism prevented African Americans from actively participating in Parham's school, at least one gained some of the school's teachings indirectly. This person, William Seymour, started his training in Ohio, and continued it in Houston before taking Pentecostal doctrine to Los Angeles. Despite some resistance from those abiding by Holiness teachings, Seymour continued his ministry seeking to bring people to a full understanding of their Christian commitment and to do so in a way that discarded race as a marker of

Figure 5.7 The Church of God in Christ. Courtesy of the Library of Congress, Prints and Photographs Division [LC-USW3-010264-C].

difference: we are all the same under Christ. Under the leadership of Charles Mason (1866–1961), the Church of God in Christ attempted to live out the doctrinal and ethical demands of the Pentecostal Movement so widely associated with the Azusa Street revival in Los Angeles led by William Seymour.

Mason, initially a Baptist minister, was ostracized in Baptist circles because of his embrace of Holiness teachings such as sanctification. However, with the assistance of Charles P. Jones and W. S. Pleasant, he established a church – the Church of God (1897) – in line with these teachings. Mason claimed to have received a revelation from God with a new name for the church – the Church of God in Christ. Shortly after this name change, Mason attended the Azusa Street revival and embraced its Pentecostal teachings. Attempting to implement these teachings in his church proved problematic, and he lost the support of many, including Jones. Over the course of several decades, using ministers sent out to preach in revival style, Mason's church grew into the largest African American Pentecostal denomination in the United States.

Like the other denominations, an increase in the number of members and physical churches resulted in changes to the administrative and programmatic structure of the denomination. This growth garnered the attention of whites and African Americans

> When the day of Pentecost had come, they were all together in one place. And suddenly from heaven there came a sound like the rush of a violent wind, and it filled the entire house where they were sitting. Divided tongues, as of fire, appeared among them, and a tongue rested on each of them. All of them were filled with the Holy Spirit and began to speak in other languages, as the Spirit gave them ability.
>
> (Acts of the Apostles 2:1–4)

alike, and both came to Mason seeking ordination into Pentecostal ministry. Like Baptist and Methodist denominations, the Church of God in Christ has maintained an interest in missions – both domestic and international – as well as some attention to issues of social justice, although the dominant concern has consistently revolved around personal salvation and the individual search for life meaning marked by holiness. In a general sense and in keeping with Seymour's ability to gain international interest, Pentecostalism found an eager audience in the Caribbean and in Brazil, as well as Europe and Africa, where Pentecostalism represented one of the fastest growing religious orientations in the twentieth century. This growth continues today.

The 1950s and 1960s marked a unique period of growth for African American churches in large part because of public attention given to church leaders involved in social justice efforts. However, during the 1970s–1980s African American churches experienced a decrease in membership for a variety of reasons. These reasons include the manner in which socio-economic and educational gains made (as a result of the Civil Rights Movement) provided other means by which to secure socio-political and economic improvement. Furthermore, there was some disillusionment with churches due to an increasing interest in black power ideologies combined with what was considered the conservative stance of so many churches. It is important to keep in mind that although there were prominent figures whose public presence might give the impression that all churches were involved in the struggle for socio-economic and political advancement, the fact is most were not. In short, during the decades after the most energetic phases of the Civil Rights Movement, African American churches – like other denominations in the United States – experienced numerical decline. This was not always acknowledged by these denominations (to do so will be to admit their declining influence), but studies during the period attest to this dilemma as being very real. Declining membership was matched in some churches by a shift in orientation with respect to the public mission of the Church, whereby some churches turned their attention to spiritual concerns and left public affairs to others. Scholars have come to refer to the decline of church participation in public issues as the "deradicalization of black churches," by means of which they lost their major focus on the socio-political welfare of African Americans. And this was matched by the "dechristianization of black radicalism," whereby efforts toward social justice became more solidly lodged

New Christianity-based Churches

- Combine Christianity with other traditions.
- Often led by charismatic leaders.
- Critique Christianity as taught and practiced in mainstream African American churches.
- Often combine spiritual growth and material success through a combination of scripture and positive thinking philosophies.

in secular organizations such as the National Association for the Advancement of Colored People (NAACP).

Churches had become too comfortable in their mainstream status, but African Americans had alternatives to these churches. The air was thick with frustration and disillusionment on the part of many African Americans with churches. However, the 1990s marked a turn in this trend as members of the African American middle-class moved back into churches. They did so for a variety of reasons including a desire to forge new relationships with African American culture; to network with other African American professionals; to provide cultural outlets for their children; and, to address a desire for fulfillment that was not addressed adequately through gaining a piece of the American dream (e.g., good education, good job, suburban home). Due to this influx of professional African Americans, it became increasingly difficult to assume the pastor was the more highly educated or capable person in the church. The presence of lawyers, doctors, businesspersons and so on meant the need for changes in leadership structures. Successful churches recognized the benefits associated with tapping into the talents of these new members, and, to accomplish this, many churches implemented different leadership structures based on a sharing of power and control regarding church business. One consequence of this new model was the ability of churches to undertake more projects without the need for the pastor to be the point person. The pastor could comfortably delegate responsibilities because of the range of talents and skills represented in the congregation. I have in mind community organizations associated with churches that are run by members, rather than the pastor, who have professional training in business and law (e.g, the Bridge Street AWME Church's "Bridge Street Affiliated Community Corporations and Programs" headed by Dr. Robert J. Williams, Jr. rather than the pastor, the Rev. David Cousins). This is not to say that such talent has not always existed in churches; rather, the late twentieth century represented such talents in greater numbers due to greater access to higher education and employment opportunities.

The status of African American Christianity has shifted over time, moving from deep relevance to a questionable presence. The ebb and flow of its importance is reflected not simply in public conversation concerning various denominations and debates regarding the role of churches such as those taking place online (e.g., Religion

Dispatches, Huffington Post, BlackandChristian.com), but also in the ways in which various church organizations reconstruct their programs, arrange models of leadership to include members with specialized degrees and talents, and adapt beliefs to reflect contemporary challenges such as HIV/AIDS. As the questions, challenges, and successes of African Americans changed from the nineteenth to the twentieth century, churches shifted to reflect their perspective on the conditions of African American collective life. This re-thinking and re-presentation of African American churches has not done away with questions concerning their role in African American public life. If anything, the past few decades have entailed intensification of these questions.

African American Jews

Most of the new religious developments during the twentieth century play off Christianity in some way – either critiquing its basic doctrines or transforming these doctrines. However, in addition to this positive and negative attention to Christianity, there were also African Americans who rejected Christianity and embraced Judaism. For some, this meant an embrace of Judaism in line with the American Jewish community as represented by Orthodox, Conservative, and Reform traditions. The number of African American Jews is not clear; however, estimates range from fewer than 50,000 to 200,000. For others, an embrace of Judaism required alterations in line with the challenges of black identity in the United States. Grounding for this latter position is found in earlier appeals to the Hebrew Bible and framings of African Americans as being similarly positioned to the Children of Israel. Like the latter, African Americans have faced suffering, have been removed from their homes, and forced to wander the "wilderness" (i.e., plantations supporting the system of slavery). Furthermore, like the Children of Israel, African Americans awaited an exodus from their oppression. This perspective, for example, is found in many of the spirituals and it also found a home in sermons related to the development of African American communities as having special connotations and special meaning. Most prominent amongst late nineteenth- and early twentieth-century leaders behind configurations of Judaism is Prophet F. S. Cherry (1870–1965), who organized a group in New York City popularly known as the "Black Jews," but more properly known as the Church of the Living God, Pillar of Truth for All Nations. Prominent in his teachings is the belief that African Americans are the descendants of the Jews mentioned in the Hebrew Bible. Like others, Prophet Cherry sought to reconstitute African American identity in more positive terms by associating central biblical figures with blackness. Hence, he understood Jesus to be black like African Americans. As such, they, Black Jews, are the chosen people of God; they are those favored by God; and, they are those who are meant to occupy God's kingdom on earth. For some African American Jewish groups in the United States there was an interest in moving to Israel as fulfillment of God's plan for their restoration to the "Promised Land." However,

Figure 5.8   New York City's first black rabbi, Wentworth A. Matthew, leader of Harlem's
Ethiopian Hebrew congregation. Courtesy of NY Daily News/Getty Images.

this was not the case with all. Unlike other groups, Cherry's community gives little attention to Christian interpretations of the Bible and instead relies primarily on the Talmud, which is the central text of Judaism giving attention to the basic elements of religious life and practice such as ethics and the history of the Jews. The efforts of Prophet Cherry were followed by similar ministries, such as that of Arnold Ford who studied the Talmud in a much more systematic and sustained fashion than most. While Ford's work took place over a short period of time, it did inspire Wentworth Matthew who developed a congregation in 1919 called the Commandment Keepers Congregation. He, like others before him, used Judaism as a way to rethink African American identity, to separate it from the racist history of the United States by connecting African Americans to a different land and people.

African Americans were really associated with the Israelites referenced in the Bible. While these communities made claims to an identity connected with the land of the Hebrew Bible, the Hebrew Israelites founded by Ben Ammi extended the argument by relocating members to Liberia and then Israel as of 1969. He, unlike others, argued that his people weren't Jews but were Hebrews, and this distinction revolved around his embrace of only the Torah and not the other materials accepted by the Jews. Although he would modify this distinction with time, he and the Hebrew Israelites remain committed to belief and practice consistent with a particular take on Judaism.

African American Jewish organizations

- Often argued African Americans are the chosen people.
- God and Jesus are black.
- Selective in which texts associated with Judaism are embraced.
- At times seek relocation to Israel.

Institutionalized humanism

As various formations of God-centered traditions emerged and fought for followers, humanism remained a persistent reality within African American communities. African American literature during the first six decades of the twentieth century – particularly the "Harlem Renaissance" – gave voice to humanist sensibilities as writers such as Richard Wright (1908–1960), Lorraine Hansberry (1930–1965), and Alain Locke (1886–1954) expressed the opinions and beliefs of African American atheists and humanists. The promotion of humanism in literature continued through the end of the twentieth century by means of the publications and speeches of figures such as Alice Walker (1944–). However, during the twentieth century this presence also took more organized and institutional form primarily through African American involvement in social protest organizations such as the Black Panthers, the NAACP, the Student Nonviolent Coordinating Committee associated with the Civil Rights Movement, the Communist Party, and so on. African Americans remain a small but active membership in the Humanist Movement through membership in the American Humanist Association, the Center for Free Inquiry's African Americans for Humanism, and other national, regional and local organizations. In addition, some African Americans expressed their humanist sensibilities and beliefs through membership in the Ethical Culture Society movement and the Unitarian Universalist Association.

As of the 1940s there were efforts on the part of African Americans to establish congregations within the Unitarian Universalist Association (UUA). The two most prominent ministers attempting this were Egbert Ethelred Brown (1816–1902) in New York and Lewis McGee (1893–1979) in Chicago. Brown's work produced few results and with time he lost financial backing by the UUA in part because of his limited success in establishing a viable congregation but also because the Association wasn't certain that the attainment of "non-white" members was very important. More successful, however, was McGee who established the Free Religious Fellowship in the late 1940s, an organization that survived his retirement. During the 1960s and 1970s the debate concerning issues of race within the Association gained more public attention and resulted in both moments of growth and some setbacks as African Americans became disillusioned with the slow pace of change. Nonetheless, the Association today maintains an African American presence in the pews, ministry,

Twentieth-century humanism

- Its ideas become articulated in a growing body of fiction and non-fiction literatures.
- Associated with organization such as the Unitarian Universalist Association as well as non-church related communities such as the American Humanist Association.
- Struggle to have issues of race and racism recognized within humanist circles.

and denominational leadership. As one example, William Sinkford became the first African American president of the Association in 2001, and he served in this capacity until his retirement.

All these developments – new denominations, new religious movements, and reconstruction of existing traditions – took place as nineteenth-century social regulations gave way to new restrictions on the relationship between African Americans and political life. The pseudo-sciences provided justification for discrimination by suggesting that the size of the African American's skull, the look of his/her face, and other dimensions of the physical look served to make reasonable practices meant to exclude that population from full participation in the life of the country. In response, each tradition or religious community in its particular way sought to wrestle with the new challenges to identity and life meaning given rise by the altered dynamics of what it means to be African American in the United States.

Key points you need to know

- Twentieth century witnesses tremendous expansion of religious options, each in competition for members.
- The importance of African American churches is debated as some focus on spiritual renewal and others combine that with social justice work.
- Religious leadership changes to reflect the skills of new members and the changing foci of religious organizations.
- Pentecostalism becomes the fastest growing religious orientation in African American communities.
- The global reach of African American religious traditions gains momentum.
- Many of the social functions of religious organizations are taken over by non-church affiliated groups.
- Membership of African American churches declines during several decades of the twentieth century, and when African Americans return they do so for some reasons that aren't connected to spiritual commitment.
- Black identity and black nationalism become major areas of doctrinal and practical concern.

Discussion questions

1. Why did many African Americans become disillusioned with churches, and what resulted from this?
2. What is meant by the "deradicalization of black religion"? Give an example of how this occurred in the twentieth century.
3. What did African Americans find appealing about Buddhism as presented by Soka Gakkai International-USA?
4. What was the impact of Pentecostal teachings on African American religion?
5. What are some of the reasons African Americans embraced traditions such as "the way of the saints"? What were some the frustrations associated with an effort to participate in the tradition?

Further reading

Brandon, George. *Santeria from Africa to the New World: The Dead Sell Memories.* Bloomington, IN: Indiana University Press, 1993.

Brown, Karen McCarthy. *Mama Lola: A Vodou Priestess in Brooklyn.* Berkeley, CA: University of California Press, 1991.

Chireau, Yvonne and Nathaniel Deutsch, eds. *Black Zion: African American Religious Encounters with Judaism.* New York: Oxford University Press, 2000.

Dannin, Robert. *Black Pilgrimage to Islam.* New York: Oxford University Press, 2002.

Essien-Udom, E. U. *Black Nationalism: A Search for Identity in America.* Chicago, IL: University of Chicago Press, 1962.

Jacobs, Claude F. and Andrew J. Kaslow. *The Spiritual Churches of New Orleans: Origins, Beliefs, and Rituals of an African-American Religion.* Knoxville, TN: University of Tennessee Press, 1991.

McGreevy, John T. *Parish Boundaries: The Catholic Encounter with Race in the Twentieth-Century Urban North.* Chicago, IL: University of Chicago Press, 1996.

Morrison-Reed, Mark D. *Black Pioneers in a White Denomination*, 3rd ed. Boston: Skinner House Books, 1994.

Sanders, Cheryl. J. *Saints in Exile: The Holiness-Pentecostal Experience in African American Religion and Culture.* New York: Oxford University Press, 1996.

Williams, Angel Kyodo. *Being Black: Zen and the Art of Living with Fearlessness and Grace.* New York: Penguin, 2002.

Part II

Major themes in African American religion

6   *Worldly change, or a new world?*

In this chapter

As the previous several chapters noted, much of what we know about African American religion (particularly black churches) revolves around the outcomes of a tension between an "other-worldly" orientation and a "this-worldly" orientation. This raises a few questions: Is African American religion concerned with saving souls or changing the socio-political and economic arrangements of life for African Americans? What is the final result of a religious life? Such questions are of concern within the religious context of other communities as well. However, in this chapter an effort is made to answer these questions with respect to African Americans.

Main topics covered

- How religious institutions distinguished types of responsibilities to their communities
- Arguments made to justify the main positions on institutional obligations
- The impact of the social, political, and economic developments of the work performed by religious institutions
- Ways in which institutional growth was affected by the types of services provided

The early functions of African American religion

Thinking back to Chapter 1, it is clear that religion seeks to accomplish something. The ability of religious traditions to promote greater life meaning, to wrestle with the large questions of life, has remained central over the centuries. Its purpose is to provide greater life meaning, to help its adherents respond to the huge questions of life such as who we are, what we are, and, why we are. This has always been the purpose of religion, and it is likely to remain the primary purpose. Religious traditions that accomplish this in relationship to the pressing issues of the day grow and gain status. Those that fail to provide compelling responses to those questions in ways that satisfy the needs of the moment fail to advance and die off. However, open to discussion is the particular range of needs a given religious tradition highlights and the type of answers to life's questions it provides. In a word, does the tradition primarily promote the securing of heaven as the objective of its work, or does its work give more significant attention to the improvement of life for its members on earth? Regarding this question, one thing is certain: perspectives on the ultimate reward for a religious life shift over time.

During the period of slavery, forms of African American religion provided a way for enslaved Africans to survive the hardships of life. This involved both ways to think about themselves as fully human and as valuable to God and the world – and this took place through either a turn to the importance of their physical body, in terms of the value of their soul, or in some combination of the these two. Through this rethinking of their worth, African American religion provided a critique of slavery and dehumanization by pointing out the hypocrisy of slaveholders who claimed to be Christian but whose behavior was brutal and without the compassion exemplified by Christ. So, in the spirituals they reminded listeners "everybody talkin' 'bout Heaven ain't going there." At times religious pronouncements were more aggressive in that religion provided the tools to physically fight back against slavery by assuring enslaved Africans that their enslavement was wrong and that the shedding of blood to secure their freedom was consistent with the will of God. The most visible examples of this position include slave revolts, or even more subtle attacks on slaveholders through the use of conjure and hoodoo to harm them if not kill them. At other times, religion provided a way for enslaved Africans to rationalize their condition and look beyond it for a reward after their physical life was over. What emerges during this period is a tension, a type of conflict between opinions – with some arguing religion is concerned with a better existence beyond this world, and others that provide much more attention to improving life on earth. The question can be put simply as this: what to make of heaven? The more institutionalized traditions often contained both opinions – with one dominating at any given point in their history. For example, some Christian leaders pushed followers to believe what took place in this life paled in comparison to the rewards they would receive in heaven, if they lived a good spiritual life. Others, like Henry McNeal Turner of the AME Church, were much more committed to active struggle against slavery and they understood their Christian faith and their churches as a way of achieving a better life. Heaven wasn't so much of a concern for radical leaders like Turner. African-based traditions, while working through a spirit world, concerned themselves with improvement of life circumstances within the context of the physical world. Yet, even this appeal to spirit forces seems to be in services of earth-based questions and concerns. There does not appear to be great concern with salvation, in part because unlike Christianity, there is no sense of original sin that requires work to overcome. Instead, the work of African-based traditions involves an effort to create balance in life through the proper relationship of physical forces and spiritual forces, but all this work for balance was meant to enhance the welfare of our physical existence. This is not to say African-based traditions have no sense of a realm of existence beyond this physical world. They certainly do. Yet, the involvement of African Americans in these traditions tends to highlight these traditions' impact of human life within the context of this physical world. Finally, regardless of the particular tradition, it appears within African American religion in general there has been a tension between a set of responsibilities – running from strict concern within spiritual life, to a combined concern with the spiritual and physical needs of African Americans, to expressions of religion that appear much more grounded in the physical wants and needs of practitioners.

Pre-Civil Rights Movement

- Tension between concern with spiritual life and physical justice.
- Churches privilege the soul through moral and ethical codes to control bodily desires.
- Other churches support slave rebellions, political policies, and educational opportunities as their priority.

New needs and religious response – Civil Rights Movement

This tension remained in place after slavery's end and was perhaps intensified by what was supposed to be a new context of freedom. African Americans, after the Emancipation Proclamation ended the system of slavery, still encountered discrimination and they often turned to religious traditions to help them during these tough times. Heightened by the disappointments of the Great Migration, as African Americans moved into cities looking for opportunities, religious institutions felt the pressure of new and old members wanting assistance with a full range of needs. Some churches responded by extending their programs and offering their resources to meet the physical needs of those coming to them for assistance. Taking the form of job training, educational opportunities, classes to improve social skills, and so on, for these churches their teachings gained a social dimension whereby they understood Christian compassion to include a full range of services. Other churches, either because of limited resources or because of their doctrines and creeds, expressed a concern only with the spiritual life of African Americans. They offered opportunities for African Americans to find salvation and they provided the tools necessary to help Christians live more Christ-like lives, but they expressed little interest in providing for the socio-economic and political needs of those around them. Instead they suggested that the demands of secular life were of limited consequence when one considered that salvation would mean eternal happiness once this physical life ended.

African American churches worked to establish themselves first within a country defined by racial discrimination and then within the context of a country struggling to re-think itself in light of African Americans as free citizens. When reflecting on this, many scholars privilege the story of churches as organizations concerned with the needs of African Americans in the world through a spirituality combined with mundane programs. Others provide a more balanced perspective by highlighting the existence of both an "other-worldly" perspective and "this-worldly" perspective often within the same churches. However, it is also the case that this debate concerning the proper activities and focus of churches was often forgotten by the mid-twentieth century because the popular US imagination begins to focus on the energy of the Civil Rights Movement and the manner in which it appears to be headed by religious leaders and discussed through the use of Christian vocabulary. For many, the role of some churches in the civil rights struggles of the twentieth century exemplifies the orientation of African American Christianity. And Dr. Martin Luther King, Jr. (1929–1968), is typically understood as the best representative of the activist church concerned not with heaven but with life on earth.

Based on his formal education, and commitment to engaged faith, Martin Luther King, Jr., made use of the church as a base from which to structure and populate a host of protest activities all geared toward the securing of full inclusion in the life of the Nation for African Americans. His doing this as a minister of an African American church only enhanced the assumption that churches were rightly concerned with the socio-political and economic needs of African Americans. He spoke in these terms, and who could ignore interviews regarding and photographs of strategy meetings and recruitment sessions taking place within churches? Everything seemed to point to changed physical life circumstances rather than an appeal to a better life after death. Even the songs and slogans associated with the Civil Rights Movement are drawn from and couched in religious language. King was not alone because other ministers and their churches paved the way through localized protest for King and the national movement to step in. Participants in the Civil Rights Movement such as Fannie Lou Hamer (1917–1977) spoke during interviews and meetings about the importance of her faith for her efforts on behalf of African Americans. It, according to Hamer, was her commitment to Christ and the Church that provided much of the energy and commitment marking her civil rights and economic work despite the potential threat to her own safety.

The importance of religious organizations and institutions for civil rights activism is also suggested through negative encounters. For example, the bombing of the Sixteenth Street Baptist Church of Birmingham, Alabama in 1963 killed four young girls and pointed out how those opposed to the equality of African Americans marked churches as both real and symbolic centers for civil rights work.

And attacks on churches in part because they represented for many a prime location – again practically and symbolically – for struggle against injustice continued

Figure 6.1   Martin Luther King. Courtesy of the Library of Congress, Prints and Photographs
Division [LC-DIG-ppmsc-01269].

Civil Rights period

- Nation of Islam rejects participation in the Civil Rights Movement.
- Debate concerning church involvement results in a schism creating the Progressive National Baptist Convention as a church organization committed to social protest.
- Humanists' views represented in the movement.
                               (SNCC and the Black Panther Party).

beyond the civil rights struggle. For example, defacing of churches in the 1980s and the burning of African American churches in the 1990s speak to such assumptions concerning these organizations: white supremacists reasoned destruction of these important institutions would send a loud and clear message against equality, and this message would go to those most likely associated with efforts to produce different life options for African Americans.

Figure 6.2 Congress of Racial Equality conducts march in memory of youngsters killed in Birmingham bombings (1963). Courtesy of the Library of Congress, Prints and Photographs Division [LC-U9-10515-6A].

> Anybody in the South knows that the strength of the black community is our churches. When they start to burn our churches, they're trying to take away our strength.
>
> (Pamela Berry, quoted in Ron Nixon and Dennis Bernstein, "Mississippi Burnings: Who's Torching Black Churches, and Why Hasn't the Massive Investigation Cleared the Smoke? *Vibe Magazine* (October 1996): 98)

It is also important to remember that, even according to Dr. King, most churches did not actively support the movement: they did not provide financial resources and did not physically participate. Instead, the movement relied on a small but committed group of activist ministers and churches.

Conflict between the two approaches – spiritual renewal or physical freedom – is presented graphically through the schism encountered by the National Baptist Convention USA, the Church organization of which Dr. King and his church were a part. There had been debate within the Convention concerning whether or not it should – as an organization – take an active role in the Civil Rights Movement, and which strategies should be used. The president, Joseph Jackson, rejected this type of approach – direct confrontation and demonstrations – to civil rights advocated by King. However, King and his supporters favored the Convention playing a lead role consistent with the civil rights strategies promoted by King. A failed attempt to remove Joseph Jackson from the presidency of the Convention resulted in a backlash that ultimately could only be addressed through the departure of Dr. King and a like-minded group, who in 1961 formed the Progressive National Baptist Convention with a full commitment to an aggressively direct approach to civil rights. Others not active in the movement consistent with the model provided by Dr. King were not unaware and were not necessarily disconnected. For example, some Christians holding to this perspective prayed for change, assuming the final condition of humans was tied to the will of God and not human action. One could argue that some Christians used prayer and other spiritual practices as struggle against injustice just as others used physical protest and resistance.

During the same period of time, Sunni Islam was growing in the United States and provided a response to the dehumanization perpetuated by "Jim Crow" regulations. Sunni Islam re-framed African American social, moral, and religious sensibilities by connecting African Americans to a worldwide community of Muslims. For example, the work of Darul Islam with African American prisoners was taking place during the Civil Rights Movement, and might be understood as that community's effort to reconstitute black life through rigorous work in prisons and the providing of proper understanding of faith for African Americans. Darul Islam understood adherence to one's Islamic faith and close association with only those who also held to the faith as a way around "Jim Crow" discriminatory practices. Darul Islam, that is to say, argued for limited separation, from those not of the Islamic faith. Yet, the Nation of Islam provided a different model. The Honorable Elijah Muhammad, the leader of the Nation of Islam, argued that its members should not participate in the US political process. This is because he believed the United States would be destroyed, and the original inhabitants of the Earth – black people – would again rule. Why, then, worry about the political workings of a nation that was bound to end within the near future? African Americans might, through their non-violent direct action, secure some rights but that wouldn't change the overall nature of this country, nor would it prevent its eventual destruction. No, African Americans would simply be wasting time trying to fit into a country that is incapable of loving them when time would be better spent learning the true knowledge of themselves and preparing through proper discipline and training for their future greatness associated with the return of Allah (aka Master Fard Muhammad). While reflecting some of the sensibilities associated with Christian talk of heaven – e.g., a new world for the faithful – it is a vision grounded in the physical workings of society and it takes place on earth.

According to the Nation, African Americans had been brainwashed by Christianity to believe they need inclusion in this country. This perspective, however, was combined

Figure 6.3   Elijah Muhammad surrounded by members of the Fruit of Islam at a convention in
Chicago. © Bettmann/CORBIS.

with a deep regard for African American life expressed through the rhetoric of self-
defense. Yet, the Nation's members were never involved in direct conflict. There
weren't members charged with use of weapons in self-defense, or physical harm to
others in the capacity of defending themselves. Violence was a reality only within the
community. For example, the Fruit of Islam as the disciplinary unit of the Nation was
often associated with violence against members as a way of correcting wrongdoing,
but not against those outside the Nation of Islam organization. One might consider
the Nation's tough talk and efforts in the direction of African American nationalism,
but it did nothing that resembled the direct confrontation marking some African
American churches and their ministerial leadership. Members of the Nation of
Islam were taught to protect themselves against attack, but this active safeguarding
of African American well-being did not extend to participation in the democratic
process, not even in voting. The Nation of Islam further justified this stance through
its demand for African Americans to have their own land, their own economic
system, their own political structures. To accomplish this, the Honorable Elijah
Muhammad demanded the United States provide land and resources sufficient to
25 years, enough time to get started on solid footing this new nation within a nation.
This approach downplayed the politics of one nation for that of another created by
and for African Americans. What is somewhat odd about this situation involves
the Honorable Elijah Muhammad's deep concern that members of his organization,

particularly its high profile minister, should not say anything negative about political leaders such as President John Kennedy. He wanted to avoid unnecessary challenge of and animosity toward his organization. Yet, this seemed matched by ongoing critique of white racism and a veiled threat that members of the Nation of Islam would meet violence with an appropriate degree of violence. This they said marked a necessary appreciation for African American life and the right of US citizens to protect themselves against potential harm to life or property. Furthermore, while not explicitly involved in the Civil Rights Movement, there were ways in which the public presence of key members such as Malcolm X pushed forward the less charged rhetoric of Dr. King and as a result made the demands of the Civil Rights Movement as presented by church leaders more attractive. Not participating in the sit-ins, protest marches, etc., associated with the Civil Rights Movement, did not prevent Malcolm X from commenting on those activities and encouraging the "powers that be" to work with King so as to avoid having to deal with him. Before his split with the Nation of Islam, Malcolm X would begin to show signs of frustration with the Nation's policies. He was growing tired of critiquing churches and the civil rights struggle, but offering little concrete activity of his own. The rhetoric of struggle was becoming thin for Malcolm X, but for as long as he remained in the Nation he followed the teachings of the Honorable Elijah Muhammad and avoided direct involvement in politics and social justice activities associated with the Civil Rights Movement.

Many religious organizations avoided direct confrontation over issues of racial injustice. Father Divine and Sweet Daddy Grace, for the most part, addressed such issues through providing resources for their membership and shaping their organizations in ways meant to offer aid. If anything, Father Divine considered himself to be building a new society, a new 'heaven' on earth in the form of the peace mission. But non-violent direct action was not the hallmark of the ministries of these two. African American Buddhists found in that tradition a posture toward life and an understanding of dignity that informed their activism – to the extend they were involved – but Buddhism itself within African American communities did not have the Civil Rights Movement presence of African American churches. Furthermore, a focus on physical needs and wants ran contrary to Buddhist teachings on the nature of suffering and the way in which suffering ends. It ends when one surrenders desires and wants. African-based traditions also provide an intellectual base for understanding religion as having felt consequences in the physical world, and their appreciation for human life also contributed to this thinking. Yet, these traditions did not provide an infrastructure and organizational base for social justice activity during the Civil Rights Movement. Unlike these traditions, although their numbers were small, African American humanists were active and visible in the civil rights struggle. From members of the Black Panthers such as Huey Newton, to the leadership of the Student Nonviolent Coordinating Committee (SNCC), like James

Figure 6.4　Black Panther Convention, Lincoln Memorial: people gathered with a banner for the Revolutionary People's Constitutional Convention (1970). Courtesy of the Library of Congress, Prints & Photographs Division [LC-DIG-ppmsca-04303].

Forman (1925–2005), many humanists understood themselves to have an obligation for involvement in the struggle for justice in large part because there are no cosmic sources of assistance. There is no heaven in place to serve as an alternative to a transformed set of life options on earth. Humans are responsible for their condition and only humans can correct their condition.

Members of the Black Panther Party often maintained civil relations with churches because they understood these churches provided quick and efficient ways to spread information and secure people to help with their breakfast programs for students and other programs, but this did not mean they embraced the church's teachings including its particular modes of protest and perceptions of heaven.

Instead, Black Panther leaders such as Huey Newton (1942–1989) in some of his writings maintained distance from belief in God as a source of aid with the human struggle against power and for justice.

Humanists such as Forman (who is explicit in his autobiography about his atheism) also gave little attention to divine assistance with human struggle, instead committing himself to social justice struggles during the Civil Rights Movement. He had questions about the involvement of churches, believing as he did that church teachings had an internal flaw – belief in a concerned God and the Black Church's connection to the religious practices and concerns of a country marked by a legacy of slavery – that prevented proper activism. This type of frustration with the strategies offered by churches in the Civil Rights Movement was not his alone. Many, including the late Stokely Carmichael (Kwame Ture, 1941–1998), expressed a similar disillusionment with Christianity as a source of sustainable political protest. Instead of a continued allegiance to Christianity, Carmichael proclaimed a need for "black power," as the alternative to American racism and this had nothing to do with the Christian faith. It was a secular call for African American control over the life and destiny of African Americans.

Post-civil rights: what now?

The Civil Rights Movement resulted in a variety of advances on socio-economic and political fronts for African Americans and others. African American churches and church leaders received a good deal of credit for this, and some of these leaders sought and gained political offices as a way to further their social justice work. This included civil rights activist, Reverend Jesse Jackson's (1941–) bids for the Democratic nomination for the presidency of the United States in 1984 and 1988. Some within church circles remained assured that the proper concern for Christians was not simply heaven, but a more just and healthy existence on earth. Others continued to debate this, suggesting that heaven is the ultimate goal of the gospel message. With denominations representing the latter perspective growing after the Civil Rights Movement while other African American denominations declined in membership, the importance of each claim was put to the test. Furthermore, what appeared to be the changing fortunes of African Americans raised anew questions concerning the purpose and function of religion. The appeal of heaven as the end product of the religious life remained in place for many, while others were more concerned with the ability of religion to offer tools for transforming the circumstances of their ordinary, mundane lives. Some churches worked to support an other-worldly agenda while others put in place activities and community programs meant to address earth-based concerns. This is not to say that churches concerned with mundane issues did not appreciate the Christian assumption that people have souls needing attention. No, they continued to recognize that humans are more than their bodies; yet, they understood that their work must involve more than just attention to the soul as if bodies don't matter. That is to say, religious organizations with a "this-worldly" direction understood the health of the soul and the restoration of proper relationship with God as a source of energy for their earth-based work. They read in the story of Jesus Christ a deep concern with the physical conditions of life, and they sought to mirror that. In other words, their work in the world made their souls deserving of connection with God after death. On the other hand, many of those who privileged the soul saw attention to its needs as the end in and of itself, and work in the world could easily serve as a distraction and a danger to the welfare of their soul. In either case, morality and ethics remained important, while the target of our actions and perspective on what is right and wrong differs depending on which of these two goals dominate.

Post-Civil Rights Movement

- Christian leaders once in the Civil Rights Movement gain political offices.
- Nation of Islam changes it policy on involvement in secular affairs, giving it priority status.
- The White Office of Faith-Based and Neighborhood Partnerships developed to add churches interested in social service programs.

The "Charitable Choice" regulation put in place in 1996 gave religious organizations interested in social services as part of their outreach an opportunity to secure federal dollars. One can imagine how this might impact the tension between this-worldly and other-worldly orientations. An old argument used by some churches, for example, for not doing more work on secular issues involved limited resources. Now those resources could be secured through the United States government. This did not necessarily mean churches changed their thinking on the significance of heaven, but it did mean opportunities to expand services for churches that saw work in the physical world as being a high priority. Fifteen years after "Charitable Choice" was initiated, a more robust option was initiated with the creation of the White House Office of Faith-Based and Neighborhood Partnerships. Many activists and citizens – more than a few being humanists and atheists – have complained that this department is inconsistent with the constitutionally imposed separation of church and state: it seems only churches are receiving this money, and are they using it to spread their teachings? Others have applauded what it means in terms of more sustainable efforts for social improvement on the local level.

The ongoing existence of this office adds a wrinkle to the question of the proper role of religious organizations by complicating the sources of either position – spiritual development or physical renewal. Are churches involved because of the

Figure 6.5   President Barack Obama signs the executive order establishing the White House Office of Faith-Based and Neighborhood Partnerships (2009). Courtesy of http://www.whitehouse.gov/.

money available? Does the availability of this money affect the spirituality of religious organization and put them under the domination of government? One thing is for certain – the debate regarding the purpose of religion was amplified and engaged by those inside and outside religious organizations, including politicians and attorneys.

Much of this debate took place within the major African American denominations, while other, smaller groups began a process of decline during the late twentieth century. For example, the death of charismatic figures such as Father Divine and Sweet Daddy Grace greatly impacted the ability of those organizations to maintain a high profile in the public arena. Father Divine's wife continued the work he started, but has not mustered the same growth and the same involvements. In like manner, passing away five years before Father Divine, Sweet Daddy Grace's church continues in a variety of locations and it still attracts visitors, but without the same level of impact. Furthermore, Buddhism continued to remain viable, having supported the justice-related activities of African Americans for much of its time in the United States, but without a significant presence in these larger and more energetic debates; and African-based traditions remain of real interest to a growing group of African Americans but with no more influence on this debate than Buddhism. Unlike Christianity and Buddhism, the African-based traditions have no sense of humanity as flawed in ways that can support the same sense of perpetual struggle making so much of their doctrine and practices necessary. To the contrary, these African-based traditions recognize the need for involvement on the physical level and use their resources for this purpose but without a visible presence in worldly activism. In this way, for most churches and other religious traditions, the questions were asked in new ways because of the changing circumstances encountered by African Americans in the aftermath of the Civil Rights Movement.

The twentieth century witnessed major changes in the perspective of Darul Islam as some of its members moved in the direction of Sufism, while others remained Sunni in their religious orientation. Yet, the tension resulted in major shifts in the organization of Sunni Islam in the United States. The Nation of Islam also experienced a split revolving around perception of Islamic practice – on the role of religion and the activities of the religiously motivated in the world. As was noted before, the death of the Honorable Elijah Muhammad ushered in many changes as his son, Wallace Deen Muhammad, moved the organization in the direction of Sunni Islam. Minister Louis Farrakhan's revival of the Honorable Elijah Muhammad's approach to Islam initially started with few alterations. However, with time, some of the more charged elements of the teachings – such as the idea that white Americans are evil by nature – had their importance rendered symbolic (e.g., white supremacy and racism are evil). Farrakhan maintained a commitment to the teachings regarding the return of Allah and the Honorable Elijah Muhammad in the "Mother Ship," an advanced space craft that would be used to destroy all peoples on earth except those who embraced the teachings of the Nation. There is a sense in which the timeframe for this event shifts – so many African Americans left to reach with the truth about their history and their purpose. And, for members of the Nation the consequence of this return isn't a distant heaven within a different realm of existence, but rather it involves a purged earth and the development of a new society run by the "original people," the members of the Nation. So in certain ways, the Nation of Islam promoted a type of heaven as the purpose of their work, but this involved transformed, physical arrangements. The Honorable Elijah Muhammad provided the initial workings of this doctrine, but without attention to any involvement in the current structures of political society. However, under the leadership of Minister Louis Farrakhan, as the twentieth century moved towards its close, the Nation of Islam promoted activities meant to gain greater participation in the life of the United States for African Americans. In fact, Farrakhan wrote a book – *A Torchlight for America* – that outlines political policies, educational policies and so on – arguing that the book can be used to save the United States from destruction. One must wonder what impact this new approach has on the significance and timing of the redemption of the members of the Nation through the return of their original leader and their God. Despite such questions, now there is a more intimate connection between redemption and physical life, a blurring of the line between an "afterlife" and the present existence of people.

Key points you need to know

- The question of what religious organizations should privilege was tied to their doctrine and creeds.
- The Great Migration resulted in new needs and new methods of naming and meeting African American spiritual and physical needs.
- Religious organizations often changed their opinions on whether to privilege the soul or social transformation.
- The Civil Rights Movement centered the conversation concerning what religious organizations should be doing.
- Religious organizations were at times the target of those seeking to maintain the political status quo.

Discussion questions

1. What caused the 1961 schism within the National Baptist Convention USA?
2. What changes did the Nation of Islam make to its approach to heaven or earth-based transformations?
3. What is the White House Office of Faith-Based and Neighborhood Partnerships? Why are some opposed to it?
4. What role did humanism play in the Civil Rights Movement? And, what did humanists such as Huey Newton say about churches?
5. What reasons did churches give for avoiding social activism? What reasons did they give for promoting social activism as the core of their mission?

Further reading

Baldwin, Lewis V. *The Legacy of Martin Luther King, Jr: The Boundaries of Law, Politics, and Religion*. Notre Dame, IN: University of Notre Dame Press, 2002.

Carson, Clayborne. *In Struggle: SNCC and the Black Awakening of the 1960s*. Cambridge, MA: Harvard University Press, 1995.

Cone, James H. *Martin and Malcolm and America: A Dream or a Nightmare*. Maryknoll, NY: Orbis Books, 1992.

Evans, Curtis. *The Burden of Black Religion*. New York: Oxford University Press, 2008.

Farrakhan, Louis. *A Torchlight for America*. Chicago, Il: FCN Publishing Co., 1993.

Frederick, Marla F. *Between Sundays: Black Women and Everyday Struggles of Faith*. Berkeley, CA: The University of California Press, 2003.

Forman, James. *The Making of Black Revolutionaries*. Seattle, WA: University of Washington Press, 1997.

Harris, Frederick C. *Something Within: Religion in African-American Political Activism*. New York: Oxford University Press, 2001.

Joseph, Peniel E. *Waiting 'Til the Midnight Hour: A Narrative History of Black Power in America*. New York: Henry Holt Co., 2007.

Marable, Manning. *Malcolm X: A Life of Reinvention*. New York: Penguin Books, 2011.

Pinn, Anthony B. *The Black Church in the Post-Civil Rights Era*. Maryknoll, NY: Orbis Books, 2003.

Ross, Rossetta. *Witnessing and Testifying: Black Women, Religion, and Civil Rights*. Minneapolis, MN: Fortress Press, 2003.

Savage, Barbara Dianne. *Your Spirit Walks Beside Us: The Politics of Black Religion*. Cambridge, MA: Harvard University Press, 2008.

7 Religion, race, and racism

In this chapter

Issues related to race and racism shape certain dimensions of life for all communities in the United States, and this is certainly the case with respect to African Americans. Earlier chapters note the importance of these two social constructions. This chapter, however, pushes the discussion along by exploring the ways in which African American religion has defined the dilemma of racism and how it has worked to address the damage caused by racism.

Main topics covered

- Changes in the nature and look of race
- Religious traditions' understanding of the nature of the human
- Impact of visual culture on religious communities' presentation of race
- Changing presentation of racism in the United States
- Practices of religious communities related to race and racism

Race

The importance of race has been at the very least implied in each of the other chapters. This is because of the ways in which race and racial differences have shaped social arrangements, politics, cultural production, and economic opportunities in the United States. However, this negative relationship to difference was not always the case. Historians tell us that the initial encounters between Europeans and Africans were marked by recognition that they did not look the same, that they dressed differently, enjoyed different activities, and arranged their social and economic lives differently. Yet, during these encounters, prior to the initiation of slavery, differences between the two groups were not understood as suggesting that one group was superior to the other. Instead, they were different and this lacked socio-political ramifications. However, the emergence of the slave trade fostered a need to differentiate Africans and Europeans more aggressively using the language of superiority and inferiority. It is important to remember that race is not biological but rather it is a social construction, a way of categorizing peoples that has no real relationship to their humanity. However, it does provide an easily identifiable marker of difference, one upon which other social practices and policies can be placed. This was certainly how race functioned within the period of the slave trade. Those involved in the slave trade took advantage of the difference in appearance between Africans and Europeans; they privileged themselves in terms of the look of their physical body and labeled Africans inferior.

This story of the slave trade raises an important question. How could Europeans who moved to the Americas for religious freedom treat others with such inhumanity? Even for those who moved to the Americas for economic and political reasons, how could they justify the slave trade and justify the dehumanizing of Africans? Many opposed the enslavement of Africans, and would come to be called "anti-slavery" advocates or "abolitionists." However, those who justified slavery made use of a variety of arguments to sanction their treatment of Africans. First, European slave holders remarked that there were physical differences between Europeans and Africans that pointed to deeper and more substantive inferiorities. That is to say, assuming they were the standard for civilization and humanity, some Europeans argued that because Africans did not look like Europeans they also lacked intelligence, full humanity, and therefore they were of less importance. In short, those sympathizing with slavery at times argued that what they perceived as a lack of beauty in Africans was accompanied by a general inferiority that justified their enslavement. After all, the argument went, Africans were not fully human the way Europeans were human. Advocates of slavery understood differences in the culture and social habits of Africans as being clear signs of this inferiority – difference equals "otherness" and inferiority. Philosopher Cornel West (1953–) labels this process the "normative gaze," and by this he means Europeans used the Greek body as the examples of the most beautiful, most intelligent and most culturally sophisticated human. And they believed those who most closely resembled the look of the Greeks also most closely resembled the Greek's beauty and intelligence. They looked more like the Greeks, and by extension, they were of more importance and more value than Africans who did not resemble the Greek body-type. Or so went the argument. This way of thinking freed supporters of slavery to trade human bodies with few outward signs of regret, offering an increased comfort with holding Africans in bondage as their property throughout the generations.

This argument of inferiority was given religious sanction as well. Supporters of the slave system reasoned that God selected them for greatness and gave them the Americas to establish themselves as God's chosen people. In this regard, the North American colonies represented a "city on a hill" established by God's glory and for

God's people. To the extent Africans were viewed as being religiously different as well as physically and intellectually different, supporters of slavery argued Africans were not God's people but were rather to be used by God's people to fulfill God's will. After all, the Bible did not condemn slavery but instead placed groups at the service of God's people – in this way physical difference and religious difference justified slavery. For biblical support of this argument, the story of Noah and his son Ham was used at times.

The curse of Ham

Noah was the first tiller of the soil. He planted a vineyard; and he drank of the wine, and became drunk, and lay uncovered in his tent. And Ham, the father of Canaan, saw the nakedness of his father, and told his two brothers outside ...When Noah awoke from his wine and knew what his youngest son had done to him, he said, "cursed be Canaan; a slave of slaves shall he be to his brothers."

(Genesis 9:20–22; 24–25)

As the story goes, after the flood initiated by God to destroy sinful humans and re-establish the world, Noah along with his family – who had been selected and preserved from the flood – began life anew. As part of this work, Noah planted a vineyard and became drunk on the wine he produced. While drunk, his son Ham, who went and told his brothers what he'd seen, discovered Noah naked. Because it was a sign of disrespect to look at one's naked parent, Ham's brothers walked backwards without looking at their father, and covered him up. When he awoke and discovered that Ham had seen him naked, he cursed Ham's son Canaan – proclaiming that Canaan was to be a slave to his brothers. It was argued that Ham and his son were the ancestors of Africans and as a result the enslavement of Africans took place through God's will expressed by Noah.

This argument for the slavery of Africans is referred to as "the curse of Ham." When challenged on their treatment of Africans, they then easily pointed to scripture and argued that they were simply acting in ways consistent with the Bible and the will of God. They were doing nothing wrong, but rather they were fulfilling God's plans for humanity in that dark people – Africans as the children of Ham – were destined for servitude, and their color is a marker or sign of this destiny.

The end of the slave system did not wipe out a perceived need to continue arguments for the racial inferiority of African Americans. Rather, it simply meant a shift in the purpose intended for these reasons. It was no longer premised on a need to keep Africans enslaved. Now it was a matter of preventing them from having and exercising

Figure 7.1   The Curse of Ham. © INTERFOTO / Alamy.

Arguments used to justify slavery

- Africans were different and therefore inferior.
- God favored Europeans and gave them the Americans to build a new society.
- The Bible indicated that the children of Ham – African – were slaves because God approved of their servitude.
- Slavery gave Africans an opportunity to encounter and accept the Christian faith.

all the rights and privileges held by white Americans. This new intent benefited from technological shifts that allowed advances in how arguments supporting the inferiority of African Americans were constructed. During the nineteenth century, the "pseudo-sciences" developed, so called because we know that these scientists operated out of their cultural and social biases rather than through scientific, objective attention to data. Nonetheless, at the time, researchers such as Louis Aggasiz at Harvard University claimed that scientific procedures such as measuring the size of the head demonstrated that white Americans had greater capacity and that people of African descent not only looked inferior but also, through phrenology (i.e., study of an assumed connection between brain size/shape – by means of the skull – and character), could be scientifically proven to have limited intellectual capacity. Whereas during the period of slavery, religion and interpretations of sacred texts took the lead in development arguments for the inferiority of African Americans, during the nineteenth century the pseudo-sciences such as phrenology played that role. In either case, African Americans were classified racially as being inferior aesthetically and medically. The pseudo-sciences were combined with cultural production that depicted African Americans as physically unappealing and threatening. African American women were often depicted as Jezebels or Mammies, either oversexed animals or sexless servants. And African American men were depicted as buffoons or threatening beasts. Many of these images would survive into the twentieth century, and while scientific rationales for racism were more difficult to make, they did not go away completely. As a consequence of these arguments and cultural depictions, African Americans, although free, continued to experience restrictions on their mobility, limited economic opportunities, almost no political involvement, and the constant potential of violence against them.

It was assumed that African Americans, although free citizens, were incapable of full participation in the life of the country. Those making this argument ignored the negative impact of slavery and continued discrimination on educational achievement, job opportunities, and family structures, and instead simply suggested that the condition of African Americans resulted not from discriminatory policies and practices – after all, they were free – but from their inherent insufficiencies. Even efforts to help African Americans during the twentieth century often traded on such assumptions. For example, the Moynihan Report, a document produced by politician Daniel Moynihan was meant as a mid-twentieth century corrective for the plight of African Americans. Yet, it noted that the family structures and social arrangements of African Americans were based on pathologies.

This 1965 report, coming on the heels of several significant civil rights gains, was meant as a further corrective and not as an argument supporting discrimination. However, it assumed that white family structures and social arrangements were normative – the standard. In this way, it tended to blame the victims of discrimination for their plight in that it did not appreciate the coping mechanisms developed by African Americans but instead labeled them a problem to be addressed: the women are breeding beyond the capacity of the community to address the needs of the children; fathers not in the home leaving women in charge and, for Moynihan, this compounded the difficulties and inhibited African American life options. He correctly points out the damage done by slavery and continued discrimination. Moynihan

Moynihan Report – "Tangle of pathology"

Obviously, not every instance of social pathology afflicting the Negro community can be traced to the weakness of family structure. If, for example, organized crime in the Negro community were not largely controlled by whites, there would be more capital accumulation among Negroes, and therefore probably more Negro business enterprises. If it were not for the hostility and fear many whites exhibit toward Negroes, they in turn would be less afflicted by hostility and fear and so on. There is no one Negro community. There is no one Negro problem. There is no one solution. Nonetheless, at the center of the tangle of pathology is the weakness of the family structure. Once or twice removed, it will be found to be the principal source of most of the aberrant, inadequate, or antisocial behavior that did not establish, but now serves to perpetuate the cycle of poverty and deprivation.

(Quotations from "The Negro Family: The Case for National Action,"
Office of Planning and Research, United States Department of Labor,
"The Moynihan Report," 1965)

suggests that improvement for African Americans should involve a mirroring of white family structures as opposed to questioning the way in which making white American behaviors the standard of conduct re-enforces subtly white supremacy and suggests a continuing division that allows for continued discrimination.

Although not his aim, the report fostered an environment in which African Americans could be categorized as the problem of the welfare state, abusive of handouts, and a strain on the resources and ethics of the nation. Racism has been so deeply embedded in the fabric of life in the United States that it is not easily uncovered and removed. It flourishes through socio-political, economic and cultural justifications of difference in people as a negative thing and continues to thrive within religious traditions where, from the period of slavery to the present, it often receives a type of trans-historical justification through religion doctrine and creeds. Nonetheless, African American religious traditions have made it a prime target of their thinking and activities from the period of slavery to the present.

The impact of this situation is clear and extends beyond the twentieth century. According to the Annie E. Casey Foundation, in 2010, 66 percent of African American children (under 18 years of age) are in single-parent homes – typically headed by the mother. This is compared to 24 percent of non-Hispanic whites. Furthermore, according to others, roughly 70 percent of African American children are born out of wedlock, as opposed to less than 30 percent of white children and 43 percent of Hispanic children. These statistics with respect to African American families too easily connect to other troubling developments. For example, a significant

Figure 7.2 Daniel Moynihan. Courtesy of the Library of Congress, Prints and Photographs Division [LC-DIG-ds-01515].

percentage of high school dropouts come from single-parent homes. The economic implications are clear in that the "Neighborhoods and the Black-White Mobility Gap" (Economic Mobility Project founded by the Pew Charitable Trust) study points out the financial hardships facing many African American families in that growing up in neighborhoods with high rates of poverty increases the likelihood that the child will become an adult with limited income resources. For instance, in 2009, the median net worth of African American households was only $2,200, and this is compared to a median net worth of $97,900 for white households. The fact that a much smaller percentage of white children spend their childhood living in high poverty areas than do African American children has remained consistent for several decades. In fact, the rate of African American children exposed to high levels of poverty from 1955 to 2000 has been almost four times that of white children. The consequence of this situation is "downward mobility" – a substantive decrease in economic well-being. African American churches and other religious communities over the years have recognized this dilemma and they attempted to combat it. For example, church doctrine encourages two-parent households and typically discourages divorce, and ritual practices such as "Father's Day" are meant to encourage the involvement of men in the lives of their children. Furthermore, the outline African American lectionary (http://www.theafricanamericanlectionary.org) used by many ministers to prepare sermons and develop worship has information available that targets these particular issues and provides churches with creative ways of thinking about and addressing issues related to African American families. In fact, there is an annual "Strengthening the Family" lectionary entry meant to help churches talk about challenges to families. Trinity United Methodist Church in Chicago offers an example of how attention to the family is brought into the ministerial concerns of a congregation. Concerning its ministry to married couples the Church announces: "The Married Couples' Ministry is a fellowship of couples aiming to strengthen marriages, while providing and receiving support from other couples. We also strive to illustrate a positive image and the importance of the covenant we made with God and our mates. We pray that this ministry will not only be a blessing to your marriage but that your testimony will strengthen the marriage bonds of other relationships." In addition, outreach programs offered by churches often give attention to financial support, counseling, affordable housing and educational opportunities meant to enhance the economic health of African American families. Christian churches are not alone in working to address the dilemmas resulting from challenges to families. The Islamic Society of North America, for instance, has information on its website that addresses domestic violence as a threat to the stability of households, and key in its presentation of this issue is attention to the Qur'an as being opposed to abuse within relationships:

> Families need to maintain open lines of communication between all of their members; regular family meetings where everyone is allowed to express themselves without any recriminations are helpful. Marriage must be seen as a partnership, and marriage contracts should specify a commitment to an abuse-free and violence-free family. The parents must ask of their children only that which is good and which conforms to Qur'anically based concepts. Extended families must stop covering up abuse, violence, and incest in the name of "preserving the family honor." Above all, the family, like the individual must keep Allah as its focus.

Redefining race and its significance

From African-based traditions to African American churches, religious communities responded to the construction of African Americans as inferior based on race. For most of these traditions the response has something to do with the very creation of all peoples. For example, African American churches have argued for a single creation of humans by God, consistent with the image of God. Christians reference this as *imago Dei*: God created humans in God's image; therefore all humans are of the same substance and have the same relationship to God. Based on this, there can be no inferior or superior human beings. African-based traditions typically argue for the integrity of humans from the point of creation as well. In all these cases, there is nothing about the creation of humans or the look of any particular group of humans suggesting a divine stain of inferiority. Some within churches made an effort to attack directly the reading of scripture used to justify slavery. They argued, for example, that the story of Ham does not promote the inferiority of Africans because it is not Ham who is cursed, but Canaan, Ham's son. And, in response to the traditional interpretation of this scripture, critics question the idea that God would obey the whims of a drunken man. Furthermore, they argue that the Christ Event of the New Testament supersedes Hebrew Bible moral and ethical arrangements, and Christ makes no distinction between groups of humans. It is not that these various traditions do not acknowledge the difference in the physical look of different groups of humans. They do; however, they see these differences as having no impact on the beauty or importance of a given group, and they certainly don't see racial difference as justification for poor treatment.

A more radical stance on the topic was taken by a few within African American churches, figures such as Henry McNeal Turner (1834–1915) of the AME Church who argued, in 1895, that "God is a Negro." Turner's goal was to counter all the religious images and conversations that presented God as resembling white Americans. Turner reasoned such a proclamation was the natural extension of the idea humans are made in the image of God. To follow this to its logical conclusion, each community should think about God and depict God as resembling them in God's features and commitments. He argued one reason African Americans weren't making substantial gains is because they were content to think about what is best in the Universe – God – as resembling them in no particular way.

Most African American Christians were offended by Turner's proclamation, and this would be the case until the Civil Rights movement and the Black Power philosophy of the 1960s. At that point more and more ministers decided that negative color symbolism had to stop. No more associating "black" with evil, dirt and so on; and no more assuming "white" reflects purity and goodness. And in the realm of religion they would affect this change by altering the songs they sang: No more singing songs that depict white as symbolic of salvation, as found in lyrics drawn from a popular song in many churches:

> What can wash away my sin? Nothing but the blood of Jesus; what can make me whole again? Nothing but the blood of Jesus. Oh! Precious is the flow that makes me white as snow; No other fount I know, nothing but the blood of Jesus.

Even the Bible posed a problem that had to be corrected through translations that did not embrace the superiority of whiteness through a negative depiction of blackness. Problematic passages included this one from Psalms 51:7: "Purge me with hyssop, and I shall be clean; wash me and I shall be whiter than snow." Here, like other passages in the Bible, white is presented as the color of goodness and purity; and, as Cornel West has remarked it did not take long before the negativity of a color

Figure 7.3   Henry McNeal Turner. Courtesy of Time and Life Pictures/Getty Images.

became associated with particular bodies. So, the negative depiction of the color black soon became the assumption that people of African descent are also evil and soiled based on their color. To counter this, some ministers included in their services more elements – such as clothing, artwork, and worship elements such as libations to the ancestors – associated with blackness and an African heritage. During the 1960s it became common to find members of churches dressed in clothing associated with West Africa, and to include Afro-centric teachings and rituals into their services. So, for example, many churches adopted rites of passage programs for young men and women that were meant to resemble the way in which West African young people had the phases of their lives celebrated. In addition, Kwanzaa (an African American holiday – December 26–January 1 – celebrating African life principles and heritage) was added to the list of holiday celebrations alongside Christmas. Occurring around the same time as Christmas, Kwanzaa provides an avenue for African Americans to acknowledge their connection to the values and ethics of Africa.

Those embracing this Afro-centrism platform typically followed the materials offered by Maulana Karenga (1941–), an activist and university professor who developed Kwanzaa as part of a larger push to get African Americans to recognize

Figure 7.4 Kwanzaa stamp. Courtesy of iStockphoto.

their African roots. The larger philosophy undergirding this is called "Kawaida." Having been a part of the Black Power Movement, Karenga concerned himself with uncovering information concerning African values and philosophy to provide people of African descent an alternative to the Europe-dominated approach to life that oppressed African Americans through theories of racial inferiority and racial superiority.

Interesting about the appeal of Karenga's Kwanzaa and larger program of Kawaida for churches is the failure to recognize the human-centering intent undergirding his work. That is to say, Karenga is concerned with removing practices based on myth and replacing them with solid information about human values and ingenuity. However, picking the components of his platform that fit their Christian sensibilities, this shift toward a more Afro-centric approach to religious thought and rituals was meant to change the way race was understood and to counter racism as it was embedded in some of the practices of not only white churches, but also black churches. With respect to the latter, the presence of a preference for whiteness was called "internalized racism" – the idea that some African Americans accepted their second-class status. To attack internalized racism and its consequences, some

Principles of Kwanzaa

- *Umoja* (unity) – To strive for and maintain unity in the family, community, nation and race
- *Kujichagulia* (self-determination) – To define ourselves, name ourselves, create for ourselves and speak for ourselves
- *Ujima* (collective work and responsibility) – To build and maintain our community together and make our brothers' and sisters' problems our problems and to solve them together
- *Ujamaa* (cooperative economics) – To build and maintain our own stores, shops and other businesses and to profit from them together
- *Nia* (purpose) – To make our collective vocation the building and developing of our community in order to restore our people to their traditional greatness
- *Kuumba* (creativity) – To do always as much as we can, in the way we can, in order to leave our community more beautiful and beneficial than we inherited it
- *Imani* (faith) – To believe with all our heart in our people, our parents, our teachers, our leaders and the righteousness and victory of our struggle.

(From the Official Kwanzaa Website:
http://www.officialkwanzaawebsite.org/NguzoSaba.shtml)

pushed against being ashamed of blackness. Instead they celebrated their blackness and African heritage, and used both as a way to think about the proper look of their doctrine and worship. Some churches also rethought the look of their buildings, and in an effort to better connect to blackness as positive and based on a desire to better connect with Africa, built new edifices that looked like African huts and other structures associated with communal life in West Africa. In this way, the thinking, practices, values, and aesthetics of the church all gave a different value to African Americans embracing race as a positive marker of importance and life meaning.

The language used reflected this – no more negative color symbolism – and the style and content of worship and community services encouraged this rethinking of race as a positive. These ministers attempted to root out internalized racism through the means already mentioned but most importantly through the images of God and Christ presented. Both were presented as black, looking like the members of the black churches where the stained glass windows and paintings were found. Jesus was given an Afro hairstyle, brown skin, African clothing; and Mary the Mother of Jesus was also depicted as an African American woman. Not all accepted this black power influenced change, and churches moving in this direction lost some of their older members; but they also gained the attention of a younger crowd looking for a way to express their black pride and their religious commitment. It is also interesting that this embrace of Africa-associated practices brought these churches a step closer to the African orientation represented by African-based traditions.

Churches that did not embrace Afro-centric thinking and that did not feel comfortable changing the look of Jesus and God found other ways to rethink race. First, appealing to passages of scripture that speak to equality before God provided one approach to countering anti-black racism. Wearing one's best clothing also gave black bodies a different look, a look that ran contrary to racist depictions of African Americans. Even after the Civil Rights Movement and the resulting increase in educational, economic, and political opportunities, racism still placed limits on African American leadership roles. While racism prevented African Americans from exercising many positions of leadership in the larger society and prevented them from securing some economic opportunities because of race, even the most conservative African American churches afforded African Americans leadership opportunities that promoted a greater sense of their importance and abilities. This was a safeguard against discrimination in that African Americans could display their creativity and skills in a relatively safe environment when the color of their skin kept them from using their talents in many ways outside these churches. Regardless of what they thought about black power and its religious potential, many churches sought to provide a space in which African Americans would feel less impingement on their lives from racism. For some of these, images of Jesus Christ in their churches remained white, but this did not prevent them from embracing the value of black bodies on certain levels such as their social importance, their integrity, their capacity for good works, their beauty consistent with their creation in the image of God and so on.

African Americans within historically white denominations also raised questions concerning the nature of race and racism within their churches. African American Roman Catholics argued for, and in some instances demanded, greater participation in the leadership structure of the Church and pushed the Church to recognize its racism. African American Catholics organized and became attached to new church-based organizations meant to advance the cause of African American Catholics. The same effort to force change on issues of race through new programs and church-based organizations took place in Presbyterian churches, Episcopal churches, and so on. However, perhaps the most aggressive attack on racism within churches (and Jewish Synagogues) took place in the late 1960s through the presentation of the Black Manifesto issued by the Black National Economic Conference held in Detroit, and read by its representative James Foreman at Riverside Church in New York City in 1969.

Drawn up based on conversations at the conference, the Manifesto began with recognition that African Americans were part of a community that had been exploited for centuries. Furthermore, this exploitation benefited white Americans including white churches and Jewish synagogues. The document continues by outlining reparations to be paid to African Americans by these religious institutions in a total of $500,000,000. The money would be used to develop infrastructure

Figure 7.5   James Forman during the campaign to raise $500 million from the religious organizations of the United States to indemnify the black population for slavery and subsequent hardships endured (1969). Courtesy of Pictorial Parade/Getty Images.

in African American communities such as a bank to provide funds for farmers, the development of African American-owned publishing companies to produce materials relevant to African Americans, and the establishment of a university free from racism that would train African Americans to think and be productive with respect to the needs of their community. In addition, the money would be used to develop programs and institutions to provide job skills and to provide organized support for African American laborers as well as programs to teach and train those depending on social services for support. Furthermore this money would also be used to grow economic ventures and opportunities that would allow African Americans to continue building financial infrastructure in their communities, including ventures to advance the global reach of African Americans particularly in relationship to Africa.

While few thought the amount of money requested could be secured, the energy and passion behind the Manifesto did result in many denominations providing

Black Manifesto

We are therefore demanding of the white Christian churches and Jewish synagogues which are part and parcel of the system of capitalism, that they begin to pay reparations to black people in this country. We are demanding $500,000,000 from the Christian white churches and the Jewish synagogues. This ... is not a large sum of money and we know that the churches and synagogues have a tremendous wealth and its membership, white America, has profited and still exploits black people. We are also not unaware that the exploitation of colored peoples around the world is aided and abetted by the white Christian churches and synagogues. This demand for $500,000,000 is not an idle resolution or empty words. Fifteen dollars for every black brother and sister in the United States is only a beginning of the reparations due us as people who have been exploited and degraded, brutalized, killed and persecuted. Underneath all of this exploitation, the racism of this country has produced a psychological effect upon us that we are beginning to shake off. We are no longer afraid to demand our full rights as a people in this decadent society.

(The Black National Economic Conference, "Black Manifesto" http://www.nybooks.com/articles/archives/1969/jul/10/black-manifesto/)

resources to African American members to meet some of their needs and to study and remove racism from church policies and procedures. The Manifesto highlighted the manner in which racism thrived in locations one would assume did not directly benefit from the exploitation of African Americans, at least this is what churches and synagogues tended to believe about themselves. Some organizations such as the Unitarian Universalist Association (UUA) prided themselves on their social justice work, but during the same period of time as the Black Manifesto, the UUA was challenged by its African American membership to acknowledge and resolve its racism. For example, it was during this period that African Americans within the UUA first began to reference themselves as "black humanists" as a way of celebrating their racial heritage and their religious orientation. And it was also in response to the Manifesto that the UUA held a meeting to address these pressing issues – "Emergency Conference on Unitarian Universalist Response to the Black Rebellion." According to reports, many of the African Americans at that meeting left to forge a more focused effort as part of the Black Unitarian Universalist Caucus. This caucus made a variety of demands, all revolving around resources and "space" for African Americans, and demanded a committed effort on the part of the Association to address its racism. The caucus also recognized and pushed the need for all effort on this front to be determined and monitored by African American members. The denomination, although torn on the issue, provided funds to enhance work on issues of race and class. There were problems and ongoing struggles, but this was the start of major organizing efforts on the part of African American UUs to be fully self-determining. By the 1970s, the UUA was also responding to this challenge by creating greater opportunity for congregations to be more involved in community activism through new urban ministry designs. Members of the Association like Mark Morrison-Reed also began documenting the long involvement of African Americans as a way of rethinking the relationship of African Americans to the denomination and the denomination to African Americans both in positive and negative terms. In recent years, the General Assembly – the major annual meeting of the UUA – issued resolutions encouraging congregations to discuss and correct for any racism, classism or other modes of oppression within their activities and patterns of thoughts. For example, on its website, the UUA has this resolution first drafted in 2006: *"Resolved, that the Delegates to General Assembly are charged to work with their congregations to hold at least one program over the next year to address racism or classism, and to report on that program at next year's General Assembly."* Despite such changes, African Americans continue to argue that even these improvements have not served to wipe out racism on the national level or within local congregations. African Americans continue to represent less than 3 percent of the Association's membership, and race-based challenges are still present in this denomination – one of the most liberal denominations in the United States.

UUA on anti-racism work

In addressing the racism that exists in these institutions and systems, including the Unitarian Universalist Association (UUA), its districts, and congregations, many programs at our General Assemblies from 1992 until 1997 addressed these issues, and members of congregations across the continent discussed how racism operates in our congregations and communities. Some of the observations of this era still hold true today:

- Many Unitarian Universalists provided important leadership in integrating our religious community.
- In our congregations white culture is considered to be the norm and People of Color are expected to assimilate into this white culture.
- The focus of much of our justice work is on the victims of racism and not the oppressors that benefit from racism.
- We need to put greater focus on the power and privilege that white people have in our racist society.

(From "The Journey Toward Wholeness Path to Anti-Racism: Many Paths, One Journey," http://www.uua.org/multiculturalism/history/jtw/index.shtml)

African-based traditions did not suffer from this problem of the visual image in that the gods resemble in appearance the devotees and the spirits are often ancestors of those involved in the tradition. The Nation of Islam, as was previously discussed, would in the twentieth century also argue that God looks like the members of the Nation; and this resemblance is a sign of the importance and value of African Americans over white supremacist arguments to the contrary. The beauty of blackness is embedded in African-based traditions in that blackness is assumed as the proper look of the gods and the spirits, and the connection held by these traditions to the continent of Africa keeps them from falling prey to the assumptions of white superiority. These traditions, although drawing elements from Native American practices and European practices, have maintained a sense of life outside the confines of American discrimination that safeguarded something of the history and self-consciousness that white supremacy and the talk of African Americans as inferior was meant to destroy. One might imagine that the movement into Darul Islam of some Black Power advocates would give the associated mosques an interest in and a means by which to address issues of black identity within the context of religious practice. The clothing and sense of community (e.g., as composed of other believers) advanced by Darul Islam certainly provided a way of pushing against the dehumanizing depictions of African Americans expressed through anti-black racism. Race remains real, but it is modified and filtered through Darul Islam's efforts to connect Muslims through relationships that extended beyond the United States to the world-wide community of Muslims with a certain knowledge and practice of the faith. For the Nation of Islam, teachings revolved around an effort to get African Americans to appreciate their beauty and their value. This took place not only through the celebration of Allah as a black man, but also through the serious attention given to the presentation of black bodies. The Honorable Elijah Muhammad demanded proper nutrition, proper appearance, and proper attention to how young men and women should present themselves and treat each other. These demands on members involved dignity at all times and in all places, over the negative depictions of African Americans offered in the media and politics. In addition, the very geography of human development offered by the Nation of Islam speaks to a re-evaluation of race; but whereas many churches sought to simply place African Americans on equal footing with white Americans, the Nation of Islam's teachings rendered African Americans superior. According to the Honorable Elijah Muhammad, African Americans are from the original people who lived in the Middle East and embraced Islam as their religion. He indicates that with time some strayed away from the true teachings of Islam and moved to new locations like North America and Africa. Those who moved to North America are referred to as Native Americans, and those who migrated to Africa are Africans. His is not the type of black nationalism one sees with Marcus Garvey, in that the Nation of Islam made no solid moves to get African Americans back to Africa, and at times the Honorable Elijah Muhammad's perspective on Africa seems somewhat negative. Yet, African Americans continued to represent a special people. Although they encountered problems and punishment for having rejected the religion of Islam, the original people – including African Americans – are more civilized and representative of what is best about the universe. This is in opposition to Europeans, he argued, who are uncivilized and mischievous. The Nation would modify this perspective over time, but the value and beauty of African Americans as the original people has remained intact as a strike against racism within the religious and political environments of the United States.

Key points you need to know

- Where there was friction within African-based traditions it tended to revolve around the language used in ritual and difficulties between African Americans and Latinos.
- The Nation of Islam addressed difficulties with race and racism in the United States by positioning African Americans as a superior people.
- Images of God and Jesus Christ as Black served as a visual critique of anti-black racism.
- Some pushed for reparations as a way of addressing anti-black racism in secular and religious organizations.
- Black humanism is first used in the 1970s as a way to describe African Americans who do not ascribe to supernatural beliefs.
- White American and African American Christians were confronted with the residue of slavery and legal discrimination within their churches.

Discussion questions

1. What arguments were used to justify the enslavement of Africans?
2. What is *imago Dei* and why is it important?
3. What is the Black Manifesto? What did it require from religious institutions?
4. What are some of the ways African American Christians have tried to fight racism and establish a strong sense of self-worth and self-determination?
5. What did the Nation of Islam say about African Americans, and how did it address issues of racism?
6. How did the Unitarian Universalist Association understand and address racism within its congregations?

Further reading

Anderson, Victor. *Beyond Ontological Blackness*. New York: Continuum, 1995.

Carter, J. Kameron. *Race: A Theological Account*. New York: Oxford University Press, 2008.

Copeland, M. Shawn. *Enfleshing Freedom: Body, Race, and Being.* Minneapolis, MN: Fortress Press, 2009.

Douglas, Kelly Brown. *The Black Christ.* Maryknoll, NY: Orbis Books, 1993.

Jordon, Winthrop. *White Over Black: American Attitudes Toward the Negro, 1550–1812.* Chapel Hill, NC: The University of North Carolina Press, 1968.

Lecky, Robert S. and H. Elliott Wright, *Black Manifesto: Religion, Racism and Reparations.* Lanham, MD: Sheed & Ward, 1969.

Massingale, Bryan N. *Racial Justice and the Catholic Church.* Maryknoll, NY: Orbis Books, 2010.

Morgan, David. *Visual Piety: A History and Theory of Popular Religious Images.* Durham, NC: Duke University Press, 1999.

Morrison-Reed, Mark D. *Black Pioneers in a White Denomination.* Boston, MA: Skinner House Books, 1994.

Muhammad, Elijah. *Message to the Black Man in America.* Chicago, IL: Secretarius MEMPS Publications, 2009.

Murphy, Joseph M. *Santeria: African Spirits in America.* Boston, MA: Beacon Press, 1993.

Townes, Emilie M. *Womanist Ethics and the Cultural Production of Evil.* New York: Palgrave Macmillan, 2006.

8   The question of gender

In this chapter

Discussion of race/racism in the United States in general and African American communities in particular has often failed to account for the dilemmas faced by African American women. This chapter explores the history of discussions of gender within African American religion, giving particular attention to developments such as "the cult of true womanhood," and the "cult of domesticity," as well as ongoing challenges related to male-dominated patterns of leadership within African American religious organizations.

Main topics covered

- How gender is understood within African American religion
- Impact of gender on the structure and activities of religious communities
- Changes to how gender plays out in the development and dispersal of leadership roles
- Innovations made by women within African American religion
- Larger social dynamics informing issues of gender in thought and practice within African American communities

Religion and the difference between men and women

Within the majority of the religious traditions dotting the landscape of African American communities, there is a shared assumption concerning the distinctions between men and women. While humanism is an exception to this rule, most theistic traditions understand the differences between men and women to stem from some sort of divine determination. And this pattern of difference originating from some sort of trans-historical process or moment of creation is played out in the social arrangements of life. For African American Christians committed to either the literal or symbolic significance of the story of the creation of humans in the Book of Genesis, there is a way in which the male is privileged. According to the Genesis account of creation, the male was created first and the female was created from him to serve as a helper for him. Their removal from the idyllic life in the Garden of Eden, according to the story, results from the female breaking God's command and convincing the man to also do so. More important than the content of this story, however, is the way in which from the first book of the Bible through the last, the story of human encounter with the Divine is told from the perspective of men. And it is told in a way meant to privilege men, and downplay the importance of women. The main figures within scripture, with few exceptions, are men. Women are appreciated to the extent they aid these men in the completing of their tasks. While this is important to mention, more damaging for women is the traditional manner in which God is described using masculine language; for example, God is referred to as "He," again with few exceptions such as when the Divine is associated with the female personification of wisdom. This is more damaging because it does not simply place men above women in human relationships, but it suggests that the very creation and nature of men is more in line with what is best about the universe – God. But in general, the Christian faith is presented in terms of men and this includes the story of Christianity's spread that highlights the role of men as disciples. And, as the Christian Tradition grew and expanded, men controlled the religious institutions, the doctrine, and the practices of the faith. This is a patriarchal presentation of the human story – one that sets up a variety of gender-related problems.

While rejecting any support for racism within scripture, African American Christians have been much slower – when it is done at all – to challenge the gender-bias within scripture and within the larger Christian tradition. In a variety of ways they have actually embraced scriptural justified discrimination against women. For instance, the household codes from Deuteronomy have been used to assign social and churchly roles to women that limited their agency within and outside churches. Again for instance, from the early formation of independent churches to the present, many have used scripture to justify disproportionate numbers of male pastors and male leadership in the church. Furthermore, some denominations have created creeds that deny women opportunities to become ordained ministers. Resulting from this is sexism within churches through which men are considered superior to women, with opportunities and rights afforded them simply because they are men. In addition, positions available to women tend to involve them serving as helpers, such as missionaries. Denominations have encouraged women to develop missionary societies through which they have helped raise money to spread the gospel domestically and internationally. Women have served traditionally as those who took care of church materials, while also caring for the needs of the ordained preachers. They cook the church dinners and prepare items such as coverings for the altar used by churches during Sunday services. In this way, the roles open to women in churches have

Figure 8.1   Surrounded by minority women at the Houston Civic Center, Coretta Scott King talks of the resolution on minority women's rights that won the support of the National Women's Conference in 1977. The minority resolution, proposed by representatives of many races, declared that minority women suffered discrimination based on both race and sex. © Bettmann/CORBIS.

mirrored what were supposed to be their caregiver's roles within the traditional family structure. For many churches, this framework for women's activities was important precisely because it was consistent with thinking on the role of women encouraged by the larger society. Readers will remember what was said in the last chapter about the Moynihan Report; well, the assumptions concerning the proper family structure are older than that 1960s report. It was assumed a man, who controlled all major decisions, headed the proper family and women were in place to raise the family through care for children and the installation of proper values and moral formation. A true woman, the argument went, stayed within the domestic arena of life and left everything else to men. This way of thinking in the nineteenth century was commonly referred to as the "Cult of True Womanhood," or the "Cult of Domesticity." However phrased, the idea was simply that women should work within the home, and men should control the public dimensions of life including church ministry. Many African American church and civic leaders, such as Daniel Alexander Payne, assumed an effort on the part of African Americans to mirror the normative family structure espoused by the larger society and its moral values would result in African Americans being accepted by this society and gain the full range of rights and opportunities afforded whites.

Gender discrimination in churches

- Male-centered biblical stories, including the creation account, were used to justify sexism against women.
- Churches combined social regulations with church doctrine to re-enforce limited opportunities for women.
- Roles for women were typically limited to supportive roles meant to complement and assist male leaders.
- Pentecostal and spiritual churches were more open to women in leadership positions than other denominations.
- A significant number of denominations began ordaining women as of the mid- to late-twentieth century.
- Some women developed their own churches and denominations rather than be bound by unreasonable restrictions on the exercise of their talents and skills.

Women and Church ministry

Because of the centrality of ordained ministry within African American churches, and the dominant authority typically held by the ordained preacher, the availability of this form of leadership is a good indicator of how gender plays out within churches. Over the course of many years, there has been an internal debate within churches concerning the validity of gender-biased thinking to the extent it limited the opportunities for women to express their Christian faith through church service. Some supported the desire for social acceptability through an embrace of the gender-roles supported by religious arguments. Others believe only God is capable of determining who is fit for the pastorate and other forms of ministry. Denominations holding to this latter perspective began ordaining women in the nineteenth century. Prominent amongst these churches was the African Methodist Episcopal Church Zion. In the early twentieth century, however, some women went further than accepting ordination in traditional African American churches. They began developing their own churches and denominations. This included many of the spiritual churches, particularly those organized and controlled by Mother Leafy Anderson and the women she brought into ministry. These spiritual church leaders were able to exercise complete authority and maintain that authority through the establishment of denominations based on their teachings and practices. Pentecostal churches, based on what they accepted of William Seymour's preaching on equality through spiritual preparation, also provided greater opportunities for women to be involved in church ministry. Whereas most African American denominations denied women the opportunity to preach from the pulpit, Pentecostal churches in general did not abide by such restrictions.

Instead they believe God selects those whom God wants to preach the Word, and the test of one's spiritual power and "calling" to preach is found in the quality of one's preaching. Did people join the church as a result of the sermon? Were Christians strengthened, and did they have their spirits renewed as a result of the sermon?

It was not until the mid-twentieth century that all the major Methodist denominations ordained women into ministry, and many of the Baptist Conventions still do not allow women to be ordained or preach from the formal pulpit. This, however, is still under discussion within Baptist circles and it is changing. Within the context of African American churches in general, it is typically the case that ordination does not mean that women are given churches to pastor. And, when they do receive churches to pastor, they are typically small churches and not the large or central churches within the denominations. There are exceptions to this, of course, and these exceptions have resulted in women finally becoming bishops within some of the major Methodist denominations at the end of the twentieth century.

Sexism has been alive within the Christian tradition and this is the case in both predominantly white and African American churches. African Americans in historically white denominations did not necessarily fare any better. For example, it is not until the 1970s that the Episcopal Church ordained women, with the Rev. Dr. Pauli Murray (1910–1985) as first African American woman ordained, and the Rev. Barbara Harris (1930–), was the first African American woman consecrated as an Episcopal bishop, and this took place in the late 1980s.

Pauli Murray's reflections on the September 1969 Special General Convention related to issues of women in Episcopal Church ministry

The longer the Church delays full recognition of women's legitimate rights as persons, the larger this alienated group will become, the greater its threat to established procedures and the more powerless will become women who are desperately trying to bring about reforms within these procedures. Although the Church now has a residue of faithful women who are still willing to do the thankless supportive work of the Church – dinners, altar guilds, choirs, mothers, etc., these needs do not satisfy women capable of leadership and the shaping of policy. Nothing less than full sharing of power in every phase of Church life will satisfy the needs and legitimate aspirations of these women. They will either share power within the Church or they will be outside the Church as part of its formidable opponents.

(Pauli Murray Papers, Schlesinger Library, Harvard University, Box 95, Folder 1666)

These tend to be exceptions to the general rule, but even these changes in the "look" of church leadership did not mean that sexism was removed from church teachings and practices. Arguments continued to be made for the inclusion of women in the full life of churches. Some suggested that African American women, because of the unique nature of their oppression due to race, gender, and class, were best equipped to develop strategies for improving life in the United States. This is because they are so very aware of the multiple ways in which people are oppressed and suffer. This was used as an argument for inclusion in the political sphere and also in the religious realm. In addition, others argued the fact that Mary Magdalene was the first to announce that Christ had risen from the dead speaks to the abilities of women to proclaim the gospel message. When this reason is given, the person usually emphasizes that the male disciples hid away during this trying time after the crucifixion, but Mary Magdalene and Mary the Mother of Jesus persisted and that is the mark of spiritual abilities and religious determination. If women could play this key role in caring for Christ during the time of the crucifixion, while also being first to announce his triumph over death, they are certainly qualified to preach the Christian faith in the contemporary world. Women, and supportive men, within a variety of denominations continue to expose and fight against sexism within the various denominations.

Sociologist Cheryl Townsend Gilkes puts a different spin on this situation. She argues that while sexism persists within churches, there are forms of power and authority that African American women have held for a significant period of time and this power and authority has important consequences. While they may not control the pulpit within these churches, as church mothers and other established figures within the church they are looked to for advice on pressing issues. In this way, they have some authority with respect to the large and important decisions made within the church. In addition, Townsend Gilkes points out that these highly visible women are also looked to when it's time to select a minister within Baptist churches, or to orient a new minister assigned by a bishop. Hence, African American women within restrictive churches are able to work beyond restrictions and exercise some control over the workings of their churches. In addition, some women have left denominations with such restrictions and have developed independent churches and their own denominations as a way of exercising their talents and skills. This, however, is more difficult within Roman Catholicism where strong regulations restrict the range of leadership positions available to women. For example, women cannot be ordained into the priesthood. Positions held by women in the Roman Catholic Church are consistent with general understandings of gender-based authority in the larger society where men are assumed to be better equipped to control both the family and public life. While there is debate within Catholic circles concerning restrictions on the priesthood as sexism and gender-based discrimination, the Church's stance has not changed because it views a hierarchy of service not as discrimination but as a practice consistent with divine regulations concerning men and women, and consistent with what scripture says about church leaders being men. A variety of international organizations have developed over the years that address the ordination of women. For example, the Roman Catholic Women Priests is an international organization committed to providing information and support to women who feel called to the priesthood within the Church. In addition, Women's Ordination Conference is one of the oldest organizations committed to changing the Church's practice regarding the ordination of women. According to its website, this work involves an effort to: "Renew church governance to be inclusive, accountable and transparent; bring about justice and equality for Catholic women; incorporate women-centered theologies into every-day Catholicism." It does this through a variety of activities including symposia, conferences, petitions, and a general spreading of information concerning this issue.

Institutions serving as home to humanists are also plagued with similar problems in that leadership tends to be male dominated, although within the Unitarian Universalist Association women do pastor significant numbers of churches. The number of ordained women has increased over the past several decades, and they now hold leadership positions on the national level. Furthermore, in the 1970s the UUA passed a resolution – "Women and Religion Resolution" – which called congregations to root out any practices and thoughts that supported sexism and limited the ability of women to be nourished within the context of the church. A commitment to the principles of justice and the posture of being "welcoming" required attention to the manner in which sexism negatively impacted the Association's ability to live out its principles. Before the end of that decade, the Association formed a committee responsible for addressing issues of gender equality across the Association in line with the "Women and Religion Resolution." The president also requested that the impact of the resolution also be felt on the level of the districts and the local congregations. According to UUA records, efforts to implement the resolution included changing the language used by the Association to describe its commitments and ethics – as found in its principles and in the materials used for worship and teaching – so that the language was inclusive as opposed to gender specific and sexist.

Women and Islam

Darul Islam, as an example of commitment to Sunni Islam in African American communities, maintained an understanding of gender roles it considered to be in line with the teachings of Islam and the social arrangement of Muslim communities worldwide. One gets a sense of this in the style of dress suggested for women, who should have their faces covered and should wear loose fitting clothing so as to avoid calling attention to their bodies. In addition, for much of its history the Nation of Islam, as was also the case for smaller Islam-based traditions within African American communities, made a clear distinction between the activities appropriate

The UUA on women, gender equality and family

Unitarian Universalism is very supportive of women and families. We believe that our first principles, respecting "the inherent worth and dignity of every person," applies equally to people of all gender and family situations. Unitarian Universalists are well-known for supporting women's rights. We consistently speak out in support of reproductive rights, including family planning, abortion, and comprehensive sexuality education. ... We actively support women in every role in our denomination, from greeting visitors to leading congregational committees to delivering Sunday sermons. More than half of all active Unitarian Universalist ministers are women. In 1863 we became the first denomination in the United States to ordain a woman with full denominational authority.

(Quoted from the Unitarian Universalist Association website: http://www.uua.org/beliefs/justice/7012.shtml)

for men and those for women. While they understood them as both vital and having an important status within the context of the proper working of the community, it was also clear that acceptable activities were based upon the gender roles considered normative by the larger society. Women were to be modest, without make-up, with limited public interactions with men who are not members of the family. In connection to this, marriage was understood as the proper arrangement for men and women, and establishment of the home – including home economics such as cooking and cleaning – was the proper sphere for women. Men, on the other hand, were to be protectors and providers – safeguarding the welfare of the tradition and of women and children. The Nation's goal was to make certain it provided proper training for young girls in areas related to caring for the home and being good wives. It wanted to avoid its female members being perceived as anything but women of high moral standing, who did not dress inappropriately and did not entertain the advances of men. And because popular culture such as movies served to provide improper examples of how to live, members of the Nation were not allowed to attend movies, or listen to American music. Instead, members developed their own sources of entertainment, ones that supported the gender roles and code of moral conduct within solid family units advocated by the Honorable Elijah Muhammad.

Because educational opportunities in the larger society could not be relied on to provide members with knowledge consistent with their religious beliefs, the Nation established the University of Islam through which young people and adults received religiously based instruction related to their faith and every other dimension of life.

For girls, the Muslim Girl's Training and General Civilization Class provided lessons concerning these other dimensions of life, which include information on

"Laws of Islam" for women

- Do not use lipstick or makeup.
- Do not wear hair up unless wearing long dress.
- Do not smoke or drink alcohol.
- Do not commit adultery.
- Do not eat pork in any form.
- Do not cook in aluminum saucepans.
- Do not wear heels over 1½ inches.
- Do not dance with anyone except one's husband.

(From Clifton E. Marsh, *From Black Muslims to Muslims: The Resurrection, Transformation, and Change of the Lost-Found Nation of Islam in America, 1930–1995*, Lanham, MD: Scarecrow Press, 1996, 44)

Figure 8.2   Lunch is served after graduation ceremonies at the Nation of Islam's University of Islam Temple #2 (Chicago, 1965). Courtesy of Robert Abbott Sengstacke/Getty Images.

how to take care of the children they would have when married, how to care for one's home, and how to take care of one's body through proper hygiene. Because the gender roles were clear, these areas of study were meant only for women. There are similarities between the Nation of Islam's perspective on women as having their proper role within the family – as producers of the Nation's population and

"Laws of Islam" for young men

- To protect organizational officials and property.
- To reinforce the doctrine and objectives of the organization.
- To prepare for the race war known as Armageddon.

(From Clifton E. Marsh, *From Black Muslims to Muslims: The Resurrection, Transformation, and Change of the Lost-Found Nation of Islam in America, 1930–1995*, Lanham, MD: Scarecrow Press, 1996, 44)

caregivers – and the role of women as "earths" in the 5 Percent Nation whereby they are celebrated for their ability to produce children. For young men, in the Nation of Islam, the regulations revolved around the need to develop the public presence of the Nation and to defend its teachings.

The discipline and strict moral code for both genders was important for the Nation because they offered protection from the "trickology" of white Americans whereby they encouraged African Americans to maintain practices and beliefs inconsistent with their true position as a special people with dignity and an ordained future as rulers of the universe. The Nation's teachings meant the advancement of African Americans and the protecting of and respect for African American women. With Minister Farrakhan's reconstitution of the Nation of Islam came a renewal of the need for men to protect and respect women and to play a positive role in their communities. The culmination of this thinking may have been the 1995 Million Man March in Washington, DC, organized by the Nation of Islam. African American men came from around the country to the capital in order to recommit themselves to the welfare of their families and their communities, and in line with traditional gender roles. A similar event was held the next year and this one included the participation of women. For the Nation, a proper sense of self will generate respect and appreciation for others, and will promote life within the context of proper gender roles. Pain and suffering within social life stem from a lack of adherence to proper roles established by Allah and low moral standards. Under the leadership of Minister Farrakhan, a change in the roles available to women took place. While still concerned with the need for women to establish a solid moral framework for the home, they were also afforded opportunities for greater leadership. For examples, Minister Ava Muhammad has served as the national spokesperson for Minister Louis Farrakhan as well as serving as one of the prominent theologians in the Nation responsible for explicating many of its doctrines and beliefs. Furthermore, she was the first woman to serve as head of a mosque in the Nation of Islam. This is a significant accomplishment in terms of women within the Nation, and puts the organization at odds with other Islamic organizations that deny women participation in the faith at this level of authority. Nonetheless, while representative of a shift in gender roles within the Nation, Minister Ava Muhammad remains an exception to the general rule that men, through a relatively clear distinction in gender roles, hold positions of leadership. In Sunni Islam in African American communities, there is also a strong distinction between men and women based on a similar placement of women within the domestic sphere of life, with men in charge of the home as well as the public representation of the faith.

African-based traditions and women

Traditions such as conjure and hoodoo that lack formal structure have fewer problems related to women exercising ritual authority, although they are far from problem free on this issue. However, it is often the case that anyone who is able to demonstrate spiritual ability can develop a clientele and secure recognized standing in the tradition. Yet, like other traditions, there are elements of practice that are gender determined and bound.

Women in Santería

- Women can serve as religious leaders and run their own communities.
- Only men can become priests of Ifa or Orula.
- Women cannot play the ritually dedicated Bata drums.

For example, the drums played during rituals in Santería are very important, and those drums constructed using the rituals that make them "Fundamento" or appropriate for ceremonies are not played by women. Some argue the reason women can't play these drums is because menstruation weakens their energy and damages the connection to the deities or *orishas*. This would suggest the restriction has something to do with the proper energy required for the drums. There is still some debate concerning whether there is merit to this argument or whether it is simply a matter of gender-bias. However, according to some practitioners, and in some instances, women can play drums that aren't "Fundamento." Yet, learning to play these drums that aren't "Fundamento" has little bearing on the ceremonial structure of the tradition because women do not play during ritual activities. However, unlike Christianity, this does not involve the same type of privileging of the male gender through a one-sided depiction of divinity. That is to say, African-based traditions entail an array of deeply significant divinities and spirits, many of whom are female, and women tend to play a major role in rituals related to these deities. Whereas Christians tend to depict God – in language, at the very least – as male, African-based traditions recognize a variety of deities many of them female. And, unlike most Christian churches, there are a significant number of women serving as religious leaders who are in charge of their own communities, and have a significant clientele reliant on their knowledge and expertise. In this way, there tends to be greater opportunities to participate in the life of the tradition and to exercise authority within ritual and belief structures than one finds within most churches.

The number of women who are religious leaders certainly outpaces what one finds within the Nation of Islam and other Islamic communities. However, there are gender restrictions with respect to one type of priesthood, although all others are open to either men or women. Such restrictions come into play with respect to the *Babalawo* – a high priest who has mastered the sacred stories and wisdom. This priest is the priest of Orula, the deity associated with the most sophisticated form of divination, using a series of palm nuts. The nuts provide arrangements of numbers that correspond to particular Odu, and these relate to particular stories, riddles, etc., that are used to aid those coming to the *Babalawo* for assistance. Traditionally, only a man can hold this position. However, there is a position reserved for women – *Iyalawo* or "Mother of Secrets" – that some argue is similar in status to that of *Babalawo*.

Others are not as convinced that these positions constitute equivalent levels of authority and power in that certain key activities are restricted to *Babalawos*.

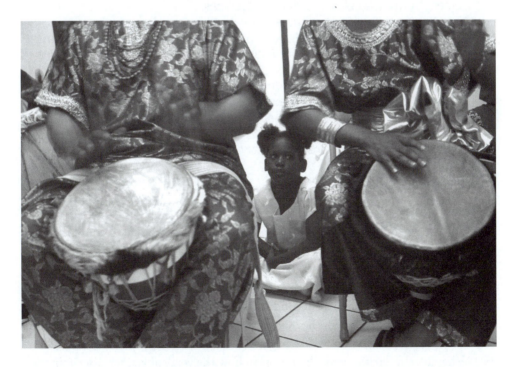

Figure 8.3   A drumming ceremony to Xemaya, the deity, earth mother. © Karen Kasmauski/ Science Faction/Corbis.

Still other practitioners see no need for comparison in that both serve important purposes in line with the development of the tradition and the welfare of the religious community. In this regard, according to those holding this last position, there is equality within the practice of traditions such as Santería in that the roles played are determined by the inner workings of the faith as opposed to being simply the result of social regulations. More to the point, all the leadership positions are vital components of the practice of the tradition. In other words, the difference in leadership positions, many would suggest, is not the result of an assumption that males are superior to females. Rather both are essential in their own way; both have inherent energy and purpose that are vital and necessary for the tradition (and the world) to function properly.

Key points you need to know

- It is often the case that the role of women in religious communities mirrors social regulations regarding the difference between the genders.
- Most churches did not begin ordaining women until the twentieth century.
- Access to ordination has not meant equal opportunities for key leadership positions such as being a bishop in Methodist denominations.
- Spiritual churches and Pentecostal churches have been more open than others to women holding leadership positions.
- The Roman Catholic Church does not allow the ordination of women.
- The Nation of Islam's national spokesperson is a woman, and she is also the leader of a prominent mosque in Atlanta; but she is the only woman holding this type of authority.
- Women in African-based traditions such as Santería are able to serve as priestesses of deities, with the exception of Orula.
- Existing limitations on the roles of women in African-based traditions are often discussed in terms of differences in energy between men and women in part resulting from menstruation.

Discussion questions

1. How was scripture used to justify gender-bias against women in churches?
2. What arguments were used to counter sexism and gain greater leadership opportunities for women within Christian churches?
3. What roles were considered proper for women in the Nation of Islam? Why?
4. What are some of the rules of conduct for women in the Nation of Islam? What about the rules for men in the Nation of Islam?
5. Why are women not allowed to play ritual drums or be priestesses of Orula?
6. What are similarities and differences in how the issue of gender discrimination has been addressed in Protestant churches and in the Roman Catholic churches?

Further reading

Butler, Anthea D. *Women in the Church of God in Christ: Making a Sanctified World.* Chapel Hill, NC: The University of North Carolina Press, 2007.

Cooey, Paula M., William Eakin and Jay McDaniel, editors. *After Patriarchy: Feminist Transformations of the World Religions.* Maryknoll, NY: Orbis Books, 1991.

Giddings, Paula J. *When and Where I Enter: The Impact of Black Women on Race and Sex in America.* New York: Harper Paperbacks, 1996.

Griffith, R. Marie and Barbara D. Savage, editors. *Women and Religion in the African Diaspora: Knowledge, Power, and Performance.* Baltimore, MD: The Johns Hopkins University Press, 2006.

Higginbotham, Evelyn Brooks. *Righteous Discontent: The Women's Movement in the Black Baptist Church, 1880–1920.* Cambridge, MA: Harvard University Press, 1994.

Rouse, Carolyn Moxley. *Engaged Surrender: African American Women and Islam.* Berkeley: University of California Press, 2004.

Tate, Sonsyrea. *Little X: Growing Up in the Nation of Islam.* Knoxville, TN: The University of Tennessee Press, 2005.

Townsend Gilkes, Cheryl. *If It Wasn't for the Women...: Black Women's Experience and Womanist Culture in Church and Community.* Maryknoll, NY: Orbis Books, 2000.

Weaver, Mary Jo. *New Catholic Women: A Contemporary Challenge to Traditional Religious Authority.* Bloomington, IN: Indiana University Press, 1995.

9 Dreams of democracy

In this chapter

Popular understanding of African American religious activism typically draws on the political engagement of churches and other religious institutions. And much of this understanding centers on the Civil Rights Movement. This chapter, while presenting some of that story, will also give attention to the ways in which African American religion has sought greater involvement in US democracy and also complete political independence.

Main topics covered

- Manifest destiny and chosen people philosophies
- The Jeremiad tradition within African American religion
- Descriptions of the apocalypse and its aftermath
- Socialism in African American religious thought
- Descriptions of Christian nationalism
- Separation of Church and state debates

How the religious understand and present themselves

From the very beginning of the colonies there was a religious and theological assumption that those moving to the Americas were a special people chosen by God. And this special people was destined, the story goes, to develop a new nation that would conduct its affairs consistent with the will of God. Seeing themselves as the "new" people of God, they painted themselves into the biblical story of the Jews, to whom God would give the "Promised Land." Colonists who came to the Americas who made the effort to escape political persecution and to practice their faith believed North America to be their promised land. This connecting of religious commitment and the establishment of a nation loyal to God was not lost on others. For example, African Americans who embraced the Christian faith also spoke of themselves as God's chosen people, a special group set aside for a grand work, and this destiny would result in the development of a new society based on equality and the fulfillment of God's will. They, the argument went, were marked for greatness exhibited in their role in the establishing of God's kingdom on earth. In general this line of thinking – a chosen people in North America would be established and live out a history of greatness in line with the will of God – is called manifest destiny. And, to the extent the United States was understood as being this special place, a "City on a Hill," this vision of religious loyalty rewarded had something to do with democracy. Of course, until the Civil War and the Emancipation Proclamation that freed the enslaved, there were no significant signs that this nation would respond to the will of God and promote the development of a society in line with Christian virtues manifest. From the perspective of free and enslaved Africans, the end of slavery and the destruction of discriminatory practices could only realize this adherence to God's plan. This did not go unnoticed and some offered a response involving not only localized socio-political revolt but also a theological challenge that pronounced the destruction of a disobedient nation. Drawing from the biblical prophet Jeremiah – who proclaimed the destruction of a people that rejected their obligations to God – this style of theological critique provided by African American Christians was referred to as the "Jeremiad."

Many individuals incorporated this critique and warning into their thinking and conversation – "change behavior or face punishment." Yet perhaps one of the most compelling examples of the Jeremiad, one that captured the popular imagination of nineteenth-century North America, was offered by David Walker (1785–1830). He provided this Jeremiad in his book titled *Walker's Appeal in Four Articles; a Preamble*

Jeremiah 1:17–19

"Get yourself ready! Stand up and say to them whatever I command you. Do not be terrified by them, or I will terrify you before them. 18 Today I have made you a fortified city, an iron pillar and a bronze wall to stand against the whole land—against the kings of Judah, its officials, its priests and the people of the land. 19 They will fight against you but will not overcome you, for I am with you and will rescue you," declares the LORD.

(Bible – New International Version)

Jeremiad

A strong statement of moral and ethical failure on the part of communities (or nations), followed by a proclamation of punishment and destruction if the failure isn't corrected.

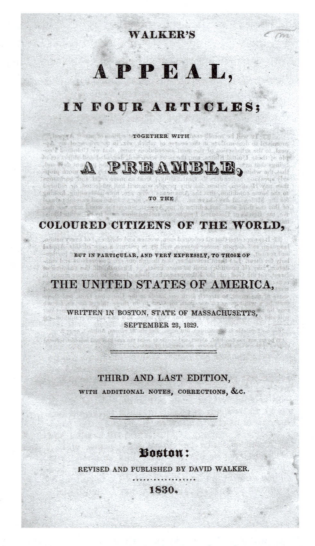

Figure 9.1   David Walker's *Appeal*. Courtesy of Documenting the American South, the University of North Carolina at Chapel Hill Libraries.

to the Coloured Citizens of the World, but in Particular, and Very Expressly, to Those of the United States of America. It was written in 1829, when Walker lived in Boston, Massachusetts; and, he distributed it by sewing the book into the lining of the clothing from his shop he sold to sailors.

Moving through the North and South in this manner, Walker's book caused uproar with slaveholders fearing the worst. To control damage they plotted his death, and offered a reward for his capture. In essence, Walker argued that the United States did not abide by its proclaimed Christian principles and as a result had no moral authority. He argued enslaved Africans have experienced pain and degradation like no others in human history – even the situation of the children of Israel under the Egyptians wasn't as brutal – and all this at the hands of a supposedly Christian nation. The socio-political and cultural arrangements of life in the country simply numbed Africans and encouraged them to accept their condition as their divinely sanctioned lot in life. Some enslaved and free Africans, he lamented, did accept slavery as the proper lot of Africans. He reasoned they were brainwashed by the slave system and embraced suffering as a consequence of their enslavement. He hoped to break Africans free of this poor thinking, to encourage them to a greater sense of their own value. More to the point, Walker encouraged enslaved Africans to revolt violently against their unjust condition. From his perspective, a fight against slavery, even if it caused death, was justified and consistent with the will of God over against unjust socio-political arrangements. Walker sought to foster a strong sense of belonging and ownership of the country in that it was built by enslaved Africans and enriched through their labor and blood. As a consequence of this connection to the development of the country, people of African descent had a greater claim to the land than white Americans. Taking the land, furthermore, is consistent with God's demand for justice and righteousness; and, to remain content with slavery is to work against the will of God. This is because only God must be served, and no human can rightly claim dominance over others. The only way to avoid the collapse of the country into violence and turmoil, and here's where the Jeremiad comes in, is to free the slaves and treat free Africans with dignity and as equals. God, he asserts, will not stand for this misery to continue indefinitely and will not allow the United States to pretend the brutality of slavery is consistent with the will of God. Continued brutality toward Africans will result in pain and suffering for whites brought about by God's wrath.

Destruction of an unrepentant nation

Americans! Notwithstanding you have and do continue to treat us more cruel than any heathen nation ever did a people it had subjected to the same condition that you have us. Now let us reason – I mean you of the United States, whom I believe God designs to save from destruction, if you will hear. For I declare to you, whether you believe it or not, that there are some on the continent of America, who will never be able to repent. God will surely destroy them, to show you his disapprobation of the murders they and you have inflicted on us ... As unexpected, strange, and wild as these propositions may to some appear, it is no less a fact, that unless they are complied with, the Americans of the United States, though they may for a little while escape, God will yet weigh them in a balance, and if they are not superior to other men, as they have represented themselves to be, he will give them wretchedness to their very heart's content.

(David Walker's *Appeal*, Bedford, MA: Applewood Books, 2008, 79–80)

Walker's offering is one of the most graphic examples of African Americans presenting themselves as determined to participate in the life of the nation, a new nation without the trappings of racial discrimination. But his argument that failure to establish such a country will result in the violent destruction of this nation extends beyond other pronouncements made during the same period. For example, the second Great Awakening mentioned earlier in this book assumed failure to abide by the will of God would result in destruction but this had little to do with the evils of slavery; nor did this assumption of spiritual renewal or the fall of the nation during the Great Awakening take on political transformation as its basic emphasis. Walker critiques Christianity as practiced by slave holders and advances a demand for democratic renewal in line with God's demand for justice and righteousness. The differences between Walker's reasoning and that of either of the two Great Awakenings contemporary to his life were pronounced and resulted in a great deal of conversation, but did not result in major changes to the nation. Some saw bloody slave rebellions and revolts around this period as evidence of the violence Walker prophesied. Others believed a spiritual change was the only lasting possibility for the Nation.

With Walker's mysterious death shortly after the publication of his book, others took up the cause and pronounced Jeremiads against the nation. Maria Stewart was one person inspired by Walker's *Appeal*, and in response to it she gave a series of lectures in Boston. In fact, she was the first African American woman to lecture publicly on political issues. Consistent with Walker, Stewart advanced the idea that the health of the nation required adherence to God's will which included proper treatment of enslaved and free Africans. Only the destruction of the slave system, an end to racial discrimination, and greater opportunities for both African men and women could preserve the integrity of the United States. A key difference in Stewart's attack, however, was the clear attention she gave to the needs of African American women. After the end of the slave system, legal race-based discrimination would prompt other Jeremiads culminating in the demands for justice within the Civil Rights Movement. In both cases – the attack on slavery and the demand for civil rights – the survival of the country was connected to the proper treatment of African Americans, in line with a sense of manifest destiny and chosen people status.

The demand for true democracy and economic opportunity

There was no underlying threat to democracy nor was there a challenge to the core elements of capitalism in these Jeremiads. Rather, it was typically the case that African Americans were demanding more participation in the workings of a post-racism United States. This push for the transformation of US political and economic life is the dominant approach endorsed by African American religious traditions, and the Jeremiad is one of the most graphic presentations of this position. Attention to this perspective typically takes the form of churches, for instance, offering educational opportunities for their communities – including grade schools, junior high, and high school options, in addition to arrangements with institutions that afford members of the church opportunities to gain college credits. In addition, churches have developed job training programs and social services programs as a way of preparing African Americans for jobs in the traditional marketplace. The perspective involves attention to correctives rather than the dismantling or rejection of the capitalist system and democracy. Hence, church programs and policies mirror the framework of both capitalism and democracy – a paid staff based on a hierarchy affecting compensation, a variety of offices each with a type of authority. Even Baptist churches, in which the minister is central and the local congregation operates independently of external controls, have a system of checks and balances such as deacons who are responsible for hiring (and firing) ministers as well as controlling other dimensions of church business.

By and large, churches have not assumed the philosophy of democracy is flawed nor that capitalism couldn't work. Instead they typically argue that humans have failed to adequately implement them. However, this problem is easily corrected, they continue, through attention to the morals and ethics of the Christian faith. This faith provides a platform upon which to rework and transform the structures of life in the United States – to make the nation truly democratic and to make available to all healthy economic opportunities. In most cases, African American Christians championed clear attention to a full exercise of democratic principles as consistent with the will of God, and as a means by which to avoid God's wrath. So conceived, what most African American Christians promote is a better United States – full inclusion for African Americans in the life of the Nation.

Promotion of a socialist alternative

A minority of Christian ministers critiqued the possibility of African Americans benefiting from participation in what passes for democracy and the aggressive capitalism marking the United States. From their perspective, there was very little about the workings of the United States that qualified as truly democratic. These figures would go further and argue that the system promoted by Jesus Christ was communal and more consistent with socialism than capitalism. Efforts to include African Americans in the economic and socio-political life of the United States failed not simply because of racism – although this is a profound factor – but also because of deep flaws in the economic and political structures of the United States. True equality, these ministers suggested, could only be achieved through the transition from a privileging of the wealthy to a deep concern with the poor and despised. One of the earliest African American ministers to embrace socialism publicly as a form of doctrine and ministry was Baptist preacher-turned-socialist worker George Washington Woodbey (1854–1920s). Having studied a variety of political perspectives, he settled on socialism as most useful and spent a great deal of time touring the country speaking about the value of socialist ideals to a variety of audiences, many of whom were impressed by his passion and his compelling ideas. From his perspective, only socialism provided an accurate understanding of the economic and political condition of African Americans and the poor in general. As a consequence, only it could address this condition in an adequate fashion by changing the relationship between groups as well as fostering a different perspective on the consumption of goods. This is because socialism helped to better understand the dynamics of class and its relationship to race, thereby allowing for a more robust challenge to discrimination and injustice.

The Nation of Islam also understood the importance of controlling one's economic arrangements and doing so in a way that advances one's humanity. But while the Nation saw the possibility of such a relationship to the means of production in the development of an alternate capitalist society, Woodbey believed only a socialist society would allow for the full development of people as more than their labor. Furthermore, Woodbey understood socialism as the resolution of issues of class, race, and gender-bias in that equality as promoted by socialism cuts across difference, and provided equal opportunity for all. Because there was no contradiction between Christianity and socialism, he assured any who would listen that socialist principles were in fact biblical principles. In this way, his brand of socialism did not threaten the existence of churches. Instead it enhanced the effectiveness of churches in addressing the deep needs of African Americans. Reverdy C. Ransom (1861–1959) of the AME Church was a contemporary of Woodbey's who also worked as an advocate for socialism. His argument was similar to that offered by Woodbey: socialism is consistent with the teachings of Jesus, and it is the best means for African Americans to secure socio-political and economic health. Whereas capitalism has supported their enslavement and subjugation, equality as an inherent value within socialism provides a different relationship to the means of production. As a consequence, socialism, when combined with the Christian faith, promotes an understanding of African Americans as more than their labor, more than tools used for the benefit of the wealthy. Ransom worked to connect the activities of the church to his socialist sensibilities despite the resistance of his denominational colleagues. The Institutional Church and Social Settlement House he developed in Chicago (1900) was a concrete example of these sensibilities at work.

Through this organization, he fostered elements of Jesus' communal approach to life in ways meant to counter the harm done to the poor and racially despised by industrial economics and capitalism. Yet, resistance by his denomination was substantial and resulted in him being assigned to a different church. The minister who replaced Ransom reoriented the church's focus so as to better reflect traditional concerns with spiritual salvation. In the long run, socialism never amounted to a

Figure 9.2   The Rev. Reverdy Ransom and wife in Chicago, *c.*1910s. Courtesy of Chicago History Museum/Getty Images.

The Institutional Church's mission

The Institutional AME Church of Chicago was not born before its time. It comes to meet and serve the social conditions and industrial needs of the people, and to give answers and solutions to the many grave problems which confront our Christianity in the great centers of population of our people. It is not a dream spun out of the gossamer web of fancy; it is not an evasion, an abridgment, or a short-cut method for the realization of Christ and the Christ life in the life of the people. It is a teaching, ministering nursing-mother, and seeks through its activities and ministrations to level the inequalities and bridge the chasms between rich and poor, the educated and the ignorant, the virtuous and the vicious, the indolent and the thrifty, the vulgar and the refined, and to bring all ages and classes of the community to contribute to the common good.

(Quoted from Reverdy C. Ransom, "The Institutional Church," *The Christian Recorder* (March 7, 1901), reprinted in *Making the Gospel Plain: The Writings of Bishop Reverdy C. Ransom*, edited by Anthony Pinn, Harrisburg, PA: Trinity Press International, 1999, 198) widespread practice within African American Christian circles. Nonetheless, it is important to recognize Woodbey and Ransom as powerful examples of an alternate vision of social transformation that questioned the nature and meaning of democracy within the context of a capitalist country.

Religion and separation of the United States

Social transformation vis-à-vis religious argument was not limited to Christian churches. Communities such as the Nation of Islam also made this argument, also using a Jeremiad framework. Unlike the argument made by most Christians – with the possible exception of those championing a move back to Africa – the Nation of Islam understood the United States to be beyond redemption, hopelessly tainted and doomed. The economic health of the United States is built on the misery of people of African descent and as such it cannot last. God will bring about its destruction, through the "Mother Plane" that is positioned in space. This ship was built by Master Fard Muhammad and, after his death the Honorable Elijah Muhammad joined him in this large plane. According to the Nation's teachings, more than 1,000 smaller ships will be released from this "Mother Plane" and they will place bombs on earth. Before the bombs destroy the earth, the righteous will be relocated to the "Mother Plane." The time for this destruction has shifted, and although the Nation hasn't paid full attention to the reasons for these changes in logistics, it is safe to assume it has something to do with the ongoing effort to equip African Americans with proper knowledge of themselves so that they are prepared for the apocalypse. After the massive bombing and the resultant purging of the earth, the original people will leave the plane and repopulate the earth, living in accordance with the teachings of Allah.

Nothing about this sense of judgment, destruction, and redevelopment speaks to a desire for a democratic society consistent with the rhetoric of the United States. When the apocalypse is combined with the Nation's separatist tendencies, democracy is clearly not the concern. Instead, under the Honorable Elijah Muhammad, the nation wanted to be excluded from the mechanics of life in the United States. For example, no taxes paid to the US government, and the development of independent businesses and social structures. One might argue that the political system promoted by the Nation of Islam is a theocracy – a society ruled by God and arranged based on the doctrines and creeds of the religious tradition.

Shortly after the establishment of the new Nation, Minister Farrakhan reported a vision during which he was brought into the "Mother Plane," where he heard the voice of the Honorable Elijah Muhammad provide instructions and sanction Farrakhan's ministry. As this episode would suggest, while Farrakhan modified aspects of the Honorable Elijah Muhammad's teachings, he maintained the importance of the apocalypse and final judgment as central elements of the tradition. However, there are a few modifications. For example, whereas the Honorable Elijah Muhammad gave little attention to the possibility of redemption for whites, Minister Farrakhan included in his teachings an opportunity for whites to delay, if not prevent, their destruction. Doing either would require an exercise of justice and peace with respect to African Americans whereby white supremacy is destroyed. While this is possible, Farrakhan argued it is unlikely whites will take advantage of this possibility. Nonetheless, Farrakhan's change in policy from a critique of white persons to a critique of white supremacy, and the opening of membership in the Nation to all interested parties speak to a different sense of black-white relations in the United States in that salvation is available to all.

The new Earth

The present brotherhood of Islam is typical of the life in the hereafter, the difference is that the brotherhood in the hereafter will enjoy the spirit of gladness and happiness forever in the presence of Allah. The earth, the general atmosphere will produce such a change that the people will think it is a new earth. It will be the heaven of the righteous forever!

(From Elijah Muhammad's *Message to the Black Man*, Philadelphia: Haim's Publications, 1965, 304)

Changes in the Nation of Islam's relationship to democracy have occurred over the past few decades. For example, Minister Farrakhan now encourages members of the Nation of Islam to participate in the political process through voting and by means of holding elected offices. Furthermore, few will forget Farrakhan's efforts to campaign for Reverend Jesse Jackson during his campaigns for the Democratic nomination during the 1980s. More than this, African American Sunni Muslims have achieved a noteworthy level of political success. For example, Keith Ellison is a congressman from Minnesota (seventh district), who was sworn into office using the Qur'an, not the Bible. Ellison was the first Muslim in Congress and also the first African American elected to Congress from Minnesota. Until Ellison's election (2007), Larry Shaw (North Carolina State Senate) was the highest ranking Sunni Muslim in the United States. Shaw served for seven terms in the North Carolina State senate, but announced the end of his service in the Senate as of 2010. Since leaving office, Shaw has maintained his involvement with the Council on American–Islamic Relations and he also hosts an issue-based internet radio program.

Turning to versions of Christian nationalism

Organizations such as the Nation of Islam promote separation from white Americans and rejection of the real possibility of democratic principles active in a large-scale manner. However, the Nation did little to outline this separation in a full sense, and some of what Minister Farrakhan would later argue suggests the possibility of a reworked democratic and capitalist system as being consistent with the demands of the Nation and the will of Allah (Master Fard Muhammad). However, Marcus Garvey does more to develop this sense of separation in the form of Black Nationalism consistent with earlier arguments for migration to Africa; but the Universal Negro Improvement Association (UNIA) is by-and-large devoid of any real theological framing or emphasis despite the presence of the African Orthodox Church within his organizational structure. Albert Cleage (1911–2000), however, promoted a mode of nationalism – Christian Nationalism – offering an alternative political system consistent, he would argue, with Christian faith and based on the needs of African Americans. Cleage (later called Jaramogi Abebe Agyeman) was the founder and overseer until his death of the Shrine of the Black Madonna (later called the Pan African Orthodox Christian Church), a Black Power influenced church that combined principles of nationalism with an African-centered reading of the Christian faith. Agyeman and this church are best known for a theological doctrine of Jesus as a physically black messiah who came to establish a particular nation of God's chosen people. African Americans are this chosen people who, rather than seeking integration, should be preparing themselves for separation from whites and the establishment of a new black nation in line with the will of God. Cleage's church was to serve as a central organizing mechanism for this nationalist movement and in this capacity it was to provide the proper theology, and rituals. In addition, it was positioned to offer alternate images in line with a new sense of African Americans' beauty and cosmic importance, and a socio-political activism in line with the demands of the new nation of African Americans as God's chosen. From his perspective, scripture, particularly the Hebrew Bible, pointed to the truth of his nationalistic theology and his brand of activism. In the late 1960s, Agyeman formally organized a nationalist movement that he defined and explained in a book titled *Black Christian Nationalism*.

Black Christian Nationalist Creed

I believe that Jesus, the Black Messiah, was a revolutionary leader, sent by God to rebuild the Black Nation, Israel, and to liberate Black people from powerlessness and from the oppression, brutality, and exploitation of the white gentile world. I believe that the revolutionary spirit of God, embodied in the Black Messiah, is born anew in each generation and that Black Christian Nationalists constitute the living remnant of God's Chosen People in this day, and are charged by Him with responsibility for the Liberation of Black People.

(Quote in Alphonso Pinkney, *Red, Black and Green: Black Nationalism in the United States*, New York: Cambridge University Press, 1976, 172–173)

Like the Nation of Islam, the Shrine of the Black Madonna does not aim to simply promote greater participation in the life of the country as currently configured around radical individualism and capitalism. There is no way for African Americans to prosper within a system initially erected on their slave labor and continued in ways dependent on their subjugation. Instead, this organization posits existence premised on cooperation amongst African Americans in light of scriptural lessons that highlight communal existence and the importance of black pride. And churches, particularly his church, provide an ideal base from which to launch this rethinking of African American life outside the confines of capitalism and the politics of racial discrimination.

There are prominent churches that fall somewhere between an embrace of capitalism (democratic dreams) and advocacy of black power nationalism. In other words, while not nationalistic in the same way as the Shrine of the Black Madonna, recent conversations have pointed out continued attention to black consciousness and the formation of independent identity as the hallmark of some churches. A prime example of this over the past several years has been Trinity Church in Chicago, once led by the Rev. Jeremiah Wright (President Barak Obama's former pastor). The manner in which the church describes itself – "Unashamedly Black and Unapologetically Christian" – gives some sense of the ways in which the marriage between black consciousness and the Gospel of Christ gels for this congregation.

Figure 9.3   Worshippers leave the Trinity United Church of Christ following services in Chicago (June 2008). Courtesy of Scott Olson/Getty Images.

While deeply aware of and committed to the welfare of African Americans in the United States, members of this church also advance a connection to the continent of Africa and a rich legacy beyond slavery. Part of this process involves reading the Bible as well as interpreting socio-political and economic developments in the United States through African American culture and African American experience. Furthermore, the "Black Value System" discussed on the church's website outlines the various commitments of the church, which include: (1) devotion to the advancement of African Americans on the level of spiritual health (embrace of God leading to salvation and a life guided by the teachings of Jesus Christ and participation in the community of the faithful as part of God's chosen people); (2) the welfare of the collective African American community; (3) the safeguarding of African American families; (4) the creation of educational opportunities as a means by which to counter racism; (5) offering young people tools and capacities necessary to thrive; (6) attention to nurturing the full capabilities of the individual; (7) promotion of a positive attitude toward work as well as a strong sense of self measured in terms of intentionality in all activities and respect for self in relationship to the larger community.

Trinity Church's mission

Trinity United Church of Christ has been called by God to be a congregation that is not ashamed of the gospel of Jesus Christ and that does not apologize for its African roots! As a congregation of baptized believers, we are called to be agents of liberation not only for the oppressed, but for all of God's family. We, as a church family, acknowledge, that we will, building on this affirmation of "who we are" and "whose we are," call men, women, boys and girls to the liberating love of Jesus Christ, inviting them to become a party of the church universal, responding to Jesus' command that we go into all the world and make disciples!

We are called out to be "a chosen people" that pays no attention to socio-economic or educational backgrounds. We are made up of the highly educated and the uneducated. Our congregation is a combination of the haves and the have-nots; the economically disadvantaged, the under-class, the unemployed and the employable.

The fortunate who are among us combine forces with the less fortunate to become agents of change for God who is not pleased with America's economic mal-distribution!

W. E. B. DuBois indicates that the problem of the 20th century was going to be the problem of the color line. He was absolutely correct. Our job as servants of God is to address that problem and eradicate it in the name of Him who came for the whole world by calling all men, women, boys and girls to Christ.

(Found on the Trinity Church website: "Mission Statement," http://www. trinitychicago.org/index.php?option=com_content&task=view&id=20)

The last several principles covered through this system speak to a critique of capitalism in line with certain elements of Cleage's nationalism and Ransom's socialism. But for Trinity Church they are worked out in light of the challenges facing African Americans in the late twentieth century and early twenty-first century. Trinity simply calls African Americans to reject efforts that promote the economic and social welfare of the individual in line with the worst dimensions of the US class system. Economic parity, one element of the church's "10-point Vision," does not require the demise of any but instead demands the well-being of all. This is not a condemnation of individual African American economic or social success; rather, it is an argument for understanding individual success as connected to the welfare of the community. Trinity Church is structured in a way reminiscent of Ransom's Institutional Church – both related to Chicago – in that it consciously serves multiple purposes through a rich array of programs and services that address a full range of needs.

Key points you need to know

- The Jeremiad was a style of presentation that critiqued wrongdoing and promised judgment and punishment if behavior was not improved.
- Some religious communities embraced capitalism and democracy, and only campaigned for the full inclusion of African Americans in the workings of these two.
- For some, socialism was more in line with the teachings of the Bible and they argued it should replace capitalism.
- Some religious communities believed neither capitalism nor socialism were productive for African Americans, but instead advocated for a nationalism based on black power and black consciousness.
- Churches and other organizations developed religious programs and outreach efforts meant to advance their particular take on the proper economic and political arrangements for African Americans.
- The response of religious institutions to issues of economics and politics was tied to their reading of scripture and their assessment of manifest destiny and chosen people status for African Americans.

Discussion questions

1. What reasons were given typically in Jeremiads for the condition of and future of the United States?
2. What is manifest destiny and how did it figure into African American perceptions of their relationship to the United States?
3. How did the Nation of Islam describe the Apocalypse?
4. Why did socialism appeal to some African American Christians, and how did it impact their sense of the church's purpose and ministry?

5.　What are some of the dynamics of Black Christian Nationalism?
6.　What are some of the elements of ministry for churches that critique the economic structure of the country, but do not embrace nationalism?

Further reading

Azaransky, Sarah. *The Dream Is Freedom: Pauli Murray and American Democratic Faith*. New York: Oxford University Press, 2011.

Bercovitch, Sacvan. *The American Jeremiad*. Madison, WI: The University of Wisconsin Press, 1978.

Cleage, Albert. *Black Christian Nationalism: New Directions for the Black Church*. Detroit, MI: Luxor Publishing of the Pan-African, 1987.

Curtis, Edward E. *Black Muslim Religion in the Nation of Islam, 1960–1975*. Chapel Hill, NC: The University of North Carolina Press, 2006.

Horsman, Reginald. *Race and Manifest Destiny: Origins of American Racial Anglo-Saxonism*. Cambridge, MA: Harvard University Press, 1981.

Howard-Pitney, David. *African American Jeremiad: Appeals for Justice in America*. Philadelphia, PA: Temple University Press, 2005.

Luker, Ralph E. *The Social Gospel in Black and White: American Racial Reform, 1885–1912*. Chapel Hill, NC: The University of North Carolina Press, 1998.

Oltman, Adele. *Sacred Mission, Worldly Ambition: Black Christian Nationalism in the Age of Jim Crow*. Athens, GA: University of Georgia Press, 2012.

Pinn, Anthony B., editor. *Making the Gospel Plain: The Writings of Bishop Reverdy C. Ransom*. Harrisburg, PA: Trinity Press International, 1999.

West, Cornel. *Prophesy Deliverance! An Afro-American Revolutionary Christianity*. Louisville, KY: Westminster John Knox Press, 2002.

10 African American religion and economics

In this chapter

Related to the politically centered concerns and activism noted in other chapters, this chapter explores the attention given within African American religion to economic development. This includes more focused attention to the economic independence advanced by groups such as the Nation of Islam as well as more recent developments such as the Prosperity Gospel.

Main topics covered

- Major church efforts to enhance the financial welfare of African Americans
- Business ventures within the Nation of Islam
- Debate regarding the relationship between scriptural ethics and material acquisitions
- Religious organizations and community renewal within urban contexts
- Challenges to economic advancement as religious obligation
- Changing attitudes towards the importance and "look" of success

Religion as economic engine

From the period of slavery to the present, African Americans have faced challenges with respect to economic quality of life. Although the period of Reconstruction after the Civil War was meant to provide African Americans with increased opportunities to participate in the political and economic life of the country, patterns of discrimination continued to hamper the outcomes associated with these opportunities. Civil rights activism during the mid-twentieth century was meant to generate once and for all legislation and other structural changes. Yet, roughly a decade after legislation such as the Civil Rights Act of 1964 made employment discrimination illegal, African Americans continued to lag behind and face significant levels of poverty and unemployment. With so many African Americans facing intense challenges, one would expect African American religion in its various forms to address economic issues. For instance, one might expect African American humanism to have an appreciation for the economic needs and motivations of African Americans to the extent its primary concern is the physical existence of African Americans. So, attention to full inclusion in the economic life of the nation would be a natural component of a concern with the full humanity of African Americans, worked out in a moral and ethical manner. This is certainly one way, for example, to think about the labor activities of A. Philip Randolph and the critique of the impact of capitalism on race offered by James Forman. Humanism is not alone in this thinking, in that African-based traditions often held and continued to exercise options for enhancing one's material life through financial gain directly or by impeding the aims of one's enemies. From the period of slavery to the present, systematic African-based traditions and more loosely configured practices such as hoodoo and conjure have provided ritual items and practices meant to enhance economic well-being within a society marked by strong patterns of economic discrimination and inequality. Put differently, African-based traditions offer adherents the means to harness the energy of the natural environment by, for example, providing an offering to one of the deities in exchange for material advantages. In fact, as we move into the late nineteenth century and the early twentieth century, newspaper advertisements by conjurers and hoodoo experts often suggest their ability to secure material success for clients. And the reputation of those advertising, as well as of those experts more subtle in self-promotion, was dependent on the gains made by their clients. Only those with a proven track record of helping people improve their status survived in the competitive environment of multiple religious tradition options. In this respect, these traditions concerned themselves with the spiritual or unseen dimensions of individual and collective life, but did so in a way that centered on providing the resources necessary for a good, physical existence as well.

Practitioners and religious leaders associated with these traditions were not alone in their concern with religious practice and belief as a mechanism for material gain. Christians also viewed this as a viable consequence of a life committed to God. For example, it is common but incorrect to assume that spirituals are concerned only with issues of salvation and connection to God as a source of comfort within a harsh world. For sure, there is this element present in many of the spirituals when one considers lyrics like, "you can have all this world, just give me Jesus." Yet, there is present also in graphic form a concern with the economic welfare of enslaved and free Africans. In fact, the spirituals are as concerned with the markers of economic advancement as they are with notions of trans-historical salvation. Lyrics such as "all God's children got shoes to wear," or songs pointing out the look of heaven – e.g., streets paved with gold – all point to recognition of a transformed life as promised by the Christian faith. And this new life entails different economic status involving the possession of prominent markers of financial wellbeing. Drawing on biblical stories concerning the Children of Israel, enslaved and free Africans understood God's favor as manifest in the physical circumstances of life. That is to say, if faithful to the will of God the Children of Israel were to receive land and financial prosperity. And, if free and enslaved Africans maintained a similar relationship to God, why wouldn't such proper adherence to the will of God not also result in their economic needs being met? For African Americans who monitored the religious claims of white Americans, there was reason to believe adoption of a faith stance similar to that held by white Americans might result in similar financial success and social status. Put another way, some embraced the Christian faith for pragmatic reasons: it appeared to facilitate prosperity. While this approach did not rule out appreciation for its ability to safeguard the soul, it did offer another secondary benefit revolving around the material nature of life. Throughout the history of African American churches both a concern with the spiritual benefits of the faith and its potential for enhancing material life were noted and accounted. For example, the Free African Society in Philadelphia – which eventually served as the basis for the development of the African Methodist Episcopal Church – functioned in many ways as a mutual aid society providing resources and information meant to improve life for its members. Similar organizations in other locations understood themselves as providing for more than just the spiritual needs of African Americans. When these organizations gave way to new churches and denominations, an effort to address the economic success of African Americans remained a grounded and persistent concern. For example, with time, many of these churches targeted education as a form of ministry. In this regard, they followed along the lines of Booker T. Washington's model of education's importance. It was unnecessary for them to agree with his social conservatism through which he advocated for separation of the races in the social arena. Compelling for them was the idea that education – long denied to African Americans in a systematic fashion – could serve as an instrument of renewal. The AME Church's Wilberforce University in Ohio, and Livingstone College affiliated with the African Methodist Episcopal Zion Church were concerned with the production of an educated clergy equipped to lead African Americans. Yet, their concern with education was not limited to this class of leaders in that these institutions became hallmarks for a general understanding of education as a means by which to gain full participation in the life of the country. This, of necessity, involved economic advancement.

From the perspective of many churches, there were deep connections between development of proper character (expressed in relationship to the Christian faith) and material advancement. This is not to say material gain, or economic advancement, was the final outcome of a good life in all cases. No, for many churches the final

Links between spiritual health and economic well-being

- Early African American Christians saw the promises of prosperity in the Hebrew Bible as applicable to them.
- The Spirituals spoke to an interest in spiritual redemption tied to material comfort and security.
- Churches saw providing education as a religious obligation and as a way to break down barriers to full participation in the life of the nation (including its economy).
- Churches understood their financial independence as an obligation to provide for both spiritual and material needs.
- Churches developed economically-centered outreach programs meant to draw in business to their communities.
- Tax status and creation of community development organizations allowed churches to secure local, state, and federal funds for business ventures.

outcome remained lodged in moral and ethical conduct consistent with their faith; but, there is no denying that this type of character and careful conduct bore "fruit" in the form of success in one's economic activities as well. Spiritual churches provide an example of how this works by means of blending Christian sensibilities and elements of African-based traditions. Within these churches it is argued believers can tap into the spirit world and use information drawn from the spirit world to enhance physical life. This can involve an increase in wealth through information provided by spirits that allows for good business decisions. Religious leaders in this tradition also provide rituals that, when properly acted out, release positive energy useful in securing resources to meet financial needs. Much of this information, spiritual assistance, and energy are drawn from passages of the Bible interpreted and applied to daily life. People might be told to read a particular passage a certain number of times each day and claim their blessings through this process. Or, they might be told to write the scriptural passage down and place that piece of paper in a specified location in order to release energy and insight. While some members of traditional African American churches have been known to make use of such rituals and practices, major denominations typically have given more attention to standard means for making gains. For instance, it has been a common understanding within mainstream African American churches that food pantries, clothing distribution, shelters, and so on address the immediate signs and markers of poverty by offering people short-terms solutions to economic difficulties.

As the resource base grew for certain churches, they expanded their activities to include development of businesses meant to increase revenue, job options, and neighborhood resources for their members. This can involve a variety of options, including the creation of affordable housing, stores selling a variety of goods, as well as small grants to help members of their communities start their own businesses.

Figure 10.1 Volunteers pack groceries. The Love Gospel Assembly has had a food bank and soup kitchen for over 25 years and serves up to 400 families a day. © Richard Levine/Alamy.

Churches involved in these activities connect their mission to the financial welfare of the communities in which they are located. In this way, African American churches use economic development as a way to revive urban communities through new infrastructure, job opportunities, and a sustainable tax base in often forgotten neighborhoods. They do this work based on the assumption that links between spiritual renewal and ownership of the means of production is consistent with the Christian faith and the will of God. That is to say, spiritual power is tied to economic power. Much of this is possible as African American churches extend their financial resources beyond the money put in offering plates on Sundays. This has involved increased utilization of banks and traditional lending opportunities – including local and national government grants and loans. Furthermore, it is often the case that churches undertake their work through community development corporations they initiate. Because these corporations are attached to churches that are "nonprofit" organizations, they can receive government grants as well as money from private sources without penalty. However, in creating these nonprofit entities and receiving public funding, churches have had to be careful to make a clear distinction between the actual church and the corporation. This helps them safeguard against the blending of resources. This is important because the legal separation of church and state places restriction on how public funds – government money – can be used and this includes an inability to use such funding to promote a particular religious viewpoint. In short, money secured from the government can't be used to advance the spiritual work of religious organizations. While churches, of course, advocate particular theological perspectives – and they remain free to do so – public money cannot be used to do this. So, it has been important for churches interested in economic advancement to properly separate monies so as to avoid accounting problems that impact the financial health of the church and future opportunities for grants and loans. If mismanaged, churches could be sued to recoup government money; or, they could lose their tax status. In addition to using public money to promote economic renewal, some religious organizations have also worked to bring companies to their communities to provide services and jobs the churches cannot provide. While we typically think of churches playing this economic role in urban areas, it is also the case that churches in rural areas have used their resources to develop business ventures including small grocery stores and restaurants as a way of meeting economic needs through employment opportunities and greater access to much needed foodstuffs.

It would be inaccurate to assume all churches are in favor of this approach to economics and church ministry. For some, too much attention to business and economic development obscures the church's primary mission, which is the saving of souls. According to those providing this critique, scripture is very clear – one can't serve both God and mammon (or wealth). That is to say, a focus – any focus – on wealth will require a surrender of important moral and ethical principles. Effort to create balance between wealth and spiritual well-being will only result in significant spiritual problems because demands made on life by the world are inconsistent with the demands made on life by the Christian faith. Yet, when given careful and close attention, even these churches recognize the need for money in order to operate. They are not free from monetary entanglements with secular life. Nonetheless, for them there is a major difference between using money to keep the church functioning and seeking wealth as a practice of one's faith. Contrary to this more conservative approach, other churches, in fact many churches, argue the theological merits of undertaking programs that promote economic well-being by asserting God wants the best for those who follow the will of God and this must include economic health. To counter readings of particular scripture passages that might suggest friction between spiritual health and economic wealth – such as Mark 10:25, "It is easier for a camel to go through the eye of a needle than for a rich man to enter the kingdom of God" – these wealth-minded churches provide contextual information on scripture. They suggest that: (1) "eye of a needle" refers to a narrow opening on a road or passage way, or more specifically a narrow gate in Jerusalem, as opposed to the opening on a needle used for sewing. Hence, this passage of scripture refers to something difficult but not impossible; (2) the scripture points to the inability to have wealth righteously without proper morals and ethics. This calls for particular use of one's wealth, and moral demands placed on how wealth is secured. What the passage, they would argue, suggests is the need for balance. And this balance is based on the recognition that wealth must not consume the person and should not take one away from obedience to God. The Christian with economic means must remain humble and free from sin. Others support economic programming offered by churches by also countering typical interpretations of the exchange between Jesus and the moneychangers in the temple (Matthew 21:12): "Jesus entered the temple area and drove out all who were buying and selling there. He overturned the tables of the money changers and the benches of those selling doves." Here's the key, the words uttered as he did this (Matthew 21:13): "'It is written,' he said to them, 'My house will be called a house of prayer,' but you are making it a 'den of robbers.'" Pastors and other church workers committed to wealth as a sign of spiritual health will often argue that Jesus is not condemning business, but rather is challenging the ridiculous rates charged by the changers. That is to say, they argue the problem in this scriptural story is the way in which money took priority over religious engagement. However, if churches remain committed to the will of God and prioritize that, economic success/business can be consistent with God's desire for the well-being of Christians committed to the church. Clearly, there is debate concerning what Jesus actually meant by "eye of the needle," as well as the proper interpretation of the exchange between Jesus and the moneychangers, and such debate isn't the point here. More important is simply the way in which many churches interpret scripture so as to support (or at least not actively hinder) financial success for followers of Jesus Christ. In short, this interest in economic health is at times tied to a theological assumption that the moral and ethical lessons of scripture can be lived out by those who have economic success. These two are not mutually exclusive. From the mid-twentieth century to the present, there have emerged graphic examples of this thinking within African American church communities.

Arguments against economic ventures

- Christians should maintain a priority for the saving of souls.
- There is a clear distinction between spiritual health and involvement in worldly ventures.
- The Bible is critical of efforts to prioritize economic success.
- Separation of Church and state regulations suggest a clear distinction between what religious organizations and "secular" institutions should do within communities.
- Often, churches do not have the mechanisms necessary to handle governmental red tape and requirements regarding public funds.

Prosperity gospel and related approaches

Although the average African American church has fewer than 300 members, the number of churches with over 5,000 members has increased over the past several decades. These extremely large churches, often nondenominational, are commonly called "megachurches" because of their size and extensive use of technology (including massive television ministries reaching millions). Many of the pastors associated with these churches are proponents of the prosperity gospel movement. Rather than arguing economic success can be used to complete the mission of the church, these ministers argue that God in fact wants Christians to be rich. That is to say, rather than wealth being a potential offshoot of the moral and ethical life, they instead suggest that wealth may be the end (not a means to an end) of the spiritual life in line with the will of God. In simple terms: God wants God's people to be wealthy, to experience major blessings, and to receive anything less means one is not living through the will of God. There are early signs of this theology within the first several decades of the twentieth century through radio, with evangelists such as Aimee Semple McPherson (1890–1944) proclaiming to packed revivals God's ability to make a felt difference in one's physical life through healing, and so on. As an early pioneer in the use of technology to spread the message of Christ, McPherson marked the way for other evangelists and pastors who would use both radio and television. The latter even generated a new term for these preachers – televangelists.

By the mid-twentieth century, televangelism and televangelists captured the imagination of an expansive audience. Many of them were theologically conservative, using television to bring people to Christ in a way meant to promote a clear distinction between the church and the world. They used secular tools – like television – but they maintained spiritual commitments that trumped the value of these tools. These ministers made appeals for money as a way to support their evangelical mission to convert the world to Christ, but they did not necessarily see financial success as the outcome of that commitment to Christ. Others such as Jim and Tammy Faye Bakker would use television as a way to generate large sums of money used to support a lavish life style – fine clothing, expensive home, and so on. Most interesting, however, is the way by which televangelists refined the process of requesting money from supporters. They extended their financial reach beyond a local congregation, thereby gaining the financial assistance of those with no physical connection to the preacher or the ministry. In addition, televangelism opened the door for a deep connection between obedience to the will of God and economic wealth marked by interpretation of scripture in light of current economic needs and wants. Both spiritual and physical areas of life were said to entail a shared marker of life lived properly: prosperity. These preachers taught that one could have the treasures of the world and a healthy soul. This simply required recognition of the source of these riches – God – and proper worship of God for God's goodness (e.g., including giving 10 percent of one's earnings to the church). Why would God deny well-being and wealth to Christians, when God is in a position to provide it, and Christians need it?

A growing percentage of Christians in the United States answer this question by saying God wouldn't deny God's people wealth. They see economic advancement as compatible with Christian commitment, if not the content of the faith. While many connect this interpretation of the Christian gospel in African American churches with the 1980s, it is really much older. One of the more flamboyant representations of this thinking is the late Rev. Ike, mentioned earlier in this book. His rituals meant to secure wealth were explicit. For example, he sold prayer cloths and other items meant to bring people good fortune; and his radio program contained testimonials from people who bought such items and claimed to receive blessings as a result. When one considers Rev. Ike, it becomes easy to decipher an element of positive thinking present in the prosperity gospel, similar to that found in the ministries of Father Divine and Sweet Daddy Grace as well as the spiritual churches. That is to say, the prosperity gospel approach to wealth and economic advancement assumes a strong link between what one thinks and what one achieves. Accordingly, it is important to maintain proper thinking with respect to a need, recognizing that doubt and fear run contrary to the will of God and that those two states of mind prevent prosperity.

Prosperity gospel

- Is also called "wealth and health" and prosperity theology.
- Although present earlier, it is typically associated with churches and preachers coming into prominence during the 1980s.
- Claims there is consistency between economic advancement and scripture.
- God wants God's people (Christians) to have the best things in life.
- While we typically associate this message with large churches – "megachurches" – it is present in churches of all sizes.
- Wealth becomes a measure of one's spiritual growth and faith.
- Tends to make extensive use of technology and online resources for their ministries.
- Remains a charged term that elicits both positive and negative commentary.

Although Rev. Ike was more creative in his presentation, he was not alone in his thinking. For example, the Rev. Fred Price's (1932–) television ministry and church – Crenshaw Christian Center Faith Dome – in California has consistently maintained a sense of the gospel being compatible with wealth. Price ministered to a variety of denominations and locations, and he marks 1970 as turning point in his personal and professional life. It was then that he had a Pentecostal experience and was filled with the Holy Spirit. From his perspective, receiving the Holy Spirit and living in accordance with the will of God produces great benefits.

Figure 10.2 T. D. Jakes. Courtesy of Thomas Michael Alleman/Liaison/Getty Images.

According to the Crenshaw Center's website, the gospel is preached in such a way as to transform the people: "Instruct so that people rise from burned-out hopes and faulty lifestyles to enjoy the privileges and promises God has for us through Jesus Christ." Although Price was chronologically first, it is likely that more people are familiar with the Rev. T. D. Jakes, pastor of "The Potter's House" in Dallas, Texas. His ministry stretches across a variety of outlets – Hollywood films, books, conferences, and church ministry. Some years ago, he was compared to Billy Graham as being perhaps the next "America's preacher" because of his growing reputation as a leading, internationally recognized preacher. In a move that would have seemed very odd some years ago, he is listed on the church website as being "a charismatic leader, visionary, provocative thinker, and entrepreneur." It is this last skill set that would have been missing from biographical statements prior to the contemporary prosperity gospel movement.

Whereas there are ways in which Jakes has softened the message of prosperity, the language of "empowerment" used within his ministry still opens to a deep connection between spirituality and material gain. That is to say, for Jakes, there is no contradiction between being a committed Christian and economically successful and self-reliant. The former – Christian commitment – makes possible the latter. Although the Potter's House, and prosperity ministries in general, tend towards an apolitical stance by avoiding controversial topics, there is an interest in provided a version of the social gospel whereby the teachings of Christ are believed to have felt consequences that require Christians to provide assistance to those in need. Jakes builds on this understanding by offering famine relief in Africa, personal enrichment classes, a prison ministry, information and assistance concerning homeownership, guidance on starting business as well as credit for these ventures.

It is possible to be concerned with economic success without preaching a version of the prosperity gospel. For example, few of these ministers build in the type of concern for liberation and social transformation present in the ministry of the Rev. Freddie Haynes also of Dallas, Texas. The mission statement of the church speaks to a persistent demand for transformation impacting the individual and the community: "The Friendship-West Baptist Church is called to be a caring community of Christians committed to developing a personal relationship with our Lord that eventuates into a ministry of evangelization, edification, and emancipation, in the Church and the community." This church understands spiritual success to have some relationship to economic advancement. Yet, it bases this on a blend of liberation theology that understands God's commitment to be to the poor and a sense of faith's function involving transformation of social arrangements. Jakes understands the importance of providing relief from the effects of impoverishment in a variety of senses, but Haynes' conversation also includes a commitment to the principles of progressive politics and activism. For Haynes, prosperity takes place within the context of a socio-politically, culturally and economically transformed society. As the church motto indicates, Friendship-West is about the business of "equipping changed people to change the world."

Although ministers such as Jakes point to an element of ministry involving the enhancement of entrepreneurial opportunities and success (e.g., economic empowerment), more solidly positioned within the prosperity gospel camp is Reverend Creflo Dollar, pastor of World Changers Church International. For example, on the website for Creflo Dollar Ministries, one of the daily devotionals appeals to scripture (Isaiah 48:17) to promote prosperity: "Thus saith the Lord, thy Redeemer, the Holy One of Israel; I am the Lord thy God which teacheth thee to profit, which leadeth thee by the way that thou shouldest go." According to Dollar, this means "God will teach you to profit according to His way of doing things. Listen to His voice and He will guide you into your place of abundance."

What Dollar intends is clear, and it is addressed explicitly on the website as part of the "Frequently Asked Questions" page:

Figure 10.3 Creflo Dollar. Courtesy of Johnny Nunez/WireImage/Getty Images.

With a name like "Dollar," does Creflo teach about anything other than money? Yes. Although Creflo Dollar is known for his messages on prosperity, he teaches a range of lifestyle issues, from marriage and family, to health, character development and discipline.

There is a blend of evangelicalism and new thought orientation on certain issues. For example, Dollar, like prosperity preachers in general, tends to be conservative on social and political issues – such as pre-marital sex and gay rights – but rather liberal with respect to reading scripture as supportive of economic advancement. Furthermore, Dr. Dollar provides clear training on the importance of wealth and how to obtain it through his School of Prosperity.

Those attending this school have keys to accessing wealth outlined for them. According to Dollar, the Bible contains all the necessary information to increase one's economic power. One must simply have faith and a relationship with God in order to unlock this information, and through speech and action gain wealth.

Creflo Dollar's school of prosperity

Are you tired of living from paycheck to paycheck? Have you ever observed a need that you longed to meet, but you didn't have the finances to help? Do you yearn to sow freely into the needs of the ministry? Do you want more out of life for you and your family? If so, you need the School of Prosperity! Even though you are to 'owe no man anything, but to love [him] ...' (Romans 13:8), having no increase renders you useless to the kingdom of God. By the same token, you can experience financial increase, but existing debt can just as easily hinder you from kingdom advancement. Dr. Creflo A. Dollar's School of Prosperity is a course designed to teach you how to fulfill your God-given destiny – to be a blessing to others and by being His distribution center. Whether you are financially comfortable or head over heels in debt, you need this course! You will learn:

- Why God wants you rich
- How to use biblical principles to make natural principles work on your behalf
- The keys to debt reduction
- How to increase for kingdom advancement
- The automatic systems for financial freedom

(From "World Changers Church International, The School of Prosperity, with Dr. Creflo A. Dollar," http://www.worldchangers.org/soponline/soplanding.html?site=CDM)

That is to say, one must talk as if one already has wealth and one must behave as if God has already given one all the riches they desire. Through these acts of faith, God will reward believers with material goods and spiritual health. Furthermore, according to Dollar and a variety of other prosperity preachers, wealth isn't simply an option one can exercise, it is the proper life for those who are committed to God and who are living in accordance with the will of God. He goes further to argue that poverty is part of the original curse on humans because of sin. There is no merit in poverty, but rather it is a part of the human condition that salvation destroys. Being a Christian committed to the teachings of the Bible means the end of poverty and the restoration of a life marked by comfort and material success – quality of life. This type of life was God's initial plan for humanity, what Dollar refers to as "total life prosperity." And again this involves material goods, economic success, but also a wholeness of life that encompasses well-being in every area. Consistent with the general prosperity gospel message, Dollar argues that it is insufficient to simply seek money; the goal isn't materialism but rather to understand material goods as only a part – one of the manifestations – of the good life promised by God to those who are faithful and Christ-like in their thinking and actions. This requires discipline in that those committed to the prosperous life must be systematic in their study of scripture and systematic in their practice of the truths found in scripture. But, it is believed when Christians train themselves to abide by the teachings of Christ with respect to total life prosperity the results are significant. One thing is clear with respect to the prosperity gospel: the process of securing prosperity is not without effort. Rather, success requires time and attention to the biblical principles; application of those principles despite "evidence" to the contrary; control of what is said and done so as to avoid speaking or acting in a way that contradicts the principles outlined in scripture; and, discipline of the body – prayer and fasting – to make certain one's entire being anticipates and lives prosperity. All this is framed by a good sense of stewardship or proper use of one's resources (including giving a tithe – or 10 percent of one's income back to the church for the maintenance and expansion of its ministries). Furthermore, wealth is a byproduct of a good Christian life in line with the will of God. It is what God provides those who are faithful to the Christian tradition, but key here is an understanding that one must be a follower of Christ first, and maintain full attention to the requirements of that faith stance. And while those living through total life prosperity are entitled to having luxuries, it is also argued within the prosperity gospel that one must be wise with resources, control spending and commit to wise investments of money in the stock market, savings accounts, and retirement accounts so that such investments do not result in debt.

Economic cooperation

Sunni Islam in African American communities' concern with the pillars of Islam builds into its workings a sense of economic compassion and concern whereby one's personal wealth is ideally extended to benefit other members of the community. That is to say, *zakat* – the paying of alms – becomes a way of seeing financial success as entailing obligation to the larger community (the other pillars are: *Shahada* – affirmation of the oneness of God and the role of Muhammad as the last prophet; *Salat* – prayer five times each day; *Ramadan* – fasting; *Hajj* – the pilgrimage to Mecca taken by every able bodied and financially-capable Muslim). Furthermore, the Nation of Islam doesn't really have a version of the prosperity gospel, although it has always expressed concern over the economic development of African Americans. Demand for equal opportunity and the desire to develop African American owned and operated businesses involves at their core an interest in advancement of African Americans as a basic element of the Nation's faith stance. Minister Farrakhan notes the general decline of the United States' economic standing and power is based on its poor treatment of African Americans, and the US economy will not improve until African Americans are treated properly. This is not to suggest, however, that African Americans should be content with a handout from the government. Rather, as the Nation of Islam believes itself to exemplify, African Americans must foster their own economic opportunities through independent business dealings that produce revenue. For example, according to the Nation of Islam, the Honorable Elijah Muhammad developed in 1964 the "The Three Year Economic Plan" as the way by which to advance African Americans. It is a self-help initiative based on each African American contributing monthly to a general fund that would be used to wipe out economic hardship – unemployment, poverty and so on. Attached to this philosophy and ethics were a variety of enterprises, in part made possible through the work of Guaranty Bank & Trust of Chicago. In 1975, this bank was advertised as being "the Bank of the Nation of Islam" and as such it was "immune to many of the economic problems that affect many banks." The Honorable Elijah Muhammad died in that year, but the plan has continued within the Nation, and proceeds from it were used in the 1990s to develop businesses such as a large farm in Georgia that produces a variety of vegetables sold through co-ops and other outlets. Farrakhan also established P.O.W.E.R (*People Organized and Working for Economic Rebirth*), which offers toiletries and other items meant to engender economic opportunity for African Americans in line with self-determination. P.O.W.E.R. played on the Honorable Elijah Muhammad's earlier call for African Americans to keep their money and other resources in their communities through the development of businesses – the farm, restaurants, bakeries, media outlets (such as Goss Urbanite Press that produced "Muhammad Speaks," as well as the many small publishing houses that produced the Honorable Elijah Muhammad's books), imports (e.g., Whiting H & G fish import project) trucking services, markets (e.g., "Your Super Market") and so on – providing products and services utilized by African Americans. This, he argued, was the way to achieve economic independence that would in turn help African Americans safeguard themselves against manipulation by the larger society.

As Christian prosperity preachers linked proper thought and action as a synergy for quality of life (including economic advancement), the Nation of Islam understood self-reliance and proper knowledge of self as necessary building blocks for the development of a strong African American community consistent with the will of God. For both Christian preachers and the Nation of Islam, tied to posture toward self and the world is the transformation of economic circumstances. From the perspective of Farrakhan, this economic plan is consistent with the teachings of the Honorable Elijah Muhammad and constitutes a necessary building block for African Americans to develop a sovereign nation in line with their greatness and status as a chosen people of God. According to the Nation, African Americans will progress as a people only when they stop using the larger society's notion of wealth and success as the benchmark for their self-understanding. For example, jobs within the economic system arranged and controlled by the dominant society cannot generate a strong sense of self-worth for African Americans. This is only developed through economic independence generating self-determination.

Key points you need to know

- On some level, African American religion has always had an interest in the economic success of its followers.
- Education was seen as a way to secure economic advancement through the attainment of needed skills and talents.
- Churches developed programs and community development organizations to address issues of poverty and urban decay.
- Twentieth-century megachurches became synonymous with the prosperity gospel movement.
- Prosperity gospel teachings linked God's will for Christians with wealth and spiritual health.
- The Bible is believed to contain the keys to prosperity for those who study it, meditate on it and in their thinking and living practice its principles of wholeness.
- The Nation of Islam developed an economic plan meant to provide all the institutions and businesses needed to create economic independence for African Americans.
- African-based traditions and spiritual churches understood economic well-being can be achieved through proper attention to and harnessing of spiritual forces.
- African American humanism understands economic development as an essential component of full humanity in that it allows for a sense of self-worth and affords resources necessary for the further development of healthy life options for all.

Discussion questions

1. Why have some churches objected to a focus on economic development?
2. Why have other churches argued economic development is essential to their mission?
3. What types of programs and activities have marked African American religion's economic development efforts?
4. What are some of the important elements of the Prosperity Gospel?
5. According to Prosperity Gospel proponents, what are some of the reasons people experience economic challenges?
6. For Prosperity Gospel proponents, what is the link between what people think about their financial circumstances and how they experience those circumstances? Are there any similarities between Prosperity Gospel churches and the Nation of Islam on this issue?
7. Why does the Nation of Islam object to participation in the US economy?
8. What does the Nation of Islam offer as an alternative to the traditional US model of economic well-being?

Further reading

Clegg, Claude Andrew. *An Original Man: The Life and Times of Elijah Muhammad.* New York: St. Martins, 1998.

Collier-Thomas, Bettye. *Jesus, Jobs, and Justice: African American Women and Religion.* New York: Alfred A. Knopf, 2010.

Gardell, Mattias. *In the Name of Elijah Muhammad: Louis Farrakhan and the Nation of Islam.* Durham, NC: Duke University Press, 1996.

Harrison, Milmon F. *Righteous Riches: The Word of Faith Movement in Contemporary African American Religion.* New York: Oxford University Press, 2005.

Lee, Shayne. *T. D. Jakes: America's New Preacher.* New York: New York University Press, 2007.

Martin, Darnise. *Beyond Christianity: African Americans in a New Thought Church.* New York: New York University Press, 2005.

Mitchem, Stephanie Y. *Name It and Claim It?: Prosperity Preaching in the Black Church.* Cleveland, OH: Pilgrim Press, 2007.

Pinn, Anthony B. *The Black Church in the Post-Civil Rights Era.* Maryknoll, NY: Orbis Books, 2002.

Walton, Jonathan L. *Watch This! The Ethics and Aesthetics of Black Televangelism.* New York: New York University Press, 2009.

11 *Liberation theology*

In this chapter

One of the most notable developments in religious thought over the past 40 years is liberation theology. This chapter provides basic information on the development of liberation theology – including its relationship to religious communities, and the re-thinking of basic theological categories (e.g., sin) it offers. This discussion develops in such a way as to give attention to both Protestant liberation theology and Catholic liberation theology. Furthermore, readers are provided with a sense of the relationship of liberation theology in African American communities to Latin American liberation theology.

Main topics covered

- Prototype liberation theology ideas prior to the twentieth century
- Shift from social gospel to liberation theology during the civil rights struggle of the twentieth century
- Development of black theology of liberation
- Development of womanist theology of liberation
- Shortcomings and successes of black and womanist theologies
- Future of black and womanist theologies
- Relation of black and womanist theologies to other forms of liberation theology (e.g., Latin American liberation theology)

A feeling for resistance: from slavery to the social Gospel

African American theologians responsible for contemporary liberation theology argue that many root ideas in their work are easily uncovered in the thought of enslaved and free Africans in the early years of their presence in North America. They argue enslaved Africans who embraced the Christian faith spoke about God as a liberator through Christ, and connected their spiritual progress to their physical freedom from oppression. Furthermore, in connecting themselves to the biblical Children of Israel they spoke of their God as one who takes seriously the suffering of the people, and one who takes the side of those who have been marginalized and oppressed. These perspectives on God and Christ were combined with a sense of redemption revolving around life within the context of the socially, politically, and economically arranged world. Embedded in this, of course, is a critique of injustice and at times soft challenge to the structures of oppression that ruled the day. These arguments all represent dimensions of what we now call liberation theology. These early positions point to an underlying assumption found within current liberation theology: faith must do work. That is to say, commitment to Christ doesn't require a turn away from the world but rather demands a determination to change the world.

This message is embedded in much early African American Christian thought and it is often coded in order to circumvent the restrictions endemic to the slave system. However, there were some challenges, often violent in nature that marked out this demand for justice in explicit terms. But outside those examples – the Denmark Veseys, Nat Turners and Gabriel Prossers of the slave period – the early African American church tradition had to be more careful in its presentation of Christianity as a life changing force. Yet, the effort of ministers and laypersons to promote social and economic transformation speaks to an understanding of religion as having felt material consequences when it is at its best. Opening their doors to a variety of non-spiritually centered needs such as education, political discussions and so on also suggests attention to the whole person as religious obligation. Hence, from their initial formation through the nineteenth century, many churches recognized the intersection of everyday life and spiritual life. In so doing, they noted the ways in which poor physical conditions made appreciation for religious engagement difficult: does hunger prevent concentrated prayer? If so, mindful of this, domestic mission work, particularly on the heels of the Civil War, engaged the spiritual formation of new Christians but also made an effort to place concern with the condition of the soul into a larger framework of socio-political and economic considerations. They recognized that newly free African Americans needed a way to break from continuing discrimination as part of their life. Those participating in this type of ministry justified their work by pointing out Christ's engagement with those most in need and his desire to bring a comforting word of transformation that recognized the physical challenges faced by the people of God under the authority of oppressors. Churches embracing this type of orientation during the twentieth century often framed their theological thinking in terms of the growing social gospel (or social Christianity) movement.

Initiated in large part as a Christian response to poverty at the turn of the century, the social gospel turned to the ministry of Jesus Christ for signs of how to respond to current conditions. It became clear that Christian commitment required strong attention to the socio-economic existence of the needy. That is to say, Christianity properly lived had social implications. Figures such as Walter Rauschenbusch (1861–1918) developed a form of theology responsive to such needs in that it outlined a connection between individual salvation and social issues – the obligation of the faith to address social life in order to be Christ-like. Sin, in this respect, did not focus solely on individual moral failures as had been the case traditionally; rather, sin for the social gospel had to do with the fostering of life conditions that destroy people through poverty – poor housing, inadequate employment, and so on. Christianity so conceived did not promote passivity and contentment with the current conditions of life, but rather – like Jesus Christ – it was revolutionary because it promoted radical shifts in the quality of life on earth. There is a political and "earthy" quality to the social gospel that offended some who preferred a more spiritualized reading of Jesus' ministry and what he required of his followers. Yet, for others the social gospel and its presentation of a social Christianity provided the best response to the growing discomfort and suffering marking life in the United States during the late nineteenth century and early twentieth century. It allowed people to exercise their moral convictions in a way that affected and influenced the world outside the walls of churches, and in this way, the movement gave churches relevance beyond the limited audiences of their congregations. This platform, it should be noted, didn't replace a personal experience of conversion. No, social gospellers believed salvation was necessary; however, addressing individual sin had to be matched by strong attention to social sin such as poverty. This sense of religion and the theology supporting it gave churches new conversation partners, including politicians and activists who normally had little to do with church practices. Spreading quickly in the North in places like New York City, the social gospel promoted a new approach to the Christian's self-understanding and work in the world – one that did not require such a clear distinction between the "sacred" and the "secular." The meaning of the Gospel message for life circumstances became the way to interpret current events. And it was through an understanding of God as always present through Christ who is working with humans to foster a better life that social Christianity advocates conducted their work.

The social gospel message

- Jesus's ministry entailed attention to the physical conditions of life and involved the disregarded and abused.
- The Kingdom of God is not simply a non-physical relationship to God.
- Being a Christian involves more than individual salvation.
- Difficulties in the world are a result of personal and social sin.
- To be Christ-like is to commit energy and church resources to improving people's social condition.
- Churches must provide an array of services and information.

However, there were some issues with this new movement. It gave much needed religious and theological attention to issues of poverty and the other challenges of life in urban areas –health and social risks of industrialization and significant immigration from Europe. Missing, however, was attention to issues of race. In a very real sense, the social gospel movement saw all the poor and disadvantaged as being white Americans and white immigrants. In addition, there were some within this movement, such as Josiah Strong (1847–1916), whose theological thinking was in fact racist. For example, in thinking about the historical advancement of people of European descent he argued other groups – such as Native Americans and Africans – were inferior peoples whose purpose was to aid in the advancement of God's preferred people (i.e., people of European descent). He was not without sympathy in that those of European descent – "Anglo-Saxons" – were to convert and aid these weaker and inferior groups. Strong offers an extreme example of racism within the movement, whereas most simply failed to consider racism as one of the social challenges affecting life in the United States and therefore requiring action on the part of the followers of Christ.

While many African American churches had a community-minded agenda, not all embraced the more socio-politically aggressive dimensions of the social gospel movement. These figures preferred instead to have social outreach as an offshoot of spiritual development as opposed to the social gospel's more decided privileging of social outreach as the basic framing of a Christ-like existence. In essence, it was much too liberal a theological perspective for some. This points to an ongoing tension within many African American churches in which a somewhat conservative theological stance on major issues such as the nature of the human confronts recognition of social injustice and a need to address it from within the churches. As long as spiritual salvation remained the priority, churches were often able to maintain their conservatism and provide services to the larger community. If and when these services took on new levels of importance and meaning, it was necessary in many cases to also adjust their theological claims and assumptions. The tenacious hold on the social nature of religious life marked by the social gospel produced a tension that many addressed by downplaying social Christianity. For others, the social gospel was the proper perspective. It simply required a wider focus on the nature and meaning of social sin.

Whereas the general social gospel movement gave little to no attention to the plight of African Americans in a post-civil war United States, there were African American preachers who incorporated issues of racism into the social gospel agenda. They did not remove poverty as a condition needing the attention of committed Christians. Rather, they argued the situation of poverty, industrialization and the meaning of massive immigration from Europe into urban areas had to be considered in connection to the nature and meaning of race and practices of racism impacting the country. Like their counterparts, they opened their churches to educational opportunities, to fighting crime, to lobbying for green space and for recreational activities, as well as efforts to improve health conditions within crowded urban tenements. The welfare of Africans Americans became something of a litmus test for these ministers on the general spiritual and physical health of the United States as a whole. Figures such as Richard R. Wright, Jr., of the African Methodist Episcopal Church, during the early twentieth century maintained a commitment to keeping the Christian faith relevant to the lived circumstances of African Americans. However, social Christianity within African American communities hits its high point during the civil rights movement when figures such as Dr. Martin Luther King, Jr., the Reverend Ralph Abernathy, and a host of others applied its principles to the struggle for full inclusion in the life of the nation.

Although the tension mentioned earlier regarding the liberal nature of this approach against the generally conservative posture of many churches resulted in friction, some African American congregations understood non-violent direct action as a significant indicator of their commitment to the teachings of Christ. King and others like him went so far as to argue that one's allegiance to Christ and to the Church is directly related to one's willingness to risk all for the sake of social justice: to care for suffering humanity is to care about Christ. As biblical justification for this stance, many African American social gospel advocates pointed to 1 John 4:20: "If anyone says, 'I love God,' yet hates his brother, he is a liar. For anyone who does not love his brother, whom he has seen, cannot love God, whom he has not seen." Social Christianity tied together this New Testament service to humanity as devotion to God and the Hebrew Bible proclamation concerning the nature of ministry (Isaiah 61:1–3):

> the Spirit of the Sovereign Lord is upon me, because the Lord has anointed me to preach good news to the poor. He has sent me to bind up the brokenhearted, to proclaim freedom for the captives and release from darkness for the prisoners to proclaim the year of the Lord's favor and the day of vengeance of our God, to comfort all who mourn …

These passages of scripture provided biblical authority, if not mandate, for social gospel work. Based on this rationale, Christians committed to the social gospel during the 1950s and 1960s left their sanctuaries and took up positions on protest lines, sit-ins, and marches associated with the demand for equal rights.

Pushing for social transformation as suggested through the social gospel involved some gains during the civil rights movement, and church leaders took credit for them. However, even before the assassination of Dr. King, there was a growing level of discontent with the social gospel approach. While liberal, and there was benefit to this, it wasn't radical and revolutionary enough for some. The gains were slow in coming, and did little to alter the general privileging of white Americans and "whiteness" undergirding so many US policies and programs. For some, the struggles

African Americans and the social gospel

- Exposed racism found in the teachings of some social gospellers.
- Included race as a social sin to be addressed through the gospel of Christ.
- Linked the condition of African Americans to industrialization and urban decay.
- Extended community engagement already present in the "this-worldly" orientation of some churches.
- Was resisted by some churches and church leaders who questioned the flirtation with socialism found in the work of some African American social gospellers, and rejected what they considered a hyper-occupation with social sin over against the need for personal salvation.

of the civil rights movement also required a re-thinking of the nature and general power structures of the United States, as well as the role religion played in supporting an unfair distribution of power. There was a growing suspicion that the social gospel approach wasn't angry enough with the conditions shaping life for African Americans and, as a result, it couldn't effectively harness the frustrations of a generation coming of age during the civil rights movement. Willingness to embrace pain and suffering, to nonviolently absorb white supremacist violence, was not appealing to all. Those taking this position argued such a stance was counterproductive in that it marked a failure to recognize fully the humanity of African Americans. From the perspective of the most critical, this social gospel approach involved surrender to the most damaging dimensions of the faith and society. In concert with this process of re-thinking the social gospel was an effort to read the Christian tradition as well as the workings of the United States from the perspective of African Americans. And by extension it involved effort to privilege the experience, history, and cultural production of African Americans for what these say about God and God's presence in the world. True and lasting transformation, this disgruntled group claimed, would not be achieved until African Americans appreciated fully the depth of the link between God and African Americans. Everything about their lives had to be interpreted through recognition of a special connection to the Divine. White Americans could not be allowed to hide behind a version of the Gospel message that did not demand they surrender power as Christian obligation. This required more than simple charity, more than a sense of commitment that safeguarded privilege based on race. Yet, as was often made clear: even the most liberal churches were guilty of benefiting from the misery of others. And, African American denominations did not escape a similar critique in that they were often charged with being more concerned with their middle-class and mainstream status than radical activity that would change the power dynamics of life in the United States. Some people left churches because of their disillusionment with its theology and limited range of community activism for social justice.

On top of this, some ministers and academics took seriously the critique of the United States offered by Malcolm X and combined his social theory with the activist Christianity of Dr. King. They saw an opportunity for greater and more aggressive activity on the part of churches, but they understood that type of activism could only take place in response to a different theology. Within most black churches, they reasoned, was a form of theology that was passive, that couldn't withstand the most aggressive challenges of social injustice. This theology, although better than theologies that were completely silent on issues of a socio-political and economic nature (e.g., "other-worldly" theologies), did not fully appreciate how pregnant the late twentieth century was with disillusionment and suspicion concerning the church and the democratic process. The time was ripe, and questions emerged that a growing number of ministers and academics wanted to address. What happens when black power combines with Christian commitment? What does religious commitment look like if Jesus doesn't require believers to turn the other cheek when confronted with racist violence, but rather demands they strike back? Perhaps Jesus was/is in fact a black revolutionary concerned with the liberation of the oppressed at all cost, and requires the same level of commitment from those who claim to be his followers? What happens when synergy between Malcolm X and Dr. King is used as the basis of a theology for African Americans? Is there a connection between black power and the power of Christ?

Black theology

Ministers and academics who found such questions compelling and essential met in 1966. The group was called the National Committee of Negro Churchmen (NCNC), and this was later changed to the National Conference of Black Churchmen (NCBC) to better reflect their embrace of blackness and black power. Despite a different name, the task remained the same, as they wanted to make the churches relevant to a community demanding black power.

An outgrowth of their meetings was a written platform through which they meant to bring black power and the Gospel of Christ into productive synergy. To the surprise of many, this group of church leaders – 300 men representing a dozen denominations – downplayed the unrest in African American communities culminating in the riots of the 1960s. And instead, they argued the basic cause of violence in the United States is the lack of justice marked by the nation's unwillingness to live out moral and ethical precepts ordained by God. Addressing this dilemma meant correcting the failure of churches to act on the principles of the faith, and the NCBC wanted to do this by forming an organization based on contributions from black churches responsible for supporting financial efforts to improve the quality of life for African Americans in urban areas (i.e., to address the frustrations precipitating the riots). But this wouldn't be enough in that an effort also had to be

NCBC St. Louis Meeting and the call for a new theology – 1968

At the St. Louis meeting, composed largely of black caucus representatives, a number of speakers suggested that a major goal should be the creation of a fully developed black theology. Among other things, this theology might include the relation of the struggles of the Negro to the Biblical experience of the Jews as God's chosen people, and the black man's demand for justice to Jesus' ethical teachings. It might also justify, on a more practical level, the artistic presentation of Christ as black – something that has been done in a number of Negro parishes. A more sophisticated black Christianity, it was argued, would transform the Negro's religion, which since slavery days has been based on the hope of salvation in the hereafter, into a faith more relevant to his present social and economic concerns.

(Quoted from "Churches: Is God Black?" *Time Magazine*, Friday, November 15, 1968)

made to help African Americans in predominately white denominations organize and gain greater voice in denominational decisions. Action was useful and was needed; but transformation of Christianity vis-à-vis a black Christianity required a theological base. In short, it required a new theology robust enough – in tune with the nature and meaning of African American life – to guide progressive and black-power inspired activism. In 1967, the organization commissioned a subgroup of its membership to begin outlining such a theology. The statement offered by this subgroup was given more robust form in its 1969 statement of what it labeled black theology of liberation.

1969 Pronouncement of a black theology of liberation

All theologies arise out of a communal experience with God. At this moment in time, the black community seeks to express its theology in language that speaks to the contemporary mood of black people ...The word 'Black' in the phrase was defined by the life and teachings of Malcolm X – culturally and politically embodied in the Black Power Movement. The term 'theology' was influenced by the life and teachings of Martin Luther King, Jr. – religiously and politically embodied in the Black Church and the Civil Rights Movement. The word liberation was derived from the past and contemporary struggles for political freedom and the biblical story of the Exodus, as defined by the Black religious experience in the United States.

(Quoted from the NCBC 1969 statement on Black Theology's basic tenets)

Many church leaders and academics played a role in the crafting of these two initial statements on this nascent black theology. However, James H. Cone (1938–) is most widely and regularly recognized as being its main architect. Cone tells that he'd spent a few years prior to this work attempting to do traditional theology highlighting the European tradition of Karl Barth and others. Yet, he found nothing inspiring about this effort; and this frustration with his work with normative theology was amplified by his growing disillusionment with his denomination (the AME Church) and the African American Church in more general terms. African Americans were suffering, facing brutality and dehumanization, and churches had little to say that was progressive, powerful, and that made a difference in the life options available to African Americans. The critique of the churches offered by NCBC and the organization's request that he play a prominent role in drafting their initial thoughts on theology served as a source of inspiration, and an opportunity to make relevant his training. This was the perfect storm of existential need, intellectual capability, and religious desire to make a difference. Work on these two black theology statements was followed by Cone's publication of *Black Theology and Black Power* (1969), the first liberation theology text published in English in the United States. This book was followed the next year by a more systematic presentation of his main theological arguments. The title of this second book, *A Black Theology of Liberation*, provided a clear statement concerning the emergence of a new way of doing theology and a new set of responsibilities and possibilities for Christian churches interested in proving themselves relevant in the aftermath of the systematic civil rights struggle. Through these two books, along with subsequent projects, Cone shifted the theological agenda of the United States in ways that generated a great deal of impassioned conversation in a variety of quarters and communities. Some denounced his work as simple political ideology without clear theological merit and content and without notable connection to the Christian faith. Others read his work, and recognized their concerns and beliefs expressed in those pages. Either way, it was difficult to remain neutral regarding this new type of theology. It demanded a response.

Cone argued any effort to build a theology appropriate for addressing the needs of African Americans cannot take as its starting point the perspective and assumptions of European theologians and white Americans. Rather, it must be framed in terms of African American need and African American resources. He proposes as the source material for this theological discourse African American experience, African American history, African American culture, the best of the Christian Tradition, and Scripture. The latter two are to be read and interpreted through a hermeneutic of suspicion – recognition that white Americans have manipulated these two for their own purposes such as the safeguarding of white supremacy and African American inferiority. And it must also be read in light of African American need for liberation along with God's demand for justice. In a move that gained him a great deal of attention, Cone proclaimed God is ontologically black. That is to

Figure 11.1 James H. Cone. © 2009 Colgate University/Andrew M. Daddio.

say, God is so identified with the mission of liberation for African Americans that God's very being – who God is – is defined by blackness. There is a link between African Americans and God. As a consequence of this connection, God sides with the oppressed. That is to say, God requires the liberation of African Americans from racism, and anyone claiming to be a Christian had to be involved in this push for freedom. To avoid siding with African Americans seeking freedom is to fail to live out the principles of Christ. He further argued that a theology appropriate for this mission must be done differently from what had been the case in prior years. It must be contextual. Put differently, this theology is done by and for a particular community – the African American community. Drawing heavily on the Exodus as key evidence of God's concern with the oppressed, the theology Cone proposed assumed Jesus Christ is a black revolutionary, whose posture toward the world gave priority to the dismantling of privilege and a deep regard for those most in need of deliverance.

In a move that ran contrary to much dominant thinking on the issue, Cone suggested violence is a legitimate tool in the struggle for liberation in that only the oppressed can determine the proper understanding of their plight and the mechanism best equipped to free them. Oppressors do not get to decide the agenda. What was

God is Black and we must become Black

Those who want to know who God is and what God is doing must know who black persons are and what they are doing. This does not mean lending a helping hand to the poor and unfortunate blacks of society. It does not mean joining the war on poverty! Such acts are sin offerings that represent a white way of assuring themselves that they are basically 'good' persons. Knowing God means being on the side of the oppressed, becoming one with them, and participating in the goal of liberation. We must become black with God!

(Quoted from James H. Cone, *A Black Theology of Liberation*, 2d ed. Maryknoll, NY: Orbis Books, 1986, 65)

proposed in black theology pushed beyond the social gospel in that it pointed out the manner in which simple fixes to the system did little to break the stranglehold of racism on African Americans. The social gospel allowed white Americans to set the agenda, to preserve their privilege, rather than surrendering their advantages. True Christian commitment, Cone argued, required more than this. It demanded radical change. He gave no real consideration to redemption taking place outside the context of human history. The Kingdom of God, instead, is understood in black theology as involving social transformation – a reconstitution of life options within the context of human history. Talk of a trans-historical event, accordingly, can be a distraction from the real work and from the true outcome of a life well lived. Talk of heaven served to pacify African Americans, but it does little to address the nature of God's will and God's presence within human history. Connected to this, Cone gave little consideration in his theology to personal sin; rather he, like social gospel advocates, concerned himself with social sin – socio-economic, political and cultural oppression as the definition of sin. It is important to note that black theology's critique was not simply of white Americans. Cone also critiqued African Americans, arguing that simply because one is physically black does not mean that one is supportive of the cause of liberation. On a related note, Cone raised questions regarding the actual concerns of African American churches, arguing that most of them are not concerned with the liberation of African Americans but instead are willing to maintain the status quo for their own benefit. They, most black churches, he continued, are ill-equipped to embrace black theology and as a result they are irrelevant to the will of God as it is connected to the liberation of the oppressed. Hence, African American churches are not representatives of Christ on earth simply because they claim Christianity and provide a few social services.

Others were involved in this early phase of the development of black theology. And while most agreed with the basic outline offered by Cone, there were objections to some of his more charged points. For example, J. Deotis Roberts (1927–) argued for a deep connection between liberation and reconciliation. That is to say, Roberts believed Cone's approach did not allow for the development of new social arrangements based on right relationships between African Americans and white Americans. And only simultaneous attention to liberation and reconciliation would afford this type of new society. Others such as historian Gayraud Wilmore pushed Cone to provide more attention to the grounding of his theology in African American source materials as opposed to the theological thinking of Karl Barth and other Europeans that seemed to ground his first two books. That is to say, in essence, Wilmore asked whether a black theology for African Americans be drawn more solidly from materials such as the spirituals, slave narratives and other documents that tell the Christian story from an African American perspective. Furthermore, ethicist Preston Williams challenged Cone to take into consideration the economic and political diversity of African American communities. For example, he asked, what does one do with the African American middle-class in this theology of liberation?

Perhaps the most intense critique came from William R. Jones, whose 1973 book – titled *Is God a White Racist? A Preamble to Black Theology* – raised questions concerning the manner in which moral evil and God's relationship to human suffering are worked out in black theology. He argued that black theologians such as Cone make unsafe assumptions concerning God's commitment to the welfare of African Americans. Jones suggested that the history of African Americans in the United States could be read in more than one way. It could point to God's demand for justice, but it could also just as easily point to God's lack of concern with African American liberation and God's deep regard for the prosperity of white Americans. And, the ongoing success of white Americans might be evidence of God's favor. By extension, perhaps the ongoing oppression of African Americans speaks to God's disregard for them and, therefore, maybe God is concerned with the genocide of African Americans. After all, appeals to the ministry of Christ do little to change this situation in that the Christ Event – if one believes it in a literal sense – takes place long before the enslavement of Africans in the modern period. How, then, can it be God's response to the oppression of African Americans?

In highlighting these possibilities, Jones meant to point out the need for more focused attention to the reasonableness of claims made by black theology. However, Jones also used these questions as a way of introducing an alternate theological possibility: rather than attention to God, he argued for a secular humanism as the proper orientation for African Americans. This approach – still religious from Jones' perspective – was more consistent with the historical development of African Americans and avoided the more troubling dimensions of black theology's arguments. Some found it (and continue to find it) difficult to think of a theology that does not involve a God or gods. Yet, Jones has argued such a theology is possible, but it involves

Does Jesus Christ speak to the liberation of African Americans?

In point of fact, does not the continued suffering of blacks after the Resurrection raise the essential question all over again: Is God for blacks? We must not forget that black misery, slavery, and oppression – the very facts that make black liberation necessary – are all post-Resurrection events.

(William R. Jones, *Is God a White Racist? A Preamble to Black Theology*, Garden City, NY: Anchor Books, 1973)

greater attention to humanity and draws from the non-theistic cultural materials found in African American history – materials such as the blues and the literature of figures such as Richard Wright and Nella Larsen. God, he notes, isn't a requirement for theology despite a strict definition of the term theology (god-talk). Required instead is some sense of an ultimate concern and an ultimate orientation, and the human effort to understand and articulate the experience of both. Jones suggests that much about African American religion (and theology) already revolves around an enhanced attention to humanity – what he calls humanocentric theism whereby humans have "functional ultimacy." That is to say, humans "are the measure of all things" – or, humans have significant (but not complete) autonomy and freedom. His humanist theology simply extends this, making anthropology the driving force for dialogue, as it wrestles with how humans move through the world in light of the continuing presence of disproportionate suffering encountered by so many. This position was debated and continues to be a source of conversation. Yet, while still a minority opinion within African American theological discourse, others – including Anthony Pinn – have worked to advance a humanist alternative to theistic black theology. This non-god based theology speaks, he argues, to and from the humanist religious orientation within African American communities, and is as vital and vibrant as theistic black theology.

Correctives were made by Cone that addressed many of these critiques, and black theology continued to develop through the work of two additional generations of black theologians – many of them trained by Cone. What one finds is a general agreement with the framing of black theology – its preferred source materials, critiques, and aims – but with some modification to its details. For example, philosopher of religion Cornel West for several decades now has critiqued black theology's lack of a social theory that adequately understands and explains the socio-economic and political dimensions of life. That is to say, according to West, black theology calls for a transformed society but fails to provide a blueprint outlining the look of this new society. He calls for attention to Marxism for its critique of capitalism and for the general social theory it affords those attempting to urge a new appreciation for the humanity of African Americans. Others have questioned Cone's preoccupation with ontological blackness as the marker of proper relationship to God and justice. It, for the second and third generation of black theologians, suggests a very limited sense of what it means to be black – restricting participation in the African American community only to those who share Cone's (and black theology's) assessment of race without consideration to the diversity of opinions and life experiences represented in the African American communities. Perhaps a more inclusive way to map out what it means to be African American and concerned with justice is the question asked by those offering this critique. This corrective entails a larger continuum of African American struggle beyond a narrow sense of race and racism, and a matching expansive sense of proper praxis (thoughtful or informed activity). This critique or corrective is based on a more nuanced understanding of African American history, a more expansive sense of what liberation is and from what African Americans need to be liberated. It also pushes for attention to new strategies that extend beyond Civil Rights movement approaches that informed the first generation of black theologians – e.g., James Cone, J. Deotis Roberts, Major Jones, Albert Cleage.

While the vast majority of participants in the development of black theology have been Protestants, it is important to remember that African American Catholics have also contributed to this discourse. Catholic thinkers have also offered a modality of black theology response to the needs of African American Catholics. Although more committed to the church's doctrinal base than African American Protestant theologians would want to see, they are actually consistent with what tends to be a general regard for African American church tradition within black theology. In like manner, African American Catholic theologians claim the Catholic tradition and African American experience as major source materials for their work. Like their Protestant colleagues, the framers of African American Catholic theology recognize Christ's requirement that we embrace both his passion and commitment to those who suffer, becoming in the process deeply connected to the struggle for change. Being Christ-like in this respect should bring us closer to the fight for liberation. It does not close us off into a private world of individualized salvation and redemption. In this regard, the passion of Christ plays a prominent role in the way African American Catholic theology frames participation in the redemption of suffering peoples, and this is exemplified by saints such as Moses the Black, St. Benedict the Moor, St. Josephine Bakhita, and St. Martin de Porres. This attention to the saints as exemplars of proper conduct separates African American Catholic contributions to a liberation theology from those made by African American Protestants. Yet, the manner in which Christ and the saints point to the ontological blackness of God echoes the position first pronounced in the Protestant form of black theology. And, again like their Protestant counterparts, the biblical witness regarding this connection of Christ to suffering people and those who work with the suffering to bring liberation is of paramount importance. Finally, in both instances, black theology has pushed institutional churches to step-up and commit to liberation work, or be denounced as oppressive and irrelevant.

Both black theology's Catholic and Protestant frameworks have gained academic and public attention over the past four decades. Debates concerning its fine points and alterations of its arguments in light of shifts in the socio-economic, political, and cultural arrangements of African Americans have taken place over these same years. Numerous books and articles dealing with it are published each year. And undergraduate and graduate level curricula include attention to black theology. Professional organizations such as the American Academy of Religion – the largest organization in the United States devoted to the study of Religion – have several longstanding units devoted to this subject. Furthermore, graduate students receive Ph.Ds in the study of this theological discourse and news networks such as CNN invite guests to discuss its major points, and so on.

Womanist theology

In the late 1970s African American women pointed out black theology's inherent sexism. From their perspective, black theology simply perpetuated the sexism present in African American churches. These churches questioned the importance and equality of women by denying them leadership positions, fostering doctrine that labels women the source of humanity's initial departure from the will of God – all meant to paint women as not deserving all the consideration given men in the public arenas of life. And, black theology rendered African American women completely invisible. How was this done? Whereas black theology argued African American history and African American experience are critical to the construction of a theology adequate for the liberation of African Americans, these same theologians gave virtually no attention to the experiences and history of African American women. In this way, they perpetuated the oppression of women even as they considered themselves working to restore and re-direct toward greater liberation-minded activism. How could churches that claimed a mission to liberate the oppressed not recognize their sexism as a moral evil to be exorcised? And, how could theologians who projected themselves as offering a corrective to the failing of African American churches on issues of liberation from oppression not see the need to hold these churches (and themselves) accountable for oppression of women – who make up roughly 70 percent of African American church membership? When describing the nature of oppression, black theologians and churches failed to recognize that more than half of the African American population suffers from more than racism in that they are oppressed due to class and gender-based discrimination. In this way, within black theology only black men mattered. This gender-bias was even used when naming God, in that God was referenced as "HE," thereby restricting the presence of God to the male gender. These African American women asked why the trans-historical, superhuman force, called God would need to be described using male gender. There was nothing necessary or essential about this naming of God; instead it was simply another sign of male dominance and the workings of a patriarchal system even within the context of religious thought and life. African American women argued that to be black and female was to suffer from triple jeopardy: racism, poverty, and sexism. A theology could only be liberative if it took seriously as its starting point the reality of African American women's experience and their telling of that history.

This initial critique of black theology and an effort to provide a corrective in line with the voices of African American women was offered by the Rev. Dr. Pauli Murray, who called into question the limited focus of both black theology and feminist theology. She argued for a middle ground, a blending of the critique of racism offered by the former and the challenge to sexism offered by the latter. While Murray wrote several papers addressing this critique, Frances Beale, Theresa Hoover, and Jacquelyn Grant offered more comprehensive projects. Jacquelyn Grant followed an early essay on the topic with the publication of her dissertation, one of the early book-length treatments – *White Women's Christ and Black Women's Jesus: Feminist Christology and Womanist Response* (1989). Maintaining the importance of Jesus Christ for the doing of theology meant to transform social arrangements toward liberation, Grant argued the experience of women required a certain approach to understandings of Christ that centered on Jesus' physical work to free the oppressed from injustice. The year before Grant's book, Katie Cannon published *Black Womanist Ethics* in which she solidly grounds this alternative approach to theologizing liberation in the writings of African American women authors such as Zora Neale Hurston. In this text and an earlier article, Cannon connected the naming of this new theological discourse "womanist" based on the definition of womanist offered by novelist Alice Walker. It is definition of the term that highlights assertiveness, confidence, the demand for visibility and voice on the part of African American women.

Womanist scholars, in general terms, have embraced the structure for theologizing offered in Cone's first publications. The Christian Tradition, African American history, African American experience, scripture, and African American cultural production are vital. However, missing from their perspective is sufficient attention to how women in general and African American women in particular fit into and shape these source materials. Mindful of this and modeled on the work of Grant and Cannon, much of the early work for womanist scholars in ethics and theology was the uncovering of African American women's stories and experience as well as their viewpoints and opinions on the nature and meaning of religion and liberation. This involved attention to the literary traditions of African American women, the narratives offered by women, examination of the under-explored efforts of women within the context of African American church activism, and other forms of intellectual and ethical engagement with the history of African American women.

Womanist defined

"Womanist. 1. From womanish (Opp. of 'girlish,' i.e., frivolous, irresponsible, not serious.) A black feminist or feminist of color. From the black folk expression of mothers to female children, 'you acting womanish,' i.e., like a woman. Usually referring to outrageous, audacious, courageous or willful behavior. Wanting to know more and in greater depth than is considered 'good' for one. Interested in grown-up doings. Acting grown up. Being grown up. Interchangeable with another black folk expression: 'You trying to be grown.' Responsible. In charge. Serious.

2. Also: A woman who loves other women, sexually and/or nonsexually. Appreciates and prefers women's culture, women's emotional flexibility (values tears as natural counterbalance of laughter), and women's strength. Sometimes loves individual men, sexually and/or nonsexually. Committed to survival and wholeness of entire people, male and female. Not separatists, except periodically, for health. Traditionally universalist, as in: 'Mama, why are we brown, pink, and yellow, and our cousins are white, beige, and black?' Ans.: 'Well you know the colored race is just like a flower garden, with every color flower represented.' Traditionally capable, as in: 'Mama, I'm walking to Canada and I'm taking you and a bunch of other slaves with me.' Reply: 'It wouldn't be the first time.'

(Quoted from Alice Walker, *In Search of Our Mothers' Gardens: Womanist Prose*, New York: Harcourt, Inc., 1983, xi)

With time, many black theologians acknowledged the flaws in their work, confessed the gender-bias of their work, and sought correctives. However, this did not fulfill the agenda womanist scholars set out. They wanted to systematically construct a theological and ethical platform for liberation that was more inclusive, that recognized the "web-like nature of oppression," and that had the capacity to attack simultaneously multiple forms of injustice. For example, Katie Cannon argued in the book mentioned above that African American literature offers insights into ethics that have contemporary benefits. She highlights a "quiet grace," for instance, exemplified by African American women, that offers some sense of how these women maintained their self-worth within the context of a death-dealing world. This is to say within the daily lives of African American women the careful scholar uncovers strategies for addressing issues of injustice and forging creative paths toward liberation – paths and strategies ignored when attention is strictly given to African American men and their experiences of life in the United States.

Delores Williams, another pioneer in the development of womanist scholarship, offers a theological assessment of African American women's experience. In her

Figure 11.2 Alice Walker. Courtesy of MDCarchives.

book, *Sisters in the Wilderness: The Challenge of Womanist God-Talk* (1995), Williams constructs an alternate reading of the Christ Event. Again, for both black theology and womanist theology and ethics, the story of Jesus Christ is central. However, Williams argues that the traditional interpretation of Jesus Christ's ministry privileges the idea of Jesus as a suffering surrogate for the world – the One who takes upon himself the sins of the world. By extension, Christians are obligated to try to be Christ-like and for African American women this has meant taking on the role of surrogate. Williams sees African American women being forced into this oppressive role during the period of slavery as they were required to care for others at the expense of their sense of self-importance and worth. This involved taking care of the domestic needs of slaveholders, and also enduring rape as white Americans could abuse black bodies without great penalty. This surrogate role continued after the period of slavery in a somewhat "voluntary" manner as African American women found jobs as domestics outside the home while also being encouraged to see their domestic service to their own families as God's design for their lives.

Both types of surrogacy – forced and voluntary – meant the subjugation and oppression of African American women was rationalized often using religious language and arguments. And it was re-enforced through appeal to the ultimate surrogate Jesus Christ. Williams offers a corrective for this by highlighting several theological points, amongst them are these two:

1. The biblical story of Hagar provides a way of thinking about God's involvement with humans;
2. The value of the Christ Event is found in the ministry of Jesus, not in the death on the cross.

In terms of the first, Williams points to the story of the slave Hagar who has a child with the Hebrew Bible patriarch Abraham but eventually flees to the wilderness to avoid the wrath of Abraham's wife Sara. (It should be noted that other religious traditions have a different view of Hagar's relationship to Abraham, seeing her as a wife.) In the wilderness, Hagar encounters God who instructs her to return and promises to make a great nation of her son. Hagar follows God's instructions. From this Williams gathers several points, including the idea that God provides oppressed communities with resources for survival, but these communities must secure their own liberation. What Williams proposes is a major shift in liberation theology thinking because it breaks with the assumption that God brings about the liberation of the oppressed. Social injustice and the transformation of society rest on humans to achieve. By turning attention to Hagar, Williams demonstrates the manner in which attention to the experiences of women improve the content and function of liberation theology. In essence, she argued social gospel advocates and black theologians have it wrong: the passion of Christ – the death of Christ on the cross only points to human failure, the inability of humans to appreciate a good thing, to appreciate a gift from God. There is no glory in the shed blood of Christ. Rather, it points to a negative lesson – how not to behave toward humanity. Williams points to the ministry of Christ as key. It is what he did with people, the people with whom he interacted, and what he demanded of them, that matters most. In this regard, womanist theology offered an important alternative understanding of Jesus Christ for both scholars of African American religion and practitioners of Christianity. She encouraged all to give attention to his activities and his ethics, over against what humans did to try to destroy his activities and ethics.

What Williams suggests and other womanist scholars such as theologian Kelly Brown Douglas will highlight, is the need to give clear attention to the way the bodies of African American women and men figure into how they theologize and how they understand liberation. That is to say, people are more than ideas, they have physical bodies that impact how they are perceived, how they experience the world, and the nature of oppression. Liberating the oppressed, and any theology concerned with this process, must be mindful of and work from within the context of the oppressed as being "embodied bodies," physical creatures living in a physical world.

Others heard in Alice Walker's definition of womanist and in Walker's writings about relationship to the natural environment a call for a womanist theology that appreciates ecology, that seeks to end oppression by ending human abuse of the

Womanist theology

Each womanist theologian will add her own special accent to the understandings of God emerging from womanist theology. But if one needs a final image to describe women coming together to shape the enterprise, Bess B. Johnson in *God's Fierce Whimsy* offers an appropriate one. Describing the difference between the play of male and female children in the black community where she developed, Johnson says: the boys in the neighborhood had this game with rope ... tug-o'-war ... till finally some side would jerk the rope away from the others, who'd fall down ... Girls ...weren't allowed to play with them in this tug-o'-war, so we figured out how to make our own rope – out of ... little dandelions. You just keep adding them, one to another, and you can go on and on ... Anybody, even the boys, could join us ... The whole purpose of our game was to create this dandelion chain – that was it. And we'd keep going, creating till our mamas called us home.

Like Johnson's dandelion chain, womanist theological vision will grow as black women come together and connect piece with piece. Between the process of creating and the sense of calling, womanist theology will one day present itself in full array; reflecting the divine spirit that connects us all.

(Quoted from Delores Williams, "Womanist Theology: Black Women's Voices," *Christianity and Crisis* (March 2, 1987))

earth. Scholars such as theologian Karen Baker-Fletcher suggest that ending oppression of groups such as African American women requires a more general shift in attitude toward life and our environment. If we cannot appreciate the world that sustains us, we have no hope of appreciating the life forms sustained by the earth – and this includes marginalized and oppressed humans. Think of it this way: environmental destruction is often connected to other means of discrimination. Environmental racism highlights strategies whereby toxic chemicals, raw sewage treatment plants, air-polluting highways in the United States are often placed in communities populated by "people of color." This is another sign of the web-like nature of oppression. Yet, it was typically the case that when black theology addressed environmental destruction it did so with the assumption that the problem was a result of white supremacist attitudes played out through destruction of natural surroundings – another sign of white domination. However, some womanist scholars turn to Alice Walker who clearly notes environmental destruction is a human problem, with a clear human root. From the perspective of the earth, as Walker says and womanist scholars affirm, we are all the cause of the earth's destruction. This turn to the environment as a topic of concern within liberation theology is another dimension of discussion developed by womanist theologians and ethicists.

What was true for black theology is also true for womanist theology: not all the contributors are Protestant. Theologians such as M. Shawn Copeland, Diana Hayes, and Jamie Phelps have called for the inclusion of the voices and experiences of Catholic women in the doing of womanist scholarship. Attention to the experiences of African American women must extend to those who call the Roman Catholic Church home, and who have worked for liberation from within the doctrines, rituals, and practices of the Catholic Church. The voices of women typically forgotten when discussing the striving of Christianity to make a difference in the world as well as those who fought to correct their churches were also African American Catholic women working from within the structure of the church and also from their seats in the pews. Furthermore, Copeland pointed to the need within womanist scholarship for greater attention to the role played by Mary the mother of Jesus in the story of deliverance. For Catholic scholars like Copeland, Mary points to the presence of a strong woman, one whose work is vital to the faith. Related to this, she argues for greater attention to the full range of women whose presence in biblical literature is forgotten in male-centered discussion of the biblical text. Catholic scholars have offered greater attention to a wide range of doctrines, creeds, and categories of theological thinking. In addition, Catholic theologians have encouraged greater attention to academic resources typically dismissed in an effort to make theology 'black'. In so doing, scholars such as Hayes, Copeland, and Phelps have pointed out the utility of a range of sources that, when handled properly with the needs of African Americans in mind, help with the task of liberation.

Key points you need to know

- Some of the basic claims made in black and womanist theologies are present in the religious thought of slaves and early black churches.
- The social gospel movement was embraced by African American Christians as a way to combine their Christian commitment with their sense of social justice.
- Black theology develops as an effort to combine black power and the best of the Christian tradition – Malcolm X and Dr. Martin Luther King, Jr.
- Black theology considered the social gospel "too soft" and too content to think about the freedom of African Americans in terms acceptable to the dominant society as opposed to development of a liberation agenda that privileged African Americans.
- Womanist theology develops as a corrective to black theology in that it seeks to point out the sexism in black theology and highlight the history, experience, and voices of African American women.
- Both womanist and black theologies develop through the work of Protestant and Catholic scholars.

Discussion questions

1. Why did African Americans embrace the social gospel movement? How did they change it?
2. What gave rise to the first discussions of black theology? What organization started this conversation? What was the perception of black power in these early conversations?
3. What are the primary source materials for black theology? Do womanist theologians change these source materials? If so, how?
4. What importance does Alice Walker have for womanist theology?
5. What are some examples of the contributions of Catholic scholars to black theology? To womanist theology?
6. How is God described in black theology? What does womanist theology argue is important about the Christ Event?
7. What have been some of the critiques of black theology offered by scholars other than womanist scholars?
8. What does black theology think about violence, and what does it mean to say that God is "ontologically black"?

Further reading

Cone, James. *God of the Oppressed*, Rev. Sub Ed. Maryknoll, NY: Orbis Books, 1997.

Cone, James and Gayraud Wilmore. *Black Theology: A Documentary History*, Volumes 1–2. Maryknoll, NY: Orbis Books, 1993.

Davis, Cyprian and Diana Hayes, editors. *Taking Down Our Harps: Black Catholics in The United States*. Maryknoll, NY: Orbis Books, 1998.

Hayes, Diana. *Standing in the Shoes My Mother Made: A Womanist Theology*. Minneapolis, MN: Fortress Press, 2010.

Hopkins, Dwight. *Down, Up, and Over: Slave Religion and Black Theology*. Minneapolis, MN: Fortress Press, 1999.

Massingale, Bryan. *Racial Justice and the Catholic Church*. Maryknoll, NY: Orbis Books, 2010.

Mitchem, Stephanie. *Introducing Womanist Theology*. Maryknoll, NY: Orbis Books, 2002.

Pinn, Anthony B. *Why, Lord? Suffering and Evil in Black Theology*. New York: Continuum, 1995.

Roberts, J. Deotis. *Liberation and Reconciliation: A Black Theology*, 2nd Ed. Louisville, KY: Westminster John Knox, 2005.

Townes, Emilie. *In a Blaze of Glory: Womanist Spirituality and Social Witness*. Louisville, KY: Abingdon Press, 1995.

Part III

Issues and concerns in contemporary African American religion

12 Sex and sexuality

In this chapter

As is the case for many religious communities in the United States, issues of sex and sexuality have plagued African American religion for centuries, and the late twentieth century marked a much more public and heated debate on both. This chapter gives attention to African American religion's response to key issues such as HIV-AIDS, gay and lesbian rights, and general approaches to sexual activity.

Main topics covered

- Tension within African American religious thought on the nature and function of bodily wants and needs
- African American religious understandings of the nature and purpose of sex
- Teachings regarding sexual activity
- Perspectives on homosexuality and contemporary challenges to these doctrines
- Understandings of and responses to HIV/AIDS

Bodies and what they do

All African American religious traditions provide stories concerning how physical bodies come into being, offering narratives about how physical bodies develop, grow, and die. For many, this involves creation stories explaining how divine forces shaped basic materials into the human being. For humanism, there is no cosmic or supernatural basis for human beings, but rather the human as a bio-chemical reality is simply a recent product of evolutionary processes. In either case – stories of divine creation or evolution – African American religious traditions are fascinated with the human body. In a word, there is a physical quality to all African American religions. Rituals require the physical presence and movement of bodies – of bodies that are bio-chemical entities. Doctrines also speak at least indirectly to the body – what it is;

what it does; what it wants; what it needs; what happens to it after death. The pain it experiences and the happiness it seeks (and at times secures) is a topic for deep consideration within the religious traditions named in this book.

Practitioners of African American religious traditions often worry about bodies; for example, hoodoo, conjure and other African-based traditions provide remedies for all sorts of aches and pains experienced by bodies. They harness the powers of the physical world and the spiritual world to address the wants and needs of peoples' physical bodies. Humanism, of course, by its very definition is concerned with the nature and meaning of human life – and this life takes place through human, physical bodies. Thought and practice revolve around efforts to secure the best welfare of individuals and individuals within the context of communities. So much of African American religion is physical, amounting to a thinking through and reflection on how physical bodies best occupy time and space – what bodies mean, and what takes place when bodies through death no longer move in time and space. Every aspect of what bodies do and what they need gets some attention. For example, when African American religions label certain locations "sacred" space, it means mundane activities cannot take place in those locations. So, bodies can't exercise in church sanctuaries; and people must remove their shoes and ceremonially cleanse them before entering the space of worship in the mosque, and so on. African American religions tend to provide commentary on what can be eaten to nurture bodies – or not eaten so as to avoid defiling the body. There is attention given to what is worn on the body so as to avoid wrong thinking about the person, or to mark out special occasions and activities. How people position their bodies during worship or other celebrations also receives consideration by various African American religious traditions. One gets a sense of this through a variety of questions related to worship. How are bodies repositioned during services for different activities such as kneeling for prayer? Bodies then change position to sing, right? Aren't bodies also used as instruments to call forth spirits through the clapping of hands to the sound of the drum? Even the fluids associated with bodies are given thought and importance within various religious traditions. For example, blood has importance across numerous traditions. In African-based traditions that make use of animal sacrifices, blood entails energy that can be offered to the gods in exchange for what the human body wants or needs. For Christians, the shedding of blood by Jesus Christ is a source of their redemption in that he was sacrificed to cover the sins of the world. Furthermore, sweat in Christianity when on a preacher can be a sign of a powerful sermon in that the preacher has been active, moving in ways that produce perspiration. In addition, tears can be a sign of repentance for one's sin in that the tears might be produced through confession of fault and through a heartfelt request for forgiveness from God, and so on.

Everywhere human bodies are confronted with and by other human bodies, and in certain ways African American religions attempt to explore and explain this. Each tradition attempts to do this through community-wide beliefs concerning

How the body matters

- Conflict between the body and soul is a major concern and a prime target for ritual and doctrinal attention in some traditions.
- The body and how to regulate it is found in religious doctrine and practices.
- Body fluids have importance within most African American religions, often symbolizing power to transform lives when handled properly.
- Many religious practices are meant to provide for the needs and wants of the physical body; this is tied to an assumption that the body often works against the requirements of religious life.
- Many religious traditions have an uncomfortable relationship to the physical body, marked by suspicion and a desire to monitor and control it.

what bodies are and what they should do, and these beliefs are acted out through formal and informal rituals and practices meant to allow the believer some ability to maintain control over the often unruly and dangerous body. These rituals and other practices (e.g., fasting, penance, and meditating) monitor the body and keep it responsive to the discipline preferred within that particular tradition. Nothing troubles the relationship between the body and religion more than sex and sexuality.

Religion and sex

This is one of the more difficult subjects for most African American religious traditions. It is the one that receives the least amount of attention from religious leaders in general, and causes the most discomfort for believers. However, it is important to mention that this subject isn't contentious for all forms of African American religion. For example, African-based traditions often exhibit an appreciation for the wants and needs of the body. In fact, many of the doctrines and rituals speak to this concern for comforting and promoting the body. In these African-based traditions, there is no sense that the body has in some way betrayed the deeper spiritual needs of humanity, no sense that what the body wants runs contrary to the purposes of human life. Perhaps this is because some of the deities in these traditions were great humans whose extraordinary accomplishments resulted in them being transformed into gods. Maybe this relationship between extraordinary humans and gods promotes greater appreciation for human bodies and what they want and do. For example, these gods remain sexually active; hence, sex does not necessarily have a negative connotation. The urge for sexual contact isn't to be ignored nor denied in order to discipline the body into submission to the will of the gods. Conjure and hoodoo, furthermore, can be engaged and used for the very purpose of opening up sexual relationships. For humanism, there is no reason to debate sex in that the desire for it is a natural urge, and the only challenge is to maintain integrity and value – abiding by laws – when satisfying sexual desire. In short, African American religions recognize that bodies matter to some extent. For African American Christian churches, the topic of sex has been more difficult to resolve in part because of the way the body and the soul are understood. A tension between the body and the soul is referred to as Cartesian Dualism – named after the great thinker Descartes – has marked Christian thought and practice. For those primarily concerned with the soul, the body is a problem to be controlled, and this includes everything the body wants and desires. Many early church theologians and leaders encouraged this position and developed doctrines and practices meant to control the body. Drawing on this earlier thought, many African American churches have taught that sex is a problem: sinful outside the context of marriage, and only permissible in the context of marriage. African American Christians, like many other Christians, have come to this assessment in large part because of negative depictions of sex as competing with true devotion to Christ and righteous life. This is particularly the case in the writings associated with the Apostle Paul, who suggests those devoted to Christ and who anticipate Jesus Christ's second coming should even avoid marriage. Paul and other biblical writers give little consideration to a more positive and open appreciation for sex as presented in the Hebrew Bible. Be that as it may, African American Christians have had a troubled relationship with sex for religious reasons drawn from centuries of Christian teachings. But they have also had this dilemma because of the socio-cultural arrangements of the United States. By this, I mean the way in which US society has often stereotyped African Americans as over-sexed and dangerous. In general, African Americans have attempted to counter this negative depiction, and when this counter argument is made in the context of Christian churches, it often involves denial of the sexual-self in order to present African Americans as safe and capable of respectful and productive involvement in the life of the United States. That is to say, African American Christians often present sex as negative for religious *and* socio-cultural reasons.

Regulating sex

- Christianity often restricts sanctioned sexual activity to married couples, and requires all others to be celibate.
- Scholarship on Islam often notes that sex is not simply for procreation within that tradition.
- African-based traditions and humanism do not limit physical intimacy to married couples.
- Sacred texts such as the Christian New Testament present sex in a negative light, and as a potential distraction from the real work of following the teachings of the religious tradition.
- Some churches recognize the need to be sensitive to contemporary circumstances and to educate and equip people to have safe sex.
- Most African American religious traditions allow religious leaders/clergy to marry rather than requiring celibacy.

Even when sex is controlled and placed within proper relationships, there are still restrictions regarding activities considered acceptable by most churches. Pleasure within the context of marriage has been understood as acceptable. Such thinking continues to be rather normative within African American Christian circles. In the contemporary context, it is often the case that many, including African Americans, wait longer to marry – if they marry at all. In light of church regulations and the decreased likelihood that African American adults will marry, what does one make of church regulations? For those not married, this poses a problem involving a perpetual need to deny themselves fulfillment of certain urges. Some churches, admittedly a minority of African American churches, recognize that this strict regulation is inconsistent with contemporary needs. Furthermore, this demand often results in people hiding their sexual activity. While somewhat controversial, more socio-culturally sensitive and liberal churches recognize that doctrines alone do not address sufficiently issues of sex and sexual activity. And, therefore more must be done to protect against pregnancy and sexual diseases. To accomplish this, some churches provide sex education and offer information concerning safe sex – including distribution of condoms. Many other churches disagree with this practice, arguing that it promotes sexual activity outside marriage. The debate on this point continues as, in response, churches argue, it is better to keep members healthy and informed about their sexual activity than to maintain silence and foster unsafe practices. Despite disagreements, churches on both sides of this debate provide counseling and referrals for people suffering from domestic and sexual violence – both inside and outside the context of marriage.

Advancing a conservative take on sex is not an agenda embraced only by Christian churches. The Nation of Islam also maintains this posture toward topics of sexual relationships. Both the Honorable Elijah Muhammad and Minister Louis Farrakhan teach that sex is permitted only within the context of marriage. And, again, its primary purpose is the production of offspring to advance the "original people." Adultery – in both Protestant churches, the Roman Catholic Church, and the Nation of Islam – is considered sin. While religious leaders have been known to fall short of this requirement, it remains the moral standard, and an ethical norm. For the Nation of Islam, like African American Christian churches, the fulfillment of sexual desire is not a primary concern; it is something that must be addressed, but it takes a backseat to activities that impact one's spiritual growth. African American Sunni Muslims, while marked by different theological doctrines and sensibilities, typically share with Christianity and the Nation of Islam stances regarding sex: it is appropriate within the context of a committed relationship. Sex, like taking in nourishment, is a part of life; but it is a fact of human life requiring great control and diligent monitoring. And everything about the look and appearance of the body is meant to enforce this understanding. Clothing is to downplay sexual interest. Restriction on body movement is meant to avoid anything that might suggest sexual interest for anyone other than one's husband or wife. Regulations regarding make-up are meant to downplay sexual appeal, and so on. Avoiding the appearance of evil (e.g., situations when sexual interest might be sparked) is considered paramount. To the extent such institutional restrictions might not be enough and to avoid temptation, some religious communities also place restrictions on "worldly" entertainment such as non-general audience movies, sex-focused music, and so on.

It should also be noted that, with the exception of Roman Catholicism, religious leaders are not prohibited from marriage and sexual activity. Outside Catholicism, there is no sense that devotion to God is compromised through sexual relationships. Instead, it is believed that marriage (and one can assume proper sexual activity within marriage) is important for a variety of reasons, including: (1) it allows the religious leader to maintain a full and healthy life; (2) ministers will have a difficult time counseling people on marriage and marriage related issues if they aren't themselves married; (3) it is consistent with biblical requirements for leadership – for example, in outlining church leadership, the New Testament indicates that a bishop should be the husband of one wife.

Sexuality considered

Sex and gender do not stand alone within African American religious traditions. The situation is more complex than that. For example, the issue of sex raises other concerns, such as sexuality. However, before moving the discussion forward, it is important to distinguish between sex and sexuality. The former entails a basic impulse revolving around pleasure given and received through physical intimacy. Sexuality is in large part a cultural construction. In this regard, sexuality is connected to gender (i.e., masculinity and femininity) in that it defines acceptable sexual relationships along the lines of gender, determining with whom sexual encounters are permissible. For example, in many Christian and Islamic traditions, sexuality is defined in such a way as to disallow sexual encounters that are not between a man and woman. It is understood in this context that males have a particular sexuality that involves sexual relationships with women, and women with men. Anything other than this is considered inconsistent with the purpose and structure of human life. That is to say, proper sexuality according to Christian and Islamic traditions is heterosexuality. Think of the differences in this way: gender places human bodies into two categories – male and female and each gender has a set of social responsibilities and characteristics. Sex, much easier to understand, involves physical intimacy, and sexuality is the term used to capture how humans – as males and females – express themselves sexually in line with social restrictions placed on each gender. The first, sex, is something the physical body does/has; gender is one of the ways human bodies are distinguished and identified through expectations and assumed behaviors (e.g., girls do this, and boys do that); and, sexuality is a way by which the connection between gender and sex is understood. African American religions, for the most part, accept what the larger society says about sexuality and shares those assumptions and regulations within their doctrines and creeds. To accomplish this, they make use of religious language familiar to the followers of the particular tradition. Engaging in sexual practices and activities inconsistent with how one's sexuality is defined within the tradition and thereby allowing one's interest in sex to trump other obligations involves sin. Each tradition concerned with restrictions on sex and sexuality has its way of addressing sexual sin. Abstinence, of course, is a major tool used within Christian and Islamic circles, although African-based traditions and Humanism do not see a problem in respectful sexual activity outside the context of marriage.

Marking out the difference

- Sex is physical intimacy involving the genitals, and many African American religions place restrictions on how and with whom believers can be involved sexually.
- Gender is the way in which physical bodies are divided into male bodies and female bodies, with each category having responsibilities and characteristics associated with it.
- Sexuality defines how each gender is to relate to and respond to its sexual desires, providing a framework for understanding proper expressions of sexual desire.
- Most theistic religious traditions believe gender and sexuality are ordained by God and are part of human nature and destiny.
- Humanism stands alone in its understanding of human sexuality as strictly a matter of social construction and the sexual urge a matter of evolutionary process meant to preserve one's genetic line within the community.

African American religions and homosexuality

The humanist stance on sexuality results in a generally open and welcoming approach. For example, this is the perspective of the two organizations to which some African Americans belong – the Unitarian Universalist Church and the Ethical Culture Society. They do not privilege any particular sexual orientation or mode for expressing sexuality. All are welcome – gay, lesbian, trans-sexual individuals, and so on – and this is what they mean when saying they offer an opening, welcoming and affirming community. The assumption of humanists is that people are "wired" in a variety of ways and each has merit and value. Many African-based traditions hold a similar perspective and some, like Candomblé first developed in Brazil, privilege gay members in certain capacities in that they are believed to have a special relationship with deities and are more easily possessed by the gods. Yet, these are exceptions to the general rule in that most African American religious traditions reject homosexuality as improper and sinful.

For many Christians and Muslims, homosexuality is considered an abomination, a perversion of the order established by God and outlined in scripture. It, they argue, is inconsistent with the story of creation in which God created a man and a woman and united them. Many Christians also argue that the New Testament establishes the make-up of the proper relationship when arguing that it is for the reason of marriage that a man leaves his parents and makes a commitment and bond to a woman. Christians believe they find additional evidence for this position in the story of Sodom and Gomorrah – ancient cities that were destroyed because of their wickedness that included homosexuality. They also appeal to New Testament texts that label homosexuality a slide into moral and ethical decay marking the destruction of communities. There are ways in which this position supports and is buttressed by the larger society in which homosexuality is stigmatized and discriminated against. Reluctance to allow gays and lesbians to marry within most states within the United States is mirrored by a rejection of gay marriage within many African American religious traditions. In both contexts – religious communities and the larger society – there is the potential for and at times actual violence against gays and lesbians. The difference is the manner in which religious traditions couch action in the language of doctrine and creeds, God's will, and the demands of religious life.

For Christians, this is further complicated by the ways in which scripture is open to multiple interpretations and approaches in that it is said to be the "inspired" word of God. Islam's understanding of the Qur'an allows some flexibility but not as much as one finds within the Christian scriptures. According to Muslims, the Qur'an was given directly to the Prophet Muhammad. It is the literal word of God recited by the Prophet Muhammad, who could not read nor write. Christians hold a variety of opinions on the nature of the Bible, with a good number understanding it as the inspired word of God filtered through human cultural understandings and social perspective. The ability to interpret scripture in such a way as to be able to support any point of view prevents a clear assertion of "Truth" regarding what Christians should think about homosexuality.

There is a tension or paradox within church practice in that many churches condemn homosexuality and do so through their doctrines, sermons, and general practices. Yet, this does not mean that gays and lesbians aren't present in their congregations – in the choir and serving in other capacities. They are present but forced into a "don't ask, don't tell" position, which involves them helping to maintain the ritual activities and physical plant of the churches while hearing sermons that condemn them and their lifestyle. Or, in some cases, ministers or lay leaders will target gay and lesbian members for special spiritual care in an effort to get them saved and/or free from evil influences that result in such a lifestyle. Many of the churches condemning homosexuality assume it is a choice people make – a decision to resist God's will – as opposed to it the result of biological hardwiring. This is the "nurture" vs. "nature" debate. All this is to say, the condemnation of homosexuality

Figure 12.1 A black lesbian addresses crowd celebrating the passage of the New York State Marriage Equality Act (June 2011). © Katharine Andriotis/Alamy.

does not mean that only heterosexuals are present in churches and other religious communities. Rather, it simply means they participate in communities that do not recognize their full worth and condemn them to punishment because of how and who they love.

This, of course, isn't to say all Christian churches take this stance. There are in fact many African American churches that are open, welcoming, and affirming – arguing that God created all people as they are and that each person has the spark of God in them. Each is to be appreciated and not discriminated against, and they feel an obligation to provide information and support for gays, lesbians and others who are victimized in the larger society and in religious communities because of their sexual preferences.

God, through Jesus, has made life available to all and everyone who embraces Christ should be treated as a "brother" or "sister." Those taking this stand argue that the Sodom and Gomorrah story is about a lack of hospitality for strangers, not about sexual preferences. The towns are punished because they do not welcome the strangers who come to them, but rather threaten them with harm. Learning lessons from this story, then, Christians are required to exercise hospitality to all who come their way, all who enter their churches looking for fellowship and comfort. Furthermore, they argue that the New Testament is all about the ministry of Christ and the need for those who are followers of Christ to mirror his ethical and moral commitments. According to this reading of the New Testament, Jesus does not condemn homosexuality as a sin; rather, Jesus is critical of those who do not commit themselves to meeting the needs of those who are suffering. And, pronouncements in the New Testament that privilege heterosexual relationships given by disciples happen by "permission, not by command." That is to say, what these passages offer entails the particular thoughts of individuals as opposed to the demands of God through Jesus Christ. That is to say, according to these more liberal churches, those reading scripture for life lessons must be mindful of the fact that scripture is written within a particular historical and cultural context that does not necessarily translate precisely to our times. They developed regulations to safeguard their particular social and political structures, which have little resemblance to our current life arrangements and circumstances. There are general lessons that one can take away, these churches would argue, but scripture cannot be applied literally to the contemporary moment. And, the actual instructions of Christ promote mutual respect and compassion without regard for markers of difference. These instructions are the ones to follow, according to these welcoming churches. In addition to these welcoming churches, there are African American Muslims who work to rethink and provide a more positive response to gays and lesbians who claim the faith. While an important shift, it remains a minority approach.

> Black churches have been so poisoned by homophobia and heterosexism that some may think it blasphemous that an African-American heterosexual male Christian pastor would support same-sex marriage. I do so not because I believe it is safe, politically correct, or popular, but because I believe it is right. It is theologically right because we are all created equal in the image of God. It is historically right because those of us who have been the victims of oppression ought to be the last ones to oppress anyone else. It is morally right because all of God's children should be able to live the truth rather than be forced to perpetrate a lie. And it is legally right because same-sex couples are entitled to the same rights, responsibilities and protections under the law as heterosexual couples.
>
> (From Rev. Dr. Dennis Wiley, "Ebony Debate: Gay Marriage." Quoted from Covenant Baptist United Church of Christ website: http://covenantbaptistucc.org/?p=1294)

All things considered, the issue of homosexuality is a hotly debated topic within African American religious communities. It is safe to believe sexual orientation and homosexuality will continue to be a hot button issue within African American religious communities in the foreseeable future. Whereas some religious communities will work to secure and safeguard full participation and full rights for gays, lesbians, and others representing marginalized segments of the social and religious community, others will fight just as hard to restrict involvement and ostracize those they consider socially and sexually threatening.

Religious communities and HIV/AIDS

During the last two decades of the twentieth century a health crisis surfaced that confused and frightened the US population, and that served to further stigmatize segments of the population assumed to be the cause and victims of this new disease, HIV/AIDS. Religious communities had for some time given attention to issues of health and healthcare, from things as simple as exercise classes and blood pressure screening, to the development of healthcare clinics, to work with drug addicts through education, etc. Much of this has involved both church-sponsored programs and churches offering space for social service and healthcare service organizations to conduct their business. However, when they are not completely silent, the general attitude of many churches to sexual activity has contributed to a lack of attention to HIV/AIDS, particularly to the extent they consider it a disease affecting gays and drug users. Some go so far as to suggest that the disease is punishment from God for an inappropriate lifestyle. For many churches, HIV/AIDS has been understood as a moral issue, requiring a moral correction – sexual practices consistent with religious creeds. Other churches argue proper attention to HIV/AIDS through information and active care is a requirement outlined through the demand for justice and compassion found in scripture and marked out by the best of what churches practice. These churches understand that prevention, not judgment, is key to ending this epidemic that is killing members of the African American community and African American churches. In addition to committing their physical space and financial resources to HIV/AIDS education, prevention, and treatment, individual churches and denominations of this opinion often partner with organizations such as "Balm in Gilead." This organization provides education and also harnesses the spiritual dimension of churches by holding an annual week of prayer serving to inform church members of the disease and its impact.

In general "Balm in Gilead" maximizes use of African American church-based resources, such as partnering with church missionary societies and equipping those societies to extend their work to the victims of HIV/AIDS. While a significant church partner on the national level, Balm in Gilead is not the only collective to which African American churches belong. Many have also created collaborative organizations

Balm in Gilead and healthcare

- *Our Vision*

Faith institutions serving people of the African Diaspora are fully engaged in preventing diseases and improving the health status of those they serve and eliminating diseases, such as HIV/AIDS, cervical cancer, diabetes and other health disparities.

- *Our Mission*

The mission of the Balm In Gilead is to prevent diseases and to improve the health status of people of the African Diaspora by providing support to faith institutions in areas of program design, implementation and evaluation which strengthens their capacity to deliver programs and services that contribute to the elimination of health disparities.

- *Guiding Principles*

We believe that all people facing health challenges are welcome at the table of grace by the unconditional love of God and that their voices must be heard and respected.

We believe that faith leaders are a powerful voice for change and must be intentionally at the forefront of addressing the health challenges of the people they serve.

We believe that faith institutions are uniquely positioned to play a major role in efforts to improve the health status of people living in the communities they serve.

We believe in the Power of Prayer and its role in lives of Africans and people of African descent.

("The Balm in Gilead: About the Organization," at: http://www.balmingilead.org/about/)

of numerous churches in a geographic area that are committed to using available resources to address HIV/AIDS and other healthcare issues within their immediate surroundings. In some cases, churches have medical professionals in their membership and, as part of their expression of faith, they provide free healthcare. In other cases, churches use these collaborative efforts as a way to partner with secular healthcare organizations to provide treatment and education. These collectives as well as individual churches also assist those who are HIV positive as well as those suffering from other health challenges by providing rides to doctors' appointments, preparing meals, or helping them maintain other dimensions of their lives through support groups.

Furthermore, religious organizations such as the Unitarian Universalist Association and Ethical Culture Society that humanists call "home" address HIV/AIDS using the same mechanisms used by churches involved in education, prevention, and support. For example, what follows is a statement from the Unitarian Universalists Association on HIV/AIDS located on its website:

Figure 12.2 People from St. Charles Borromeo Church taking part in AIDS Walk New York 2010. © Tomas Abad/Alamy

The Unitarian Universalist Association has long advocated for medically-accurate, practical, comprehensive sexuality education to prevent the spread of HIV. We know that anyone can be HIV positive regardless of gender, age, income, sexual orientation, nationality, or racial group. However, groups that are marginalized within our society and our world as a whole are made more vulnerable to this disease because of the lack of resources available to them, such as education, healthcare, and finances. It is our shared responsibility as people of faith to challenge the structures and worldviews that prevent marginalized groups from realizing their own rights, power, and potential and allow this disease to flourish.

The Association attempts to live out this commitment through educational resources – such as its World AIDS Day worship packet – and strategies available to local congregations from the national headquarters.

One should not think that churches are the only organizations concerned with healthcare and HIV/AIDS. For example, the National Muslim Aids Initiative seeks to provide information to healthcare givers regarding Islamic customs (e.g., Islamic worldview, cultural sensitivity training, and social assumptions) so as to make Muslims comfortable in receiving treatment through equipping caregivers with information concerning Islam's regulations. This organization also educates

Muslims about HIV/AIDS as well as outlines means of prevention and support. Finally, it helps Muslim groups secure funding to undertake education, prevention, and support programs. In terms of particular Islamic leaders and mosques, Imam Al-Hajj Talib 'Abdur-Rashid is both leader of the Mosque of Islamic Brotherhood in New York City and works as an HIV/AIDS counselor and educator. He also participates in the African American Commission on HIV/AIDS and the Advisory Committee to the International Muslim Leaders Consultation on HIV/AIDS.

Key points you need to know

- A love-hate relationship with the physical body has historically informed how African American religious traditions address issues such as sex.
- Most African American religions maintain that sex is appropriate only within the context of marriage between a man and a woman.
- Sacred texts and tradition are used to justify perspectives on sex and sexuality.
- More liberal religious groups provide education and services to prevent sexual diseases, understanding that waiting until marriage is not a practical requirement for sexual activity.
- Heterosexuality is considered the only proper arrangement for the expression of sexual desire, and homosexuality is considered a moral problem, a sin.
- Some religious organizations work to be open and affirming communities that embrace gay marriage.
- HIV/AIDS has been one of the biggest challenges to religious organizations in that it typically brings together a range of contentious issues: gender, sex, sexuality, drugs, and health care.
- Partnerships with "secular" organizations provide religious communities with ways to secure education programs, prevention strategies, and support related to issues such as HIV/AIDS.

Discussion questions

1. Why is the issue of sex such a hot button issue for African American religious traditions?
2. What are some of the general approaches to sex taken by various religious traditions?
3. How do different traditions seek to control sex? What are considered the proper outlets for sexual interest? Why are these outlets considered acceptable?
4. What role does scripture play in how religious organizations understand sexuality?
5. Why is sexuality such a tense issue for African American religion?
6. What are some of the arguments used to support a liberal take on sex and sexuality? What are some of the arguments used to support a more conservative approach to both?

7. What have been some of the typical approaches to HIV/AIDS?
8. What are some of the common thoughts regarding the nature and importance of the human body?

Further reading

Ali, Kecia. *Sexual Ethics and Islam: Feminist Reflections on Qur'an, Hadith and Jurisprudence*. New York: OneWorld, 2006.

Copeland, Shawn M. *Enfleshing Freedom: Body, Race, and Being*. Minneapolis, MN: Fortress Press, 2009.

Douglas, Kelly Brown. *Sexuality and the Black Church*. Maryknoll, NY: Orbis Books, 1999.

Ellison, Marvin M. and Kelly Brown Douglas, editors. *Sexuality and the Sacred: Sources for Theological Reflection*. Louisville, KY: Westminster John Knox, 2010.

Gomes, Peter J. *The Good Book: Reading the Bible with Mind and Heart*. New York: HarperOne, 2002.

Griffin, Horace L. *Their Own Receive Them Not: African American Lesbians and Gays in Black Churches*. Eugene, OR: Wipf & Stock Publishers, 2010.

Harris, Anquelique. *AIDS, Sexuality, and the Black Church*. New York: Peter Lang, 2010.

Jordan, Mark. *Recruiting Young Love: How Christians Talk about Homosexuality*. Chicago, IL: University of Chicago Press, 2011.

Jordan, Mark. *The Silence of Sodom: Homosexuality in Modern Catholicism*. Chicago, IL: University of Chicago Press, 2002.

Kugle, Scott. *Homosexuality in Islam: Islamic Reflection on Gay, Lesbian, and Transgender Muslims*. New York: OneWorld, 2010.

Pinn, Anthony B. and Dwight Hopkins, editors. *Loving the Body: Black Religious Studies and the Erotic*. New York: Palgrave Macmillan, 2006.

Wadud, Amina. *Inside the Gender Jihad: Women's Reform in Islam*. New York: OneWorld, 2006.

13 Hip hop and the new "look" of religion

In this chapter

Many scholars have pointed out connections between religious experience and cultural production, arguing that the latter becomes a screen for the display of religious ideas and concerns. They also suggest cultural production provides a language for the expression of religious commitments and challenges. Clear examples of this include the manner in which religious language and themes are replete within the television programs and movies produced, for instance, by Tyler Perry and the Rev. T. D. Jakes. The intersection of film and religion is important and has received ample scholarly and popular attention. Yet, one of the most compelling examples of this intersection of religion and popular culture involves hip hop. Mindful of such arguments, this chapter offers readers an opportunity to explore the relationship between African American religion and hip hop culture.

Main topics covered

- Origins of hip hop culture
- Graffiti art and questions of life meaning
- Significance of break dancing
- Musical roots of rap music
- Expression of religious commitment in rap lyrics
- Efforts of traditional religious institutions to absorb elements of hip hop culture
- Challenges to church hypocrisy within rap music
- Presentations of hip hop as a new religion

A new generation with a new style

The rise of new theological discourses such as black theology, and the impassioned language of black power and black consciousness were not the only shifts in how African Americans understood and presented their life stories. The socio-political and economic turmoil of the decade also found expression in cultural shifts, perhaps the most compelling of these being the rise of hip hop culture. The term hip hop was drawn from a phrase used commonly by MCs (or masters of ceremonies) at the start of their rhymes. With time it became the language used to express a unique cultural form of expression composed of numerous elements each entailing a way by which young people expressed frustration with their life circumstance as well as the value and capabilities of their bodies for expression of self-understanding and self-worth. Economic problems and social restrictions produced anxiety, and young African Americans and Hispanics did not fare well in many circumstances – limited job opportunities and failing city infrastructure were particularly present in the areas of the city these youth called home. These problems were thrown in graphic relief through the introduction of crack cocaine in the early 1980s. This drug, much cheaper than cocaine and highly addictive, flooded inner city neighborhoods producing great misery for most and wealth for drug dealers. It marked an intensification of the worst aspects of human life, and served to nurture a growing sense of nihilism for young people who saw the selling of illegal drugs as a means to quick money but also an avenue for an untimely death. Yet, the response for some young people coming of age in the era of crack cocaine did not take the form of riots, nor sit-ins that marked strategies used during earlier periods of social justice work. They did not turn on themselves and each other in a physically violent manner. Levels of frustration and disillusionment were on the rise, but rather than violent reaction against their invisibility and dismissal by economic leaders, politicians and others, some of these young people reflected on their life circumstances through creative manipulations of the visual and expressive arts, through a twist on fashion, and through the development of an alternative vocabulary used in its most lyrically graphic form, rap music – a modality of musical expression with its own integrity, but also involving a style and social content that has found its way into the recordings of a host of artists such as Lauryn Hill and Erykah Badu.

These various elements – expressive culture in the form of graffiti; break dancing; an aesthetic representing a new fashion style; and the telling of stories of urban life using the alternative vocabulary and rhythm of "rap"– were the content of a new form of cultural expression. Many thought it was only a fad, a source of frustration for those who saw the graffiti on trains, walls, and other public spaces in the city; or, a source of amusement (or amazement) for those who saw break dancers on street corners, on subway platforms, or in clubs "doing their thing." But for the young people involved, hip hop culture provided a way of expressing their questions about life, their concern for the deep issues of life meaning. Through break dancing and graffiti, it was possible to express frustration and anger (as well as joy) in a more productive manner. These art forms allowed experts to create worlds with body movements and cans of spray paint used to project one's name or other images to the public. In general, hip hop culture provided and continues to offer a way to self-visualize, and force others to see, hear, and feel uncomfortable life stories but also to explore new possibilities for healthy lives in transformed societies.

Graffiti

Placing sayings or one's name on public spaces is much older than the 1970s. In fact, there is evidence to suggest it was a common occurrence within the ancient world. But even if one simply thinks in terms of the United States, one's name and how and where it is placed has held significance for an extremely long time. From enslaved Africans who marked the claiming of a name as part of their freedom, to the rejection of the "slave master's name" by members of the Nation of Islam (e.g., Malcolm Little becomes Malcolm X), to the taking on of an African name by black nationalists, the public presentation of one's name has had significance. This continued into the late twentieth century as young people stated their importance through the tagging of public spaces. And while tagging – the artistically creative way of claiming space through the writing of one's name or "tag" – is typically associated with the United States, particularly the subway cars of New York City, it is a global reality found on buildings in locations such as London, Paris, Hanover (Germany), and the list goes on.

Figure 13.1 Graffiti in Washington DC. Courtesy of the Library of Congress, Prints and Photographs Division [LC-DIG-highsm-10057].

Taki 183, a white American, is often credited with giving shape to the graffiti art movement. Prior to hip hop's acceptance as a cultural movement, the appearance of his "tag" (his name) across New York City gained media attention and resulted in published stories that spread interest in and an understanding of this form of visual art. Although initially involving bubbles and other creative shaping of letters blended to give a fluid look to words, with time simple tagging gave way to more complex images – both embedded messages and explicit stories and messages dealing with the social, political and economic dimensions of urban life. As graffiti grew in sophistication, it also required greater planning. Artists began marking out on paper their intended design and started using those sketches as the framework for the actual pieces they would create using paint. And while this required much thought, it also required speed in that the window of opportunity for completing the project before being discovered by authorities was narrow. Many benefited from the exchange of ideas within their "crews," like-minded friends and acquaintances composed of both male and female artists. The artistic techniques advanced, the messages became more complex, and the art world noticed. For example, "Fab Five Freddy," a New York artist was invited to exhibit in various galleries, and graffiti artist Jean-Michel Basquiat (1960–1988) became one of the most important artists of the late twentieth century.

Spray painting meaning

- Graffiti has a history that goes back well beyond the twentieth century.
- In the 1960s graffiti was used to announce political opinions and perspectives.
- Tagging trains and buildings involved writing one's name or symbol on public spaces.
- Complicated styles of writing one's "tag" or name along with the depiction of figures and stories developed with time.
- Tagging was against the law, but some galleries invited graffiti artists to present their work.

What does this have to do with religion, one might ask? Well, graffiti as it develops and advances becomes a means by which to wrestle with issues of life meaning through the visual arts. In the same way churches have used images, paintings, and the arrangement of words to express their commitments and their doctrines, there are ways in which graffiti has served as a commentary on the pressing life issues of its creators and admirers. That is to say, as religion is concerned with a desire for greater life meaning, graffiti provides an example of how young people have written down the stories of this struggle for meaning. It, in this way, can involve the visual expression of religious questions and concerns, even if this simply involves a strong effort to see one's importance and value in a society that seems to deny both.

Figure 13.2 Teenager dancing at the Grant Memorial. Courtesy of Tom Williams/Roll Call/
Getty Images.

Break dancing

Dance, as a way of expressing feelings and experience, is part of the very fabric of
African American life. From the early years of the slave system, gatherings featuring
dance marked off special occasions and holidays. Even within religious settings the
rhythmic moving of the body as a way of expressing a connection between the body
and the Divine was important. Voodoo is marked by dance connected to particular
gods. Being "filled with the Holy Spirit" in Pentecostalism also involves God taking
control of human bodies marked out through the movement of the body complete
with gestures, postures, and its own rhythm. These various examples of dance or
rhythmic movement speak to bodies serving as instruments for expressing concerns
and triumphs in human life. The same can be said about break dancing.

Body movement has figured prominently in hip hop culture. Through the
formation of crews, "b-boys" (break boys) and "b-girls" (break girls) twisted and
turned their bodies. They made their bodies plastic, bending, "popping and locking,"
in ways that gave them a type of fluidity. Rather than physical confrontation – riots,
property destruction, and so on – that one might expect to develop as a result of
the frustrations of life within the context of urban decay, b-boys and b-girls used
dance as a way of working through anger and through dance battles, many gained
reputation and status within their communities. This style of dance actually involves

a variety of moves and approaches all revolving around how one gives the body a rubber quality, or forces it to do gymnastic moves that seem to defy the limits of body postures. It could take place in clubs or on the street as participants often in crews or teams showed their skills one at a time. The equipment for break dancing is not elaborate – perhaps a piece of cardboard on the ground, gloves to allow the hands to slide across the floor, and a hat to allow the head to slide without pulling hair or being hampered by friction. The clothing spoke to a particular style as well, an aesthetic that belonged to these young people – but one that would change over time. Those with the best skills gained a large reputation. Although some of the appeal of break dancing would fade little more than a decade after its emergence, it gained international attention with crews developing in locations such as Japan and international competitions drawing young people from across the globe.

Rap music

In the early years of hip hop culture, it was really all about the creation of beats and the manipulation of vinyl records to produce new sounds. At parties and in clubs, DJs worked the turntables and proved their skills by keeping people on the floor dancing to the new beats they created. The break-dancer got the name initially because they danced between the beats, as the DJ was transitioning between songs. The MC, the rapper, played a similar role as a second to the DJ. The rapper kept the crowd excited through energetic and rhymed statements, particularly during these periods when the DJ had to change records. It was only with time that the roles were reversed and the MC or rapper gained the dominant position. Rap music borrows from traditions such as the toasting tradition, the poetic styling of the blues, the dozens (i.e., telling insulting stories about others, making insulting jokes about others), and other manipulations of language present within the American hemisphere. However, there are ways in which these practices are perfected in the urban environments of North America.

Telling stories about life – its hardships and pleasures – has been a part of the cultural landscape, but it took on a different tone and a different type of rhythm through rap music. Although it existed for some time prior to this, rap didn't capture the popular imagination of the United States until 1979 with the Sugar Hill Gang's single titled "Rapper's Delight." It was almost 15 minutes long and was composed of stories told about and by the three rappers making up the group. This single sold well, and gained rap music a much larger audience and significant attention. Numerous artists with differing levels of skill emerged after this, and before the end of the 1980s, it would no longer be the East Coast – places like New York and Philadelphia – controlling this new form. Los Angeles also made its presence felt. If one looks at the development of rap music from 1979 to the end of the 1980s, at least three genres dominate. The first is *status rap* music and, like "Rapper's Delight," it concerns itself with stories of sexual prowess, wealth and talent. Various artists showed their abilities on the microphone and in recordings, and tied it all to their possession of the American Dream. These rappers also demonstrated their success through gold chains and rings, expensive sneakers, and so on, all the trappings of material success. The second genre, *progressive rap*, is more socially conscious. It is more concerned with political developments that transform the life options of the poor and other victims of oppression. Associated with groups such as Public Enemy, this style of rap teaches African American history in a positive way, and seeks to raise questions concerning the status quo. The goal is to use this popular form of musical expression to instill a sense of pride and purpose that transforms life circumstances.

Many of the artists who represent this style of rap today, artists such as Talib Kweli, Lupe Fiasco, Nas, and Common, draw much of their thinking from Sunni Islam, the social critique offered by Malcolm X as well as other progressive thinkers associated with Black Power and the Black Consciousness movements of the mid-twentieth century. For them, rap provides a means by which to communicate important life lessons, to expose the socio-political and economic problems of the United States, and offer solutions that maintain integrity and a balanced perspective on the nature and meaning of success. Chuck D, of Public Enemy, even once referred to rap as the "black CNN." They, in large part, place success of the individual within the context of community. The achievements of the former should have positive consequences for the latter. The third genre of rap music is commonly referred to as *gangsta rap*. Many argue it was given this name by Dr. Dre, a former member of NWA – one of the early groups on the West Coast of the United States. It clearly drew on the public images of the mobster, or gangster lifestyle, but pulling this posture toward the world into the African American and urban contexts. Many gangsta rappers used movie characters such as Tony Montana from the film "Scarface" (1983) as a model of how the despised gain power in the world. While there were a few artists of this genre on the East Coast of the United States, it is most forcefully represented by artists in Los Angeles. This type of rap music is marked by anger and violence, an effort to change the life circumstances of the oppressed through counter aggression against the police and other forces perceived as causing the problems encountered. These artists chronicle stories of selling drugs, abuse of others, difficulties with police officers, and the trials of gang life. Status rap plays with a desire to secure the American Dream of success without clear critique of the mechanisms for achieving it. Progressive rap seeks to trouble the nature of the American Dream by exposing the damage such a formulation of life does to people. And gangsta rap attempts to secure the markers of success by taking what one wants through violence if necessary and without regard for the welfare of others.

It is important to remember that while there are distinct types of rap music, it is often the case that a given artist's album will move between the various genres.

Types of rap music

- Status rap – concerned with celebration of material success, sexual prowess, and power.
- Progressive rap – discusses socio-political and economic problems and seeks to provide solutions through information and strategies for transforming how people think and behave.
- Gangsta rap – chronicles the struggles of inner city life and embracing violence and a radical individualism that seeks to make personal gains through readily available urban mechanisms such as gang activity and drug dealing.

Yet, record labels have also pushed the more graphic dimensions of gangsta rap to the extent this music sells and secures greater revenue. And one of the struggles for artists has been to maintain the integrity of their music, to keep it "real," so to speak, over against the wishes of music executives who profit via caricatures of urban life. Some have attempted to move beyond this tension by developing their own labels that allow them to produce the type of music they are interested in producing without interference. Independence from the major labels also has financial consequences in that artists are able to keep more of the proceeds of their work.

Rapping religion

The above are three dominant styles of rap, each with its own images and stories to tell. If one carefully listens to the stories told by certain artists, one also learns that many artists are engaged with religious traditions discussed in earlier chapters. Not widely discussed but still present during the early 1990s, groups such as X-Clan promoted links between African Americans and the wisdom and knowledge of Egypt. They encouraged an Africa-centered perspective on knowledge and ethics through which African Americans would gain a sense of self and progress. Even earlier than this, however, one of the founding figures of hip hop culture, Afrika Bambaataa, celebrated the importance of Africa for a proper sense of African American history, and he advocated black pride as a key factor in the development of a strong community.

This commitment to an African worldview and hip hop as a way to transform life took institutional form through the Universal Zulu Nation he organized. It was composed of representatives from the various elements of hip hop culture, all concerned with providing an alternative life path than drug dealing and gang activity so prevalent in the inner city during the 1970s. Aware of the dilemmas of life facing their communities, artists such as Bambaataa provide an alternative source of life meaning in connection to a history and system of knowledge stemming back to the continent of Africa prior to the introduction of the slave system. In this way, some artists continued the appeal to empowerment and black consciousness first found in the Black Panther Party and other radical groups during the 1960s. This time black pride was rapped over a beat, rather than shouted through a megaphone, or chanted by a crowd gathered to confront segregation and socio-political abuse.

Prominent amongst the traditions advocated by some artists are the Nation of Islam and the Five Percent Nation. The lyrics give both explicit and coded information concerning these traditions for the purpose of converting listeners to the truth of their religion and for the purpose of testifying to the importance of their religious claims. Drawn from Nation of Islam theology are ideas that include African Americans as original people, as well as the Nation's understanding of white society and the future control of the universe by the original people. Groups such as Public Enemy reference the Nation of Islam for what that religious organization teaches concerning racial pride and clear ethics that pull African Americans away from some of the more damaging aspects of life in the United States. Those committed to the Five Percent Nation, like artist Rakim, code their lyrics with references to the god-status of African American men as well as use the language of the religious organization to lyrically dismantle the oppressive structures of life in the United States. There are still others like Mos Def who is a Sunni Muslim and who uses the music to advance the teachings of that particular faith. (Mos Def recently changed his name to Yassin Bey.) At times, this involves a critique of lax morality and ethics, and at other times his songs are laced with references to the principles of Islamic conduct as well as references to the pillars of Islam – the key beliefs and practices of Islam.

With groups like the Wu-Tang Clan there is a nod in the direction of the East that connects its lyrics and style to the history of the martial arts of Asia. There is something metaphysical about their lyrics and style, drawing as it does from the outlooks, body-mind discipline, and codes of conduct associated with Eastern traditions of spirituality and battle (martial arts). This involves a blending of ideas – some from Eastern traditions and some from the teachings of New Age-styled knowledge and practices, as well as the legacy of superheroes in comics and other fantasy stories. However, all this is funneled through the realities of their urban context and speaks to the questions and needs of an inner-city community.

Some Christian artists have often found it difficult to remain within the confines of what they consider "secular" hip hop, with its morality and ethics that often run contrary to the teachings of the Christian faith. Many artists with this perspective have branched off and now perform as explicitly Christian artists recording with Christian labels – including Grapetree Records and Cross Movement Records. They see their work as an opportunity to spread the Gospel of Christ. Meant to convert "sinners" or uplift committed Christians, this genre of rap – Christian rap – does not generate the same size audiences, and it does not result in the same level of economic success. However, for these artists, financial reward isn't the purpose; they are more concerned with using their musical talents to change lives and lead people to the Christian faith. They understand themselves to be a new wave of Christ's disciples spreading the power of Christ through stories of their conversion to the faith and the difference this change has made in the personal life and professional commitments. Some of the artists associated with this movement include DC Talk and Gospel Gangstaz. Some of these Christian artists also work to change the general look and tone of hip hop by encouraging "secular" artists to decrease their use of profane language, to move beyond what Christian artists perceive as a glorification of violence and drug dealing, and to stop abusive conversations concerning women within the music. There are other Christians involved in rap with a different perspective. They make a distinction between the stories they tell as professional artists and their personal lives. That is to say, they argue that their professional work is meant to chronicle life in the urban context for an adult audience – not children – but that it is not a representation of their beliefs or current practices. Some making this argument are Christian and see their music as distinct from the effort in their own lives to improve their communities through service and a sharing of resources as well as the example of proper morals and ethical living they exhibit in their day-to-day lives. Debates rage in certain quarters over the proper relationship between rap music and institutional religious traditions, but regardless of what side one takes in these discussions, it remains clear that churches have taken notice of hip hop culture and not all churches see it as problematic or deeply at odds with the intent of the Christian faith.

Although the birth of Christian rap in the 1980s predates this, the conversion of Run from "Run DMC" to Christianity marked a watershed moment in the connection between Christianity and hip hop. Run became the Rev. Run and he combined hip hop sensibilities with a commitment to church ministry.

Others have also followed this path, including Kurtis Blow. He is another pioneer in the development of hip hop, and he was one of the first artists to tour internationally and one of the first to reach certified gold status in record sales. Now an ordained minister, Kurtis (Blow) Walker has an online presence at "HipHopMinistry.com" as well as a church known as the "Hip Hop Church."

His brand of worship combines commitment to Christ and the culture of hip hop. From his perspective, there is no disconnection between the claims and commitments associated with Christianity and the tools for life meaning lodged in hip hop. Rev. Kurtis Walker argues that the Hip Hop Church is a style of worship that can be tailored to fit any Christian church context in that it maintains the core of the Christian faith but simply presents the basic elements of this faith in a contemporary way.

Jesus as rapper?

If Jesus was around today, he probably would be a rapper. Could you see Jesus battling Eminem? And Eminem needs help. He needs Jay-Z and 50 Cent. And just line them all up and Jesus is going to start speaking in tongues and it's a rap, it's all over.

(Quoted from "Kurtis Blow, Worshipping Through Hip Hop," NPR)

Figure 13.3 A Christian hip hop group and other members of the Hip Hop Church Choir singing and dancing in front of the altar during a service (Hip Hop Church in Harlem, New York). © Alex Masi/Corbis.

As gospel music brought new energy to churches and slowly gained wide acceptance within church circles, Christians have been slow to welcome hip hop into their sanctuaries. But a decrease in the involvement of young people in churches over the past several decades – and the rise of organizations such as the Hip Hop Church – has sparked interest in the potential for church growth found with hip hop.

Ministers interested in keeping their congregations vibrant and growing have come to see the advantages found in an embrace of hip hop. Of importance here is the way in which explicitly Christian artists have made it easy for churches to reject the more troubling aspects of hip hop culture associated with gangsta rap and instead embrace a new style of confessing one's commitment to the faith. But there were still changes that had to take place. For example, whereas it was once the case that people of all ages dressed up for a church service, many congregations now embrace a less formal attire, including the jeans and shirts so deeply associated with hip hop culture. Even break dancing has become an accepted element of church worship alongside earlier forms of liturgical dance.

Ministers and scholars alike who encourage this embrace of hip hop culture, particularly rap music, argue that it teaches something about what churches can do better in order to meet the needs of young people and it also provides important lessons on the way in which the style of worship must change to fit the tastes and sensibilities of new generations. Others argue that this is a thin process in that churches are not embracing the "true" dynamics of hip hop but instead they are picking and choosing elements of the culture to meet their particular needs and wants. The key is this; for these critics, churches are manipulating and devaluing the significance of this cultural form and making it into something it is not. Once meant to challenge the status quo, to critique comfort with the structures of life that limited the well-being of some of the most vulnerable members of society, it is now simply a way to increase church offerings by increasing church attendance. Some of those critiquing churches are not concerned only with the co-option of hip hop, but also what they perceive as the hypocrisy of churches that preach one thing – compassion, justice, and righteousness – but whose members, including preachers, act in morally and ethically questionable ways.

In addition, there are artists who provide an explicit atheistic framework, and whose lyrics express a means to forge life meaning without any supernatural claims. Prominent amongst this group of atheist rap artists is Los Angeles-based Greydon Square whose topics within his songs include evolution and the ill-effects of a religious (here meaning "theistic") approach to life. He has a significant following within atheistic circles such as members of African Americans for Humanism (a division of the Center for Inquiry).

Yet, he is not alone in that the ability of hip hop culture to serve as an outlet for atheistic, science-based information, has gained attention from a variety of quarters. There is a growing group of artists committed to this perspective, and they are developing outlets that connect them to the organizations marking the larger atheist movement – organizations such as Secular Student Alliance, Center for Inquiry, American Atheists, and so on.

Hip hop as a new religion?

For still others, hip hop culture in itself is a religious tradition – containing the necessary elements: sacred texts in the form of rap lyrics, houses of worship in the

KRS-One on the meaning of hip hop

Unfortunately, people today have grown accustomed to equating Rap music and the images portrayed in mainstream Rap music videos with the whole of Hip Hop's culture and history. This is why we teach that Hip Hop and Rap music are not the same things; that Rap is something that is done, while Hip Hop is something that is lived, and the living of Hip Hop is real Hip Hop. Others teach their opinions of 'hip hop' as a music genre however, rap (rhythmic speech) is but ONE expression that comes out of the total Hip Hop experience. For us, Hip Hop is the combination of Breakin, Emceein, Graffiti Art, Deejayin, Beat Boxin, Street Fashion, Street Language, Street Knowledge and Street Entrepreneurialism. For us, Hip Hop is the amplification of Human expression and awareness. At its core, Hip Hop is not just an art form; it is the pursuit of one's authentic being through the Arts.

(Quoting KRS-One, "What Does the 'Temple of Hip Hop' Teach? http://www.templeofhiphop.org/)

form of concerts and other performances, a system of morality and ethics. KRS-One (i.e., "Knowledge Reigns Supreme Over Nearly Everyone – given name of Lawrence Krisna Parker) is one who thinks along these lines, and he has constructed a multi-layered organization for the purpose of unpacking and disseminating the wealth of information and praxis that is hip hop.

The Temple of Hip Hop, as the organization is called, offers resources that enable true followers to 'become hip hop' through attention to the real history and knowledge of hip hop as something one lives. And to live hip hop, according to KRS-One and the Temple of Hip Hop, is to develop a full sense of one's being. In this way, hip hop promotes a route to life meaning by providing knowledge concerning the central questions of existence. Proper understanding, practice, and teaching of hip hop entails a "New Covenant" outlined on the Temple of Hip Hop website. Much of the language of this covenant is borrowed from Christianity, but it is put to a different use. It is a metaphysical document that connects to a special body of knowledge, a special connection to God, and it projects hip hop as more than entertainment or something one does. In fact, according to the covenant, hip hop is life. In this way, the Temple of Hip Hop promotes a sense of religion and offers the doctrines, practices, and ethics meant to express the experience of the religious. To aid with this, KRS-One produced *The Gospel of Hip Hop: First Instrument*, a volume that outlines many of his teachings concerning the nature and meaning of hip hop culture.

Key points you need to know

- Hip hop borrows from earlier cultural forms of expression but emerges in the 1970s as a unique set of practices.
- Hip hop culture is composed of at least these elements: graffiti art, break dancing, DJing, rap music, style of dress and speech.
- There are three often overlapping styles of rap music – status, progressive, and gangsta rap.
- Artists incorporate elements of the Nation of Islam, the Five Percent Nation, and Sunni Islam into their lyrics, based on personal commitment to these faiths.
- Christianity is represented through artists who see their talent as an opportunity to spread the message of Christ through explicitly Christian rap.
- Hip hop is the cultural basis for a new church movement called the Hip Hop Church.
- Traditional Christian denominations are beginning to incorporate elements of hip hop culture into their worship in order to attract and keep young people within their congregations.
- KRS-One's Temple of Hip Hop presents hip hop culture as a new form of religion, complete with its own covenant, ministers, doctrines, practices, and institutions.

Discussion questions

1. What are the conditions under which hip hop culture develops?
2. What is hip hop culture's relationship to earlier forms of expression, and why is it called hip hop?
3. What is graffiti art, and how has it changed over time?
4. What is break dancing, and what was its purpose?
5. How did the rapper gain prominence and what was the rapper's initial role?
6. What are three genres of rap music, and what does each attempt to do?
7. What is rap music's relationship to Islam and to Christianity?
8. Why does KRS-One consider hip hop a way of being? What does he mean by this, and what has he done to promote this way of thinking about hip hop?

Further reading

Chang, Jeff. *Can't Stop, Won't Stop: A History of the Hip-Hop Generation*. New York: Picador, 2005.

Forman, Murray and Mark Anthony Neal, editors. *That's the Joint! The Hip-Hop Studies Reader*. New York: Routledge, 2004.

George, Nelson. *Hip Hop America*. New York: Penguin, 2005.

Hodge, Daniel White. *The Soul of Hip Hop: Rims, Timbs and a Cultural Theology.* Downers Grove, IL: InterVarsity Press, 2010.

Kirk-Duggan, Cheryl and Marlon Hall. *Wake Up: Hip-Hop Christianity and the Black Church.* Nashville, TN: Abingdon Press, 2011.

Kitwana, Bakari. *The Hip Hop Generation: Young Blacks and the Crisis in African American Culture.* New York: Basic Civitas Books, 2003.

KRS-One. *The Gospel of Hip Hop: The First Instrument.* Brooklyn, NY: Powerhouse Books, 2009.

Ogbar, Jeffrey O. G. *Hip Hop Revolution: The Culture and Politics of Rap.* Lawrence, KS: University Press of Kansas, 2009.

Pinn, Anthony B., ed. *Noise and Spirit: The Religious and Spiritual Sensibilities of Rap Music.* New York: New York University Press, 2003.

Reeves, Marcus. *Somebody Scream! Rap Music's Rise to Prominence in the Aftershock of Black Power.* London: Faber & Faber, 2009.

Riza, *The Wu-Tang Manual.* New York: Riverhead Trade, 2005.

Rose, Tricia. *Black Noise: Rap Music and Black Culture in Contemporary America.* Middletown, CT: Wesleyan University Press, 1994.

Sharpley-Whiting, T. Denean. *Pimps Up, Ho's Down: Hip Hop's Hold on Young Black Women.* New York: New York University Press, 2008.

Watkins, S. Craig. *Hip Hop Matters: Politics, Pop Culture, and the Struggle for the Soul of a Movement.* Boston, MA: Beacon Press, 2006.

14 The new "Nones"

In this chapter

African Americans represent a growing segment of the non-theistic community. Having become more visible and vocal over the past few years, African American non-theists (humanists and atheists) challenge traditional forms of African American religion. This chapter presents the dynamics of African American non-theism, highlighting African American efforts to promote a secular United States. It also gives attention to the participation of African Americans in the larger Atheist Movement.

Main topics covered

- Changing demographics regarding atheism in the United States
- The nature of the anti-religious "None" perspective
- Characteristics of the humanist/atheist movement(s)
- African American participation in the humanist/atheist movement(s)
- Impact of African American atheism on the nature and meaning of religion within African American communities

Why discuss African American atheists?

This chapter, of all the chapters in this book, poses the most difficulty when attempting to think about the nature and meaning of African American religion. Even if one brackets the need for God or gods as a marker of religion – a difficult task for many – how does one categorize this brand of non-theism as a religion? This is particularly perplexing when one considers the resistance to the label "religion" by some within this grouping of non-theists. It is because of these challenges and difficulties that it is important to give some consideration to this group – non-theists outside organizations such as the Unitarian Universalists Association and somewhat hostile toward the idea of religion. The guiding idea is simple:

First, whether one explicitly uses the term religion or not, there is something about even rejection of, or suspicion regarding, theism that involves the formation of life meaning, that brings people together around shared perspectives and opinions on the nature of life. And, the forging of these connections is the basic "stuff" of religion. In this regard, even those who oppose traditional forms of religion (like African American churches) – and this is what this type of non-theist usually has in mind – their philosophy of life and the resulting system of ethics (i.e., how one is to behave in the world) serves a function similar to that which we have labeled "religion." This is not to deny their opposition to certain ways of thinking and the resulting practice when derived from supernatural claims. Rather, it is to recognize the type of life building work generated by their alternate ideas, strategies and practices.

Second, the significant growth in the number of Nones (i.e., those who claim no particular affiliation with traditional theistic organizations, some of whom are atheists) points to an important shift with regard to the look of the religious landscape in African American communities. The decline in church participation encountered by many Christian denominations when combined with the growth in non-belief points to a major development anyone interested in African American religion should note.

Third, attention to non-belief or the Nones also affords an opportunity to explore other angles and avenues used to make life meaningful. Put differently, this development offers an opportunity to think about the ways in which community formation, relationships of support and shared values, in the twenty-first century, do not necessitate physical connection with people.

Fourth, non-affiliated, non-theistic groups and those in theistic organizations do communicate and are in relationships. For instance, theists often think about their beliefs and practices in opposition to non-belief; and, Nones who don't associate with any of the traditional forms of religion often understand their science and reason-based approach to life as superior to and as a corrective to theism. In this way, what is believed in theistic circles is influenced by non-belief and the reverse is also true. Mindful of this, any book on African American religion would need to at least acknowledge how both orientations (non-theistic and theistic) influence what is meant by religion. More important than the term "religion" are the various ways in which African Americans have thought and acted with a focus on the fostering of life meaning in significant ways.

Increased visibility of humanist/atheism

There was a time when one could assume a theistic religious tradition would stand out as the fastest growing religious organization in African American communities. But according to some recent studies, "Nones" – again, those who claim no particular religious organization – now constitute the fasting growing group. Although

Why discuss this type of humanism/atheism?

- Whether the term "religion" is used or not, these humanists/atheists outside traditional communities of belief still provide ways to address thought and action revolving around a desire to create greater life meaning.
- The growth in the percentage of the African American population described as "Nones" is significant and this raises questions concerning the nature and importance of traditional forms of religion.
- The importance of social (online) media for these humanists/atheists points to an interesting growth in the use of non-physical gatherings and connections to share ideas and support common values and commitments.
- The look and function of religion in African American communities is impacted by the tension (and debates) between traditional theists and anti-religion humanists/atheists in particular.

these "Nones" – composed of a range of perspectives from deism to atheism – wouldn't necessarily consider themselves religious, at the very least one can say the fastest growing group is the community of those opposed to traditional religious organizations.

According to the Pew Foundation report titled "American Nones: The Profile of the No Religion Population (2008)," which was based on well over 50,000 interviews, since the 1990s the number of Nones has increased by more than a million each year. This is particularly true with respect to those under 30 and above 17, where Nones represent over 20 percent of the total United States population. Only 7 percent of the Nones identify as atheists, but the agnostics count for roughly 35 percent of the group. This is important when one considers that 70 percent of adults in the United States say they believe in God, and only 10 percent of the adult population claims some form of agnosticism. Of all adults in the United States, roughly 15 percent are Nones, and economic status has little to do with who does or does not claim this label. The same is the case with respect to levels of educational achievement. It is interesting to put this Pew study in relationship to the "National Survey of Youth

Who are the Nones?

'None' is not a movement, but a label for a diverse group of people who do not identify with any of the myriad of religious options in the American religious marketplace – the irreligious, the unreligious, the anti-religious, and the anti-clerical. Some believe in God; some do not. Some may participate occasionally in religious rituals; others never will.

(Quoted from "American Nones: The Profile of the No Religion Population")

and Religion (2002)." According to that study, African Americans constitute roughly 7 percent of all those who have a weak and insignificant importance attached to the idea of God. And, African Americans represented 3 percent of those who are atheists within the age range of 13–17. The percentages for Latinos/as were also small, with white youth representing roughly 80 percent of the atheists and 77 percent of those with a very limited sense of God. For these young people, and adults for that matter, religious community does not serve as the arbiter of moral and ethical lessons and conduct. They, instead, must turn to other groups for guidance and collaboration on life issues. Their social networks do not include traditional religious organizations, for the most part, but involve small, typically localized groups of non-theists. For young people during college years, campus organizations promoting "secular" values also serve as sources of support and means by which to sharpen and share their perspectives and opinions without direct conflict with theists.

As the percentage of Nones increases, traditional churches experience declining numbers – almost 10 percent over the course of less than two decades. The population of teenagers and young adults that many churches are desperate to bring into their membership are heavily represented in this category of Nones. Many Nones note that religion is important to them, but the surveys do not indicate on what level this importance is expressed. For example, it is possible that their interest in religion is for decidedly non-theistic but more pragmatic reasons: social networks, business connections, cultural learning, and so on.

The None future

In many ways, Nones are the invisible minority in the U.S. today – invisible because their social characteristics are very similar to the majority. Intriguingly, what this suggests is that the transition from a largely religious population to a more secular population may be so subtle that it can occur under the radar as happened during the 1990s. In the future we can expect more American Nones given that 22% of the youngest cohort of adults self-identify as Nones and they will become tomorrow's parents. If current trends continue and cohorts of non-religious young people replace older religious people, the likely outcome is that in two decades the Nones could account for around one-quarter of the American population.

(Quoted from "American Nones: The Profile of the No Religion Population.)

It is important to note that African Americans make-up almost 10 percent of the Nones population, and this percentage represents almost a doubling since 1990. This is significant in that most surveys highlight African Americans as more religious than other groups. Yet, with the Pew study, one finds a growing percentage of African Americans moving against this assumption. Overwhelming belief in God and other markers of traditional religiosity within African American communities make status as a None somewhat risky. This is even the case for the percentage of African Americans who do not claim to be atheists but rather just don't hold to any particular traditional mode of religion. That is to say, holding this position can still result in being separated from family and friends and being considered by others as one of questionable morals and ethics. This assumption is based on a particular type of reasoning. If people behave in ethical ways because of the teachings of their religious traditions and the requirements of God or gods, how can someone who questions or denies the existence of God be moral or ethical? Despite this line of reasoning and the hardship that can result from not being a part of an easily identifiable religious community, according to a 2007 survey those who claimed no particular religious tradition represented the third largest tradition within African American communities. It was behind only historical African American churches and evangelical churches (e.g., nondenominational churches).

It is reasonable to believe some of these unaffiliated African Americans attend traditional churches on occasions for a variety of reasons, but what about the others? What are the ways in which they work to satisfy the human desire for life meaning? We have already covered one answer to these questions by giving attention to the Unitarian Universalist Association and the Ethical Culture Society, church-styled communities where some African Americans find community and forge relationships that work to address the desire for life meaning. However, the percentage of African Americans (as well as the real number) suggests that a good number of African American Nones remain outside those particular institutions.

Outside traditional religious communities

Longing for human connections and shared commitments does not vanish for those African American Nones who do not participate in traditional religious communities. Instead, they tend to fulfill this yearning for life meaning through participation in what is generally called the Humanist Movement or in some quarters the Atheist Movement. That is to say, it is in relationship to non-theistic groups and activities that many African American non-theists find fulfillment. There are varieties of local and regional organizations that compose the Humanist or Atheist Movement(s). And they hold a variety of talks, lectures, and social gatherings as a way to connect non-theists and break free of the common assumption made by African American non-theists that they are the only ones. However, there are a few organizations that seem to dominate the national and international scene with respect to Humanism and/or Atheism, and they – in recent years – have worked much harder to make themselves attractive to African Americans. While all of these various organizations deserve some attention, I will limit this discussion to just a handful: The American Humanist Association, American Atheists, Freedom from Religion Foundation, the Secular Student Alliance, African Americans for Humanism, and Black Atheists of America.

The American Humanist Association

The 11,000 member American Humanist Association (AHA), founded roughly 70 years ago, claims to be the first and oldest humanist organization in the United States. It understands its function and purpose in this way: "The mission of the American Humanist Association is to be a clear, democratic voice for Humanism in the United States, to increase public awareness and acceptance of humanism, to establish, protect and promote the position of humanists in our society, and to develop and advance humanist thought and action." Recognizing humanism in a variety of forms – including atheism, agnosticism, and secularism – the organization works to promote humanist thinking and values within public life by supporting the separation of church and state, promoting scientific understandings of the world, and the development of programs and modes of thinking that advance life on earth. It does this through a variety of publications, local organizations, conferences, and educational materials. The leadership of the organization has worked to increase the number of African Americans who are members but who have more than a nominal presence. In addition, the AHA also provides contact materials and information concerning African American humanists as a way to foster better connections and interactions. For example, its website contains articles by humanists such as Norm Allen, providing guidance and suggestions concerning ways to manage greater relationships between African Americans and the Humanist Movement.

American Atheist

Founded in 1963, American Atheist has a similar goal of working toward a "secular" nation, guided by science and non-supernatural thinking. Framed by a desire to protect the rights of non-theists in part through a clear separation of church and state, American Atheist publishes books and journals, sponsors national and local conferences and other events meant to educate about atheism and to protest theism's intrusion into the public life of United States citizens. Through its community-based activities, American Atheist provides a form of community for many non-theists, particularly amongst those who make use of the label atheist to self-describe. A commitment to African Americans and other underrepresented groups is clear in the organization's self-understanding: "Atheists come in all shapes, sizes, colors, ethnicities, and orientations. American Atheist welcomes and seeks diversity, and we go out of our way to make sure minorities feel welcomed and empowered."

Figure 14.1 Billboard critiquing religious justifications for slavery and a celebration of humanism. © Religion News Service. Used by permission.

Freedom from Religion Foundation

The Freedom from Religion Foundation, with its roughly 17,000 members, was established in 1978 to promote the separation of church and state. From the perspective of the organization's leadership, this must include education to remove the false and damaging perceptions regarding the nature and purpose of non-theism – atheism, agnosticism, skepticism. In certain ways, its legal battles to enforce a separation of church and state – through challenges to prayer in public schools, public funding for theistic purposes, discrimination against gays and lesbians, and so on – seeks to provide a much healthier community in which non-theists and non-theistic thinking can thrive. Beyond the work of its attorneys, the Foundation provides literature and events (such as conferences) to spread information concerning the value of non-theistic thinking and the importance of developing a more "secular" public life in the United States.

Secular Student Alliance

Whereas young adults participate in the activities of the groups just discussed, they are not limited to these particular outlets. Founded in 2000, the Secular Student Alliance (SSA) provides information, activism opportunities, and social outlets for non-theist high school and college students. Extending beyond these campuses, the organization understands itself to have a unique ability based on its structure and orientation. That is to say, "through the SSA's nonpartisan nature and ability to channel young graduates into the national organizations, it built bridges among the secular community and reached new heights in the promotion of science, reason and free inquiry." The organization centers around atheistic, humanistic, or skeptical groups on high school and college campuses and advances non-theistic thinking and non-theistic values and ethics related to pressing contemporary issues of concern for young people. In addition, there are national conferences and meetings by means of which the Secular Student Alliance works to provide a meaningful space of fellowship and activism for non-theists within a society still marked by a deep regard for theism. It, like the other organizations named, has made efforts to increase diversity through invitation to and activities meant to attract African American non-theists. While often fighting against their own misperceptions of African Americans – misunderstandings that also affect the other organizations – there is an effort to move beyond a predominantly white audience.

Organizations of their own

The need for community, for participation with the like-minded, is widely recognized. As one African American female atheist remarked:

> Americans who claim to have no religious affiliation is only around 15 percent. The number for blacks is even lower, at 12 percent. So as a minority within a deeply closeted minority, we're going to have to work to gain visibility and influence. Those of us who are "out" mustn't apologize for our stance. We also need to join larger non-theistic groups.

The challenge is to find groups in which one's racial background is understood and embraced as intimately connected to one's atheism. This, many African American non-theists lament, can be somewhat difficult. These various organizations have made inroads into the African American non-theistic population. However, problems still abound in that what non-theistic thinking means for African Americans and the challenges and barriers to their public participation still go unrecognized and unaddressed in meaningful ways. To push beyond these misperceptions and misunderstandings that cause frustration, some African American non-theists encourage the formation of organizations and communities directly and primarily concerned with non-theistic thought and practice for African Americans, based on their needs and issues. Local (e.g. the Los Angeles Skeptics Group and the Harlem Center for Inquiry) and regional efforts to produce community for African American non-theists have been somewhat successful. Conferences and monthly meetings provide opportunities for African Americans to think through the proper framing

Aims of the African Americans for Humanism organization

- Incorporate an Afrocentric outlook into a broader world perspective.
- Add depth and breadth to the study of history by acknowledging the great contributions made by people of African descent to the world, with the purpose of building self-esteem among African-Americans and helping to demonstrate the importance of all peoples to the development of world civilization.
- Develop eupraxophy, or "wisdom and good conduct through living," in the African-American community by using the scientific and rational methods of inquiry.
- Solve many of the problems that confront African-Americans through education and self-reliance, thereby affirming that autonomy and freedom of choice are basic human rights.
- Develop self-help groups and engage in any humane and rational activity designed to develop the African-American community.
- Emphasize the central importance of education at all levels, including humanistic moral education, developing a humanistic outlook, and providing the tools for the development of critical reason, self-improvement, and career training.
- Fight against racism in every form.

(Quoted from the "African American Humanist Declaration," printed in *Free Inquiry*, Vol. 10, issue 2 (Spring 1990): 13–15)

of non-theism and the most useful strategies for public presentation of their beliefs. However, there are also national organizations meant to harness the energy and work of localized groups. Two of the more prominent of these national organizations are African Americans for Humanism and Black Atheists of America.

Founded by Norm Allen in 1989 and now directed by Debbie Goddard, African Americans for Humanism is concerned with spreading information about non-theism, encouraging critical thinking, and promoting a more secular society. These are the same aims as those presented by the organizations mentioned above. However, the AAH also understands the need to do this work with full recognition of the impact of race, gender and class on African Americans – as well as the isolation that can result from public pronouncement of non-theism by African Americans. Doing so – being public about non-theism – can result in a double dilemma: participation within a minority community (i.e., non-theists in a predominantly theistic country) as a minority (i.e., a member of a racial group outside the dominant arena of power and influence). Like the AAH, Black Atheists of America, founded by Ayanna Watson, concerns itself with "bridging the gap between atheism and the black community." And, it works to do so through education and community service meant to demonstrate the positive impact an atheistic framework can have on the lived conditions of African Americans.

Figure 14.2 Billboard depicting African American humanists past and present. © Religion
News Service. Used by permission.

These various organizations have been useful in building a stronger sense of
connectedness and "belonging" for African American non-theists. In this regard,
they have played a role in providing information and activities allowing African
American non-theists to wrestle with questions of life meaning – whether this
involves the huge questions of human existence or more mundane concerns with
connections to their own perspectives and opinions despite public opposition.

However, in the twenty-first century it is also important to note the ways in which
African American non-theistic communities are forming online, using social media
sites as a mechanism for connecting with other non-theists across the restrictions
of physical geography. Blogs such as "The Black Atheist" provide opportunities
for exchange meant to sharpen insights, spread opinions and connect with those
open to a similar worldview. According to the person behind the blog: "Despite the
"New Atheist" Movement of the 21st Century, the opinions of the minority atheist
community are conspicuously absent. This blog is my attempt to contribute something
to this movement which, if recent polls are any indication, is only growing." There are
also radio programs online that encourage non-theistic conversation about pressing
issues and concerns. One of these programs is the "Infidel Guy Radio," described
as "radio that rocks your rational mind!!" Started in 1999 by Reginald V. Finley,
Sr., the "Infidel Guy" website, with a reported 1 million visitors per month, has
involved conversation with leading figures in non-theistic circles as well as contains a
discussion forum for like-minded participants to share their opinions on particular
broadcasts. In the words of Finley,

The primary focus of this website is to tell the world that it's okay NOT to believe in god/s, and also, that there are good reasons why hundreds of millions around the world do NOT believe in god/s. Another purpose of this site is to provide a place where non-believers feel that they belong. In such an anti-atheist world, atheists often feel marginalized and attacked for their lack of belief. Here at infidelguy.com, non-believers can socialize, chat (voice and text), read thought provoking material, listen to and watch educational / entertaining programming found nowhere else on the web.

Furthermore, Facebook groups such as "AtheistNetwork" and "Black Atheist" have recently emerged that provide places for the formation of community. There is also YouTube programming that speaks to the interests and perspectives of a non-theistic audience. The bottom line for both online organizations and physical organizations with offices, staffs and programming is the same: foster and support non-theistic community formation.

Key points you need to know

- The percentage of Americans who do not claim a particular religious community has increased significantly over the past 20 years.
- The number of African Americans in this group has also increased, almost doubling during the same period.
- Publicly claiming humanism or atheism within African American communities can result in being ostracized and having one's morals and ethics brought into question by African Americans and the larger society: double trouble.
- Many "Nones" participate in humanist/atheist organizations that are critical of traditional religious traditions, and these organizations use meetings, lobbying, lawsuits, publications, public billboards, etc., to get their points across.
- Humanist/atheist organizations – often referenced as a humanist or atheist movement – have made efforts to increase the number of African Americans holding membership and who participate in their activities.
- Frustrated with what is often a lack of understanding concerning issues of race, some African American humanists/atheists have created their own organizations for support and advancement of their agenda – including African Americans for Humanism.
- Social media has become a significant source of community and support for African Americans who participate in online groups and discussions, or who tune into internet radio programs.
- Attention to humanists/atheists who are critical of traditional religion is helpful for an understanding of religion because information so gathered tells us something about the ebb and flow – the changes and consistencies – of what we have labeled African American religion.

Discussion questions

1. What are Nones and what has happened to their numbers of the past twenty years? What are some of the characteristics of members of this group?
2. What are some of the organizations that support humanist/atheists who are not involved in traditional churches? What are some of their activities and aims?
3. Are these humanist/atheist organizations interested in African Americans? If so, what do they do to make this known?
4. What are some of the challenges faced by African Americans who make public their humanism or atheism?
5. How have African Americans responded to humanist/atheist organizations? Have African Americans developed their own organizations? If yes, what types of things do these organizations do and what makes them different?
6. What role does social media play in the development and nurturing of African American humanist/atheist communities? What are some specific online outlets, and what do they offer African American humanists/atheists?
7. Why is it important to give attention to "Nones" in the discussion of African American religion?

Further reading

Allen, Norm. *The Black Humanist Experience: An Alternative to Religion*. Buffalo, NY: Prometheus Books, 2003.

Baggini, Julian. *Atheism: A Very Short Introduction*. New York: Oxford University Press, 2003.

Barker, Dan. *Godless: How an Evangelical Preacher Became One of America's Leading Atheists*. Berkeley, CA: Ulysses Press, 2008.

Dawkins, Richard. *The God Delusion*. New York: Mariner Books, 2008.

Epstein, Greg M. *Good Without God: What a Billion Nonreligious People Do Believe*. New York: William Morrow, 2009.

Harris, Sam. *The Moral Landscape: How Science Can Determine Human Values*. New York: The Free Press, 2011.

Hitchens, Christopher. *The Portable Atheist: Essential Readings for the Nonbeliever*. New York: Da Capo Press, 2007

Hutchinson, Sikivu. *Moral Combat: Black Atheists, Gender Politics, and the Values War*. Los Angeles, CA: Infidel Books, 2011.

Jacoby, Susan. *Freethinkers: A History of American Secularism*. New York: Holt Paperbacks, 2004.

Lamont, Corliss. *The Philosophy of Humanism*. Washington, DC: Humanist Press, 1997.

Law, Stephen. *Humanism: A Very Short Introduction*. New York: Oxford University Press, 2011.

Le Poidevin, Robin. *Agnosticism: A Very Short Introduction*. New York: Oxford University Press, 2010.

Tapp, Robert B. *Multiculturalism: Humanist Perspectives*. Buffalo, NY: Prometheus Books, 2000.

Zuckerman, Phil. *Society without God: What the Least Religious Nations Can Tell Us About Contentment*. New York: New York University Press, 2010.

Chronology

This chronology provides some important dates and developments as a way of mapping out African American religion. It is not a complete history of African American religion. Some additional information related to important dates is available in the individual chapters. The books listed at the end of each chapter, along with the list of resources at the end of the book, can help interested readers supplement the material available below.

1444	Portuguese take Africans to Portugal for the purpose of enslavement
1536	First African baptized in Roman Catholic Church
1619	First Africans arrive in North America (Virginia)
1641	Earliest recorded account of an African Church member (Massachusetts)
1669	African first baptized into Lutheran Church
1701	Society for the Propagation of the Gospel in Foreign Parts attempts to convert slaves
1730s	First Great Awakening
1773	One of the first black churches (Baptist) formed – Silver Bluff Church
1790–1830	Second Great Awakening
1796	Black Methodists form a church in New York
1807	First African Presbyterian Church founded in Philadelphia
1816	AME Church denomination formed
1822	Liberia founded
1828	Oblate Sisters of Providence is founded in Baltimore, Maryland
1829	David Walker publishes *Walker's Appeal in Four Articles; a Preamble to the Coloured Citizens of the World, but in Particular, and Very Expressly, to Those of the United States of America*
1830	Marie Laveau becomes Voodoo Queen

1831	Work of Oblate Sisters of Providence recognized by the Pope
1834	Black Baptist associations begin to form
1839	Daniel Alexander Payne writes an article in which he acknowledges the existence of enslaved Africans who are non-theists
1848	"Zion" added to African Methodist Episcopal Church in America
1854	James Healy ordained first African American priest
1863	Emancipation Proclamation issued
1864	St. Francis Xavier Catholic Church becomes first parish for African Americans
1865	System of slavery ends in the United States
1866	First state-wide Baptist convention forms
1866	Prophet Cherry organizes the Church of the Living God, Pillar of Truth for All Nations. During the 1940s, the organization moved to Philadelphia
1867	Patrick Francis Healy becomes first African American Jesuit priest
1870	Colored Methodist Episcopal Church formed
1874	Patrick Healy becomes the first African American president of a Catholic University (Georgetown University)
1875	James A. Healy becomes the first African American Catholic Bishop (Portland, Oregon)
1878	Mathilda Beasley organizes the Third Order of St. Francis Catholic order for African American nuns
1884	Samuel David Ferguson becomes first African American bishop of the Episcopal Church
1886	Augustus Tolton ordained a Roman Catholic priest
1889	Daniel Rudd begins conversation in Catholic Church on status of Americans
1889	Church of the Living God founded in Arkansas
1880	Year of the first of five African American Catholic Congresses
1893	William Saunders Crowdy begins having visions that result in the formation of the Church of God and Saints of Christ
1894	Julia A. Foote ordained a deacon in the AME Zion Church
1895	National Baptist Convention, USA formed
1897	Charles Mason and Charles Jones form the Church of God
1898	Mary Small made an elder in the AME Zion Church
1900	Reverdy C. Ransom organizes the Institutional Church and Social Settlement House in Chicago that is dedicated to the Social Gospel
1906	Asuza Street Pentecostal revival begins
1906	Roman Catholic Church organizes the Catholic Board for Mission work among Colored People
1907	Mason's Church of God renamed Church of God in Christ

1913	Noble Drew Ali establishes Canaanite Temple
1913	Mother Leafy Anderson develops Eternal Life Christian Spiritualist Church in Chicago
1915	National Baptist Convention of America formed
1919	Wentworth Arthur Matthew organizes the Commandment Keepers Congregation
1920	Mother Leafy Anderson founds Eternal Life Spiritualist Church in the Crescent City (New Orleans)
1923	Father Hurley starts Universal Hagar's Spiritual Church
1924	Islamic Mission of America founded
1930	Master Fard Muhammad appears in Detroit
1934	Master Fard Muhammad disappears
1941	Joseph Oliver Brown becomes first African American Roman Catholic bishop in the twentieth century
1941	American Humanist Association founded
1946	Francisco Mora becomes first Santería priest in the United States
1947	Lewis A. McGee founds Free Religious Fellowship
1948	Rebecca Glover ordained in the AME Church
1954	CME Church begins ordaining women
1955	Civil Rights Movement begins
1956	Colored Methodist Episcopal Church becomes Christian Methodist Episcopal Church
1959	Walter King becomes first African American initiated into Santería priesthood (in Cuba)
1961	Progressive Baptist Convention formed
1961	First African American Santería priestess initiated
1963	Four young girls killed in the bombing of a church in Birmingham, Alabama
1963	Five Percent Nation develops under the leadership of Clarence 13X
1963	Martin L. King, Jr. issues the "Letter from a Birmingham Jail"
1963	American Atheist founded
1964	Malcolm X leaves Nation of Islam
1964	First Santería drum dance in the United States
1965	Malcolm X killed
1966	National Committee of Black Churchmen formed
1968	Civil Rights Movement under King ends with his assassination
1969	Members of Ben Carter's community begin to move from Liberia to Israel
1969	NCBC issues a statement on Black Theology
1970s	Hip hop culture begins to take shape in New York City
1970s–1980s	Decline in church membership for some denominations

1975	The Honorable Elijah Muhammad dies and is replaced by Wallace Muhammad
1975	Wallace Muhammad begins to re-envision the Nation of Islam
1978	Members of Abeta Hebrew Israel Culture Center begin moving to Liberia
1978	Louis Farrakhan re-establishes the Nation of Islam under the teachings of Elijah Muhammad
1978	Freedom from Religion Foundation founded
1979	Rapper's Delight put hip hop and rap music on the map
1980s	Emergence of Christian rap groups
1980	Kurtis Blow's "The Breaks" becomes the first rap record to sell 1 million copies
1982	"The Message" released and it gives shape to progressive rap music
1982–1985	Influential movies related to hip hop, such as Wild Style and Style Wars are released
1983	Ice-T plays a role in pioneering West Coast gangsta rap with "Cop Killer"
1985	By this date, hip hop culture is global in reach
1985	Salt 'n' Pepa make their first appearance as a group
1985	Stephen Wiley's *Bible Breaks* becomes first Christian rap album released
1986	Rap-a-Lot Records founded in Houston, Texas
1987	National Black Catholic Congress convenes
1987	Public Enemy releases first album and Boogie Down Production's Scott LaRock is murdered after the release of the group's Criminal Minded
1987	UGK formed in Port Arthur, Texas
1988	Ghetto Boys release its first album
1988	MTV gives rap music its own show ("Yo! MTV Raps")
1988	NWA releases *Straight Outa Compton* containing "Fuck Tha Police," this is a major marker of gangsta rap's development
1989	Barbara Harris elected first African American woman bishop in Episcopal Church
1989	African Americans for Humanism founded
1990	African American Humanist Declaration developed
1990s	General movement of the black middle-class back into black churches
1990s	Growth in number of Megachurches, many marked by a "Gospel of Prosperity"
1991	Scarface (of Ghetto Boys) releases *Mr. Scarface is Back*
1991	Schism develops leading to development of Soka Gakkai International, USA

1992	UGK releases first album, *Too Hard to Swallow*
1994	Gotee Records (Christian Rap) founded
1995	Queen Latifah wins a Grammy for "Best Rap Solo Performance"
1996	UGK releases *Ridin' Dirty*
1999	Infidel Guy website created
2000	Secular Student Alliance founded
2000	Reverend Vashti Murphy McKenzie becomes first women consecrated as a bishop in the AME Church
2000	Christian rap artists in the Catholic Church gain some notice
2005	Slim Thug releases his first album, *Already Platinum*
2008	One Accord DJ Alliance network of Christian DJ and Radio Announcers formed
2008	Warith Deen Muhammad dies
2008	Barack Obama elected the first black President of the United States
2009	Kurtis Blow ordained
2010	Bun B's "Trill OG" is the first album in a good number of years to get The Source Magazine's 5-mic award
2010	Wyclef Jean announces his campaign for presidency of Haiti

Glossary of selected terms

African American religion   the quest to making meaning out of life. It serves as a primary way by which African Americans wrestle with the huge questions of life.

Babalawo   a priest in Santería who can perform divination.

Back-to-Africa Movement   the nineteenth-century movement to take African Americans back to Africa.

Black theology   a late twentieth-century theology that argues God is working toward the liberation from oppression of African Americans.

Blues   a form of American music developed by African Americans that chronicles the joys and problems of life. It was called "devil music" by Christians because it embraced behaviors and opinions challenged by the Christian faith.

Botánica   a shop that sells items needed for the practice of African-based traditions.

Buddha   the Enlightened One, upon whose teachings the religion of Buddhism is based.

Call and response   the back-and-forth exchange between the preacher and the congregation during which preachers' remarks are met with words of encouragement: "preach!" and "amen!"

Civil Rights Movement   the mid-twentieth century struggle to secure equal rights for African Americans.

Conjure   the manipulation of natural materials for spiritual benefit, associated with magic.

Convention   a gathering of like-minded congregations.

Cult of true womanhood   the idea that the proper place for women is in the home, and that women must be protected from the negativity of public life, such as politics. It is tied to a similar sense of women belonging in the home referred to as the "Cult of Domesticity."

Curse of Ham   an old argument used to justify slavery by saying the son of Ham, Canaan, was cursed because of Ham's wrong doing and this curse involved perpetual servitude.

Diocese   geographic area overseen by a bishop.

Divination   the process of securing information concerning one's destiny.

Double-talk   the practice of saying something that has more than one meaning.

Fundamentos   elements that represent the characteristics and functions of particular orisha.

Great Awakening   a period of energetic worship and revivals prior to the twentieth century during which many people converted to Christianity and joined churches.

Great migration   the mass movement of African Americans after slavery from rural to urban settings, from the period of the Civil War through the mid-twentieth century.

Gris-gris   material used in conjure that is believed to have great power to keep evil away. It is often associated with a small bag of dirt from the cemetery.

Hajj   the pilgrimage to Mecca required of all able Muslims.

Hoodoo   a popularized version of Voodoo that is associated with magical practices and lacks the detailed cosmology and ritual structures of Voodoo.

Hounfor   (also Oum'phor) the place of worship in Vodou.

Humanism   a system of life practice based on reason and human activity, and typically without any adherence to trans-historical beings.

Hush Arbor Meetings   secret meetings during the period of slavery where enslaved Africans would practice their religious beliefs.

Imago dei   the theological idea that humans are made in the image of God.

Imam   a religious leader in Islam. In Sunni Islam the imam is the minister who conducts Friday prayers at the mosque, preaches and looks after the spiritual needs of the congregation. In Shia Islam, however, the term means a supreme or semi-divine leader.

Invisible institution   the informal and secret meetings of slaves that represent the beginnings of more formal religious practices.

Kawaida   a philosophy of black consciousness and black progress developed by Dr. Maulana Karenga.

Kwanzaa   an African American holiday involving the celebration of African principles, such as unity, that was organized and founded by Dr. Maulana Karenga.

Manifest destiny   the belief that a group of people has a special mission or role in human history.

Megachurches   large churches with more than 2,000 members that make strong use of technology. Many of them are associated with the belief that God wants Christians to be prosperous, including economic wealth.

Middle Passage   the movement of enslaved Africans across the Atlantic Ocean to the Americas.

Mother ship   the space ship Master Fard Muhammad will use to purge the earth and restore the rule of the original people.

Normative gaze   the assumption that people of European descent are superior to people of African descent because Europeans more closely resemble the Greek ideal body and features.

Oba   a Yoruba king.

Ontological blackness   the idea that God is so identified with suffering African Americans that God's very being, who God is, cannot be separated from blackness.

Parish   a local congregation.

Peculiar institution   a reference to the system of slavery.

Prosperity gospel   the idea that proper Christian faith and knowledge of the Bible result in material gain and economic well-being for the believer, the result of God's favor.

Ring shout   a practice during the period of slavery when worshippers would gather, sing, and move in a circle until those involved received the Holy Spirit.

Root work   a form of religious practice that revolves around using natural items such as plants to harness and use spiritual energy for one's benefit.

Sanctification   the belief that, after being saved from sin, one has the ability to live a life free from sin.

Social gospel   the belief that commitment to the Christian faith must involve work to improve socio-economic and political conditions of life.

Spirit guides   figures who aid and protect humans.

Spiritualism   the religious movement revolving around rituals meant to bring the living and the dead into contact.

Spiritualists   persons who seek contact with the deceased in order to improve temporal existence.

Spirituals   an early form of American music developed by enslaved Africans in North America.

Tagging   the practice of writing messages or one's name on public spaces.

Talmud   a central text in Judaism involving rabbinic discussions of ethics, philosophy, and law.

Theism   belief in God or gods.

Voodoo   an African-based tradition drawn from West Africa and combined with elements of Christianity. It is associated with Haiti, but it has also had a long history in North America.

Womanist theology   a form of theology that argues attention must be given to the plight and experience of African American women, that God requires an end to racism, sexism, and classism.

Resources

The readings provided at the end of each chapter are important in that they provide context for various dimensions of African American religion. They also offer greater detail concerning particular developments related to the nature and meaning of religion within African American communities. But books alone can't provide a full sense of what religion is and what it means to African Americans.

The late twentieth and early twenty-first centuries also offer a range of other resources just as informative. This section of the book gives a sampling of these alternate resources and encourages readers to combine these materials with the suggested books in order to get a more complex and layered understanding of what it means to be African American and religious. An effort has been made to provide sources that cut across the themes of the 14 chapters, but this does not mean that every topic or key point is covered. What follows is far from complete, but it is enough to get readers started.

Websites

These sites provide information concerning some of the religious traditions noted within the various chapters. They can be used to gather more detailed information concerning the beliefs and practices associated with particular traditions and their leaders. When navigating through these sites, pay attention to the questions and key points given at the end of the chapters to the book.

- African Americans for Humanism: http://www.secularhumanism.org/index. php?page=index&section=aah/
- American Atheist: http://www.atheists.org/
- American Humanist Association: http://www.americanhumanist.org/
- African Methodist Episcopal Church: http://www.ame-church.com/
- African Methodist Episcopal Church Zion: http://www.amez.org/news/index. php

- African American Christians: www.theafricanamericanlectionary.org
- African American Christians: www.blackandchristian.com
- Ava Kay Jones (Voodoo): http://yorubapriestess.tripod
- Black Atheists of America: http://www.blackatheistsofamerica.org/history.htm
- Christian Methodist Episcopal Church: http://www.c-m-e.org/
- Church of God in Christ: http://cogic.net/cogiccms/default/
- Creflo Dollar Ministries: http://www.creflodollarministries.org/
- Five Percent Nation: http://www.allahsnation.net/
- Frederick Haynes: http://www.friendshipwest.org/pastor.html
- Fred Price: http://www.faithdome.org/
- Freedom from Religion Foundation: http://ffrf.org/
- Hip Hop Culture: www.holyhiphop.com
- Moorish Science Temple: http://www.moorishsciencetempleofamericainc.com/
- Mr. Deity: mrdeity.com
- Nation of Islam: http://www.noi.org/
- National Baptist Convention USA: http://www.nationalbaptist.com/
- National Baptist Convention of America: http://www.nbcainc.com/
- Oyotunji African Village: http://www.oyotunjiafricanvillage.org/?id=1
- Potter's House: http://thepottershouse.org/
- Progressive National Baptist Convention: http://www.pnbc.org/PNBC/Home.html
- Secular Student Alliance: http://www.secularstudents.org/
- The Temple of Hip Hop: http://www.templeofhiphop.org/index.php?lang=en

YouTube

Much information is available on YouTube that helps to provide context as well as details concerning particular religious leaders and their thinking. The videos listed below provide conversations concerning topics related to the book – the civil rights movement, liberation theology, teachings of various traditions, and the role of women within religious communities (particularly with respect to preaching within Christian churches, which continues to be a debated issue).

- Angela Davis on women and socio-political struggle: http://www.youtube.com/watch?v=Pc6RHtEbiOA
- Conversation with James Cone: http://www.youtube.com/watch?v=-1X5sZ6Q4Fw
- Cornel West lecture: http://www.youtube.com/watch?v=9ZzWWq_rQt8
- Dialogue of Reason: Science and Faith in the Black Community:
- http://www.youtube.com/watch?v=7diwQ5dHZ0U
- Honorable Elijah Muhammad: http://www.youtube.com/watch?v=Y9cCInC_v3Q&feature=fvst

- Jay Z on religion and other issues: http://www.youtube.com/watch?v=3KiWG3neWXY
- KRS-One, "Hip Hop Beyond Entertainment: Part One: http://www.youtube.com/watch?v=hoAXsSoEcZw, Part Two: http://www.youtube.com/watch?v=VtE5z5p1khI
- Malcolm X, "Our History Was Destroyed by Slavery": http://www.youtube.com/watch?v=ENHP89mLWOY
- Mama Lola (Voodoo): http://www.youtube.com/watch?v=DB0mUYpDeZg
- Martin L. King, Jr., "I Have A Dream": http://www.youtube.com/watch?v=smEqnnklfYs
- Moorish Science Temple: http://www.youtube.com/watch?v=6tCn1PogXQQ
- Oyotunji African Village: http://www.youtube.com/watch?v=F-dPpPzDckE
- Renita Weems: http://www.youtube.com/watch?v=0pE59r8AuEc
- Teresa L. Fry Brown: http://www.youtube.com/watch?v=sI5Ivj8RrtU
- Warith Deen Muhammad: http://www.youtube.com/watch?v=sFmb6bMUGzQ>

Facebook

Millions of people use Facebook as a way to connect, to share information about activities and beliefs that matter to them, and to communicate with the like-minded. The following pages provide information concerning some of the traditions from the book. Because information concerning humanism/atheism can be difficult to secure in certain ways, much of what follows revolves around humanism/atheism – particularly in its most 'secular' forms.

- "African Americans for Humanism"
- "American Atheists, Inc."
- "American Humanist Association"
- "African American Atheists"
- "African American Atheists Women"
- "Atheist Alliance International"
- "Black Free Thinkers"
- "Black Skeptics Group"
- "Council for Secular Humanism"
- "Freedom from Religion Foundation"
- "Humanism"
- "Humanist Chaplaincy of Harvard"
- "Institute for Humanist Studies Think Tank"
- "Moorish Science Temple of America"
- "Nation of Islam"
- "Nation of Islam Student Association"

- "Radical Humanism"
- "Secular Humanism"
- "SGI-USA, Soka Gakkai International USA"
- "Voodoo spiritual temple"

Documentaries and movies

Many of the topics and key points found in this book are explored in important and helpful ways through documentaries and films. The following is just a small sampling. Your school library, or public library, will have information concerning other possibilities.

- African presence in the Americas: "Sankofa," Mypheduh Films, Inc., 1993
- African presence in North America: "Roots," Warner Home Video, 2007
- African Americans: "Black Is…Black Ain't," Docurama, 1991
- African-based traditions: "Daughters of the Dust," Kino Video, 2000
- Black Power: "What We Want, What We Believe: The Black Panther Party Library," Eclectic DVD Dist., 2006
- Civil Rights Movement: "Freedom Riders," PBS, 2011
- Civil Rights Movement: "Eyes of the Prize," (Box set) PBS, 2010
- Civil Rights Movement: "4 Little Girls," HBO Home Video, 2001
- Hip Hop Culture: "The Hip Hop Project," Image Entertainment, 2010
- Hip Hop Culture: "Wildstyle," Rhino Home Video, 2007
- Humanism/Atheism: "The Atheism Tapes," Alive Mind, 2008
- Humanism/Atheism: "Religulous," Lion Gate, 2009
- Nation of Islam: "Malcolm X," Warner Home Video, 2005
- Nation of Islam: "The Honorable Elijah Muhammad, Saviour's Day, 1974," CreativeSpace, 2009
- Santeria: "The Believers," MGM, 2002
- Santeria: "Misterios," earthods, 2005
- Voodoo: "Voodoo Secrets," A & E Home Video, 2006
- Voodoo: "Divine Horsemen: The Living Gods of Haiti," Microcinema, 2007

Music

The importance of rap music for hip hop culture in particular, and religion as well as public life in general, is undeniable. While there are written materials available from various artists, the best way to get a sense of the themes and key points is to actually turn to the music – the sound and words – that combine to make rap music. What follows is just a small sampling related to the three types of rap music mentioned in Chapter 13.

- Arrested Development, "3 Years, 5 Months and 2 Days in the Life of..." Capitol, 1992
- Common, "Resurrection," Relativity, 1994
- De La Soul, "3 Feet High and Rising," Tommy Boy, 2001
- DC Talk, "Free At Last," EMI CMG, 2009
- DC Talk, "Jesus Freak," Virginia Records America, Inc., 1995
- Dr. Dre, "The Chronic," Death Row Koch, 2001
- Eric B. and Rakim, "Paid in Full," Island, 2005
- Fugees, "The Score," Sony, 1996
- Gil Scott-Heron, "Very Best of Gil Scott-Heron," Sony BMG Europe, 2009
- Gospel Gangstaz, "The Exodus," Native Records, 2002
- Gospel Gangstaz, "I Can See Clearly Now," Gospocentric, 1999
- Greydon Square, "The Kardashev Scale," Grand Unified Productions, 2011
- Greydon Square, "The Compton Effect," Grand Unified Productions, 2007
- Grand Master Flash and the Furious Five, "The Greatest Hits," Sanctuary, 2006
- Jay Z, "The Black Album," Roc-A-Fella, 2003
- Kurtis Blow, "The Best of Kurtis Blow," Island/Mercury, 1994
- Last Poets, "Chastisement," JDC Records, 1989
- Lecrae, "Rebel," Central South Dist., 2008
- L.L. Cool J, "All World: Greatest Hits," Def Jam, 1996
- Lupe Fiasco, "Lupe Fiasco's The Cool," Atlantic, 2007
- Mos Def, "Black on Both Sides," Rawkus/Umgd, 2002
- "Mos Def & Talib Kweli are Black Star," Rawkus/Umgd, 2002
- Nas, "Illmatic," Sony, 1994
- Notorious B. I. G., "Greatest Hits," Bad Boy, 2007
- NWA, "Straight Outta Compton," Priority Records
- Poor Righteous Teachers, "New World Order," Profile, 1996
- Poor Righteous Teachers, "Black Business," Profile, 1993
- Public Enemy, "It Takes a Nation of Millions," Def Jam, 1988
- The Roots, "Phrenology," MCA, 2002
- Run DMC, "Greatest Hits," Arista, 2002
- Scarface, "Greatest Hits," Virgin Records US, 2002
- Slick Rick, "The Art of Storytelling," Def Jam, 1999
- Snoop Dogg, "Doggystyle," Death Row Koch, 2001
- Talib Kweli, "Beautiful Struggle," Rawkus/Umgd, 2004
- Tupac Shakur, "Greatest Hits," Interscope Records, 1998
- Tupac Shakur, "Makaveli: The Don Killuminati," Death Row Records, 1996
- UGK, "Best of ...," Jive, 2003
- Wu-Tang Clan, "Enter Wu-Tang," RCA, 1993
- X-Clan, "To the East Blackwards," Fontana Island, 1990

Index